FLORIDA STATE
UNIVERSITY LIBRARIES

MAY 2 5 2001

TALLAHASSEE, FLORIDA

The Reform of Macroeconomic Policy

Also by J. O. N. Perkins

A GENERAL APPROACH TO MACROECONOMIC POLICY

ANTI-CYCLICAL POLICY IN AUSTRALIA

AUSTRALIA IN THE WORLD ECONOMY

AUSTRALIAN MACROECONOMIC POLICY, 1974–85

BRITAIN AND AUSTRALIA: Economic Relationships in the 1950s

BUDGET DEFICITS AND MACROECONOMIC POLICY

CONTEMPORARY MACROECONOMICS (*with R. S. Jones*)

CRISIS-POINT IN AUSTRALIAN ECONOMIC POLICY

INTERNATIONAL POLICY FOR THE WORLD ECONOMY

MACROECONOMIC POLICY IN AUSTRALIA

NATIONAL INCOME AND ECONOMIC PROGRESS (*editor with Duncan Ironmonger and Tran Van Hoa*)

STERLING AND REGIONAL PAYMENTS SYSTEMS

THE AUSTRALIAN FINANCIAL SYSTEM AFTER THE CAMPBELL REPORT

THE DEREGULATION OF THE AUSTRALIAN FINANCIAL SYSTEM

THE MACROECONOMIC MIX IN THE INDUSTRIALISED WORLD

THE MACROECONOMIC MIX TO STOP STAGFLATION

THE WALLIS REPORT AND THE AUSTRALIAN FINANCIAL SYSTEM

UNEMPLOYMENT, INFLATION AND NEW MACROECONOMIC POLICY

The Reform of Macroeconomic Policy

From Stagflation to Low or Zero Inflation

J. O. N. Perkins
Emeritus Professor
University of Melbourne
Australia

First published in Great Britain 2000 by
MACMILLAN PRESS LTD
Houndmills, Basingstoke, Hampshire RG21 6XS and London
Companies and representatives throughout the world

A catalogue record for this book is available from the British Library.

ISBN 0–333–77072–2

First published in the United States of America 2000 by
ST. MARTIN'S PRESS, INC.,
Scholarly and Reference Division,
175 Fifth Avenue, New York, N.Y. 10010

ISBN 0–312–22609–8

Library of Congress Cataloging-in-Publication Data
Perkins, J. O. N. (James Oliver Newton), 1924–
The reform of macroeconomic policy : from stagflation to low or zero inflation / J.O.N. Perkins.
p. cm.
Includes bibliographical references and index.
ISBN 0–312–22609–8 (cloth)
1. Macroeconomics. 2. Economic policy. I. Title.
HB172.5.P4443 1999
339.5—dc21   99–38849
                                                      CIP

© J. O. N. Perkins 2000

All rights reserved. No reproduction, copy or transmission of this publication may be made without written permission.

No paragraph of this publication may be reproduced, copied or transmitted save with written permission or in accordance with the provisions of the Copyright, Designs and Patents Act 1988, or under the terms of any licence permitting limited copying issued by the Copyright Licensing Agency, 90 Tottenham Court Road, London W1P 0LP.

Any person who does any unauthorised act in relation to this publication may be liable to criminal prosecution and civil claims for damages.

The author has asserted his right to be identified as the author of this work in accordance with the Copyright, Designs and Patents Act 1988.

This book is printed on paper suitable for recycling and made from fully managed and sustained forest sources.

10 9 8 7 6 5 4 3 2 1
09 08 07 06 05 04 03 02 01 00

Printed and bound in Great Britain by
Antony Rowe Ltd, Chippenham, Wiltshire

Contents

List of Tables		vi
Acknowledgements		ix
1	Introduction (1998)	1
2	Principles of Macroeconomic Policy in a Stagflationary World (1981)	4
3	Macromiximisation (1980)	28
4	Towards the Formulation and Testing of a More General Theory of Macroeconomic Policy (1987)	53
5	Some Empirical Evidence about the Macroeconomic Mix (1990)	71
6	Empirical Evidence about the Macroeconomic Mix in the Open Economy (1989)	87
7	Public Finance and Macroeconomic Policy (1991)	109
8	Of Budget Deficits and Macroeconomic Policy (1996)	128
9	The Dangers of Targeting the Budget Deficit (1995)	143
10	Of Wage–Tax Trade-offs and Macroeconomic Mixes (1981)	156
11	Deregulation and Macroeconomic Policy (1989)	167
12	Macroeconomic Policy in Conditions of Low, Zero or Negative Inflation (1998)	178
Appendix: Gilbertian Parodies for Economists		192
References		197
Index		201

List of Tables

2.1	Tax revenue as a ratio of GDP in OECD countries, 1965–80	21
2.2	Estimated real long-term bond rate, seven major OECD countries, 1965–80	23
4.1	Analysis of possible combinations of assumptions with three instruments	59
4.2	Estimated macro policy effects, 15 OECD countries, 1967–84	62
4.3	Sensitivity analysis of estimated macro policy effects, 15 OECD countries, 1967–84	64
4.4	Combinations of assumptions closest to those implied by the test results	67
5.1	Simulated effects of alternative forms of macroeconomic stimulus in UK models on real GDP as a percentage of their effects on consumer prices	76
5.2	Simulated effects of alternative forms of macroeconomic stimulus on real GNP/GDP as a percentage of their effects on the GNP/GDP price index, seven major OECD countries with floating exchange rate	79
5.3	Simulated effects of a rise in government outlays on real output as a percentage of their effects on prices, seven major OECD countries with floating exchange rates	81
5.4	Simulated effects of alternative forms of fiscal stimulus on real GDP as a percentage of their effects on prices, EEC	82
6.1	Simulated effects of alternative measures on change in real foreign balance for 1 per cent stimulus to real GDP, with floating exchange rates, seven major OECD countries	90
6.2	Simulated effects of alternative measures on change in 'thrift' for 1 per cent stimulus to real GDP, floating exchange rates, seven major OECD countries	91
6.3	Combinations of income tax cuts with reductions of government outlays equal to 1 per cent of GNP/GDP to give non-inflationary stimulus, floating exchange rates and fixed quantity of money, seven major OECD countries	93
6.4	Effects of alternative fiscal measures in the USA, floating exchange rates and fixed quantity of money	95
6.5	Simulated effects of alternative macroeconomic measures on UK current account balance for 1 per cent rise in real GDP	97

6.6	Simulated effects of alternative fiscal measures on the current account balance and on private investment, for 1 per cent rise in real GDP, European Community	100
6.7	Simulated effects on private investment and the current account of alternative forms of fiscal stimulus, EEC	102
6.8	Simulated effects on the EEC current account of alternative combinations of tax cuts with reductions in government outlays that to 1 per cent of GDP	104
7.1	Simulated change in rate of consumer price inflation for 100 000 rise in employment, UK	114
7.2	Simulated change in average annual rate of inflation (GNP/GDP price index) over five years, resulting from alternative fiscal measures for 1 per cent stimulus to employment, seven major OECD countries	115
7.3	Simulated change in consumer price inflation for 1 per cent average rise in employment in five years in five years after the change in policy, EEC	116
7.4	Simulated effects of alternative fiscal measures on UK current account balance for 100 000 rise in employment	119
7.5	Simulated effect of alternative fiscal measures on the current account balance and private investment for 1 per cent rise in employment, EEC	120
7.6	Simulated effects of alternative fiscal measures of stimulus on 'thrift' (private investment ± change in real foreign balance) for 1 per cent rise in employment, seven major OECD countries	121
8.1	Simulated effects of government non-wage expenditure and personal income tax cuts for a rise in financial deficit equal to 1 per cent of GDP/GNP, seven major OECD countries	132
8.2	Simulated effects on rate of inflation and real GDP growth rate of changes in government non-wage expenditures and cuts in a package of direct taxation having the same effect on budget balance, OECD	133
8.3	Simulated effect of various fiscal measures over five years, European Community	134
8.4	Simulated effects of various fiscal measures for an increase in the budget deficit equal to 1 per cent of GDP, USA	136
8.5	Simulated deviation of GDP price index from baseline in general government financial balance of 1 per cent of GDP, four Scandinavian countries	139

9.1 Simulated percentage-point differences from baseline reference scenario for effects of alternative fiscal policies (with given real interest rates), OECD, 1994–2000   153

9.2 Simulated percentage-point differences from baseline reference scenario for effects of alternative fiscal policies (with lower real interest rates), OECD, 1994–2000   154

Acknowledgements

The author wishes to acknowledge permission to reprint articles from the following journals and individuals, namely, *Journal of Economic Studies* (Chapter 3), Tran Van Hoa (Chapter 4), *Weltwirtschaftliches Archiv* (Chapters 4 and 5), *Economic Analysis and Policy* (Chapter 7), D.T. Nguyen (Chapter 8), and *The Economic and Labour Relations Review* (Chapter 9).

Comments and stimulus from Ian McDonald and Neville Norman over many years, including their comments on earlier drafts of many of these chapters, are gratefully acknowledged. They should not, of course, be held responsible for any remaining deficiencies.

J.O.N. PERKINS

1
Introduction (1998)*

The chapters in this book were written over a period of more than two decades. All except the last three have been published before, and the standpoint of the period in which each of them was written should be borne in mind. No attempt has been made to correct them for the change of date (apart from a few footnotes), though they have been edited somewhat in other respects, in the interests of greater clarity, and with some abbreviation. They thus present a development over time of the author's ideas on current macroeconomic policy issues, and naturally reflect the particular combinations of policy problems that were in evidence at the time of their writing. The application of the suggested principles of policy in a number of different contexts is intended to make the analysis relevant to a number of different combinations of macroeconomic problems in future periods.

There is some overlap of the ideas (though not the exact content) between one chapter and another. Where this overlap has been left in, it is in order that the chapters may be intelligible individually. The material that is common to two or more chapters takes the form of *a priori* argument or basic assumptions that are required for the ensuing argument. If the chapters are read consecutively it will be evident where the overlapping material comes (generally near the beginning of a chapter), where it may be skipped or used as a reminder of the assumptions.

The common thread running through the chapters is that macroeconomic policy needs to be considered as a framework of several dimensions. In the earlier chapters this consists in setting out the implications of the different effects on macroeconomic objectives of

---

* Written for this volume.

alternative combinations of monetary policy with government outlays, on the one hand, and taxation on the other. *A priori* arguments in Chapter 2 are followed by two chapters including different sorts of empirical support for the basic idea (Chapters 3 and 4). This approach contrasts with the widespread practice of considering only the dichotomy of monetary and fiscal policy (or, still worse, referring to 'monetary-and-fiscal policy' as if it were a single instrument). Simulations with large macroeconomic models for different countries are drawn upon to throw light on the effects of different policy measures upon inflation and the balance of payments for a given effect on output or employment. Subsequent chapters draw on the same models, and some others, for evidence of the effects of different fiscal measures on various macro objectives for the same effect on the budget balance.

In Chapters 5–9, the emphasis is on the need to disaggregate fiscal policy into different types of taxation and different types of government outlay. This illustrates that the widespread practice of using changes in the budget surplus or deficit (on some chosen definition) as if it were a useful indicator of the setting and the directions of effects of changes in fiscal policy is open to serious deficiencies. It is, indeed, likely to lead to misguided policies.

The chapter on the relevance of deregulation of the financial system for macroeconomic policy (Chapter 11) has a bearing on the selection of monetary policy compared with fiscal instruments.

The final chapter (Chapter 12) which is new, brings the story up to date in that it includes the application of macroeconomic policy discussion to situations where inflation may be low, zero or even negative. For some countries and in some years this is likely to be true in future. For one important country, Japan, as well as South Korea, and probably for some other countries, it appears to be true at the time of writing. 'Negative inflation' in the sense of falls in the prices of commodities and producer goods, and in the average prices of internationally traded goods appears already to be occurring at the time of writing. It is therefore important to consider how the approach to macroeconomic policy requires to be modified to cover this new situation.

It is also somewhat different from the situation prevailing in the 1930s. For – in contrast to the 1930s – unemployment is not likely to become again such a predominant objective that all consideration of the objective of holding down inflation can be put to one side. Moreover, the experience of inflation over so many years since the 1930s means that people's expectations about inflation are likely to differ greatly from what they were in the 1930s. Finally, the combination of low inflation with low unemployment (as in the USA in 1997–9) is new; and appropriate policies for dealing with it require to be formulated.

By way of some light relief there is an Appendix (pp. 192–6) with some Gilbertian parodies for economists – which have, nevertheless, an underlying serious intent.

2
Principles of Macroeconomic Policy in a Stagflationary World (1981)*

The basic approach to the discussion of macroeconomic policy that continues to be generally applied is that which was useful in the conditions that prevailed in the thirty years or so from the late 1930s to the late 1960s. During those years the principal macroeconomic problem at any given time was *either* the removal of excess demand *or* the reduction of unemployment. For the past decade or so, however, the problem of the world economy has generally been to reduce *both* inflation *and* unemployment. Yet we continue to try to apply models that are inherently unable to deal with that combination of problems, as they essentially lack one of the dimensions of the dual problem that we are facing. Consequently, policy makers relying on these models often become preoccupied with stopping inflation, which leads them to concentrate their measures disproportionately upon that objective, so that they thereby make unemployment worse. Alternatively, they aim their policy measures solely or primarily at reducing unemployment, and so are likely to make inflation worse.

In any case, the determination to 'reduce inflation (or unemployment) first' assumes a conflict between these two objectives that does not necessarily exist. Indeed, *combinations* of measures exist in principle that can deal with both problems at once.

In contrast to the currently prevailing approaches, the right question to ask in a situation of stagflation is: 'What *combination* of measures will do most to stop stagflation?' In other words, 'What combination of measures will minimise the upward pressure on the price level at any given level of unemployment?' Or 'What measures will minimise the

---

* Originally presented as a paper to Tenth Conference of Economists, La Trobe University, Melbourne (1981).

amount of unemployment with any given upward pressure on the price level?' Moreover, the same questions need to be asked whenever inflation is considered to be excessive, even if the economy is thought to be (in some sense) at 'full employment', or if it is thought to be recovering as rapidly as physically possible. For the most appropriate combination of macro measures will then be one that minimises the upward pressure on prices resulting from bottlenecks in the course of recovery.

Most of the present chapter will be directed to discussing this question. But it seems worth while first to set out the assumptions upon which something like the currently prevailing macroeconomic policies of the Western world would be justified, in order to contrast them with the assumptions on which the argument of the present chapter is based.

If it were true that the only way to check inflation were to tolerate (at least, temporarily) a higher level of unemployment than would otherwise have been chosen, one necessary precondition for something like the present policies would then be fulfilled. But one would still have to adduce good reason to believe that the social and economic costs of the high unemployment and lost output were less than those of tolerating the inflation. Moreover, the longer the high unemployment is tolerated in the hope of thereby achieving a given reduction in inflation, and the less convincing the evidence that it is having the desired result, the more persuasive would need to be the reasons to believe that there is no alternative. If the necessary price of reducing inflation is not merely a temporary rise in unemployment, but a more lasting one (as seems to be an increasingly likely outcome of present policies), the social costs of present policies would then obviously become much greater by comparison with any alternative that does not operate through high unemployment.

Yet very few people seem to be asking the obvious question about what combination of measures will do most to stop stagflation (or to minimise inflation at any given level of activity). The almost unconscious assumption seems to have grown up that all combinations of macroeconomic measures that change the level of employment (or unemployment), or aggregate demand, or (in some analyses) the quantity of money, by a given amount will have the same effect on the price level. But it is difficult to see why that proposition should have come to be implicitly accepted in most macroeconomic analysis. For, as we shall see, a number of reasons can be given for believing that alternative measures for changing employment (or aggregate demand, or the quantity of money) by a given amount are likely to have different effects on the price level over the relevant period.

One form in which one often finds this (probably unconscious) assumption that all forms of stimulus are equally inflationary is when someone analyses the effects of an easing of monetary policy, or of a rise in certain forms of government spending, and comes up with the conclusion that in the long run, this will merely raise prices. This then leads them to assume that tax cuts will have the same effect – and that any form of stimulus will then raise prices rather than output. Yet it would be necessary to argue that all forms of stimulus raised the price level *to the same extent* (for a given rise in employment) before one could conclude that no reduction in unemployment was possible by *any* package of measures. For, otherwise, a price increase can always be avoided by moving one measure in a contractionary direction to an appropriate extent while moving in an expansionary direction another measure that does not increase prices as much (for a given real stimulus).

The tragedy of the last decade or so (particularly) has been that governments have almost invariably been over-eager to provide a stimulus by easing monetary policy or by raising types of government spending that do little or nothing to hold down costs – rather than by cutting tax rates. People have consequently jumped to the quite unjustified conclusion that it is no longer possible to reduce unemployment by *any* macroeconomic measure.

In the conditions of mass unemployment in the 1930s, there was naturally no point in considering the different effects on prices of alternative forms of stimulus, as there was no inflation to worry about. Some of the forms of stimulus that have thus come to be popularly described as 'Keynesian' – easy money and high government spending – have had mainly inflationary effects in the conditions of the 1970s. But the wrong conclusion has been drawn that all of the measures that could properly be called 'Keynesian' (which ought to include tax cuts) could be expected to have the same inflationary effect.

Choosing the right combination of measures

In a situation of stagflation it *may* be true that *any single measure* that reduces unemployment will tend to make inflation worse – though when there is widespread underutilisation of resources this is not necessarily true. But even if every form of macro stimulus exerted some upward pressure on prices, provided that there is even one form of stimulus to employment that does not have as much upward effect on prices as the others, this means that there is a combination of measures available that can reduce unemployment without upward pressure on the price level.

If instrument A has less upward effect on the price level than instrument B (for a given effect in reducing unemployment), this means that if instrument A is set in a more expansionary direction and instrument B in a correspondingly more contractionary direction, the same level of employment can be established with a downward effect on the price level. By extension, therefore, a non-inflationary stimulus can therefore be given to employment by an appropriately greater movement of instrument A in an expansionary direction, coupled with an appropriately less contractionary setting of instrument B than if the aim was to hold employment constant.

If non-inflationary (and, indeed, price-reducing) combinations of measures to provide a stimulus are consequently available, it clearly becomes indefensible to tolerate high unemployment, even temporarily (still less, permanently), in the hope of slowing down the rise in prices over a given period. Furthermore, if reductions in unemployment can be achieved in ways that do not raise prices, such stimuli do not carry the seeds of their own reversal. This is in contrast to what is often expected to occur in many models, through real balance effects, and through upward pressure on money wage rates as they react to rising prices as an indirect result of a monetary stimulus.

Government spending and the policy mix

There is no necessary presumption that a relatively high level of government spending will exert more upward pressure on the price level (at any given level of employment) than a mix with a lower level of government spending. For there are many different forms of government spending on goods and services, having widely varying effects; so that the only safe generalisation about government spending is that any generalisation about government spending is likely to be at least partly wrong. When a relatively large proportion of the country's output is devoted to the production by the government of goods and services that are not sold on the market, there will consequently be a correspondingly lower output of those goods and services that normally figure in the consumer price index. Over a period when those forms of government outlay rise as a ratio of total output, measured rates of inflation, and probably also money wage demands, will consequently be higher than they would otherwise have been.

One may argue that most government spending on goods and services is of this type. But some forms of government expenditure help to hold down costs of production more efficiently and effectively than alternative private uses of the resources could be expected to do. Examples are: essential defence and police, many forms of outlay on transportation, and some services that might be provided by the market (but usually are not), such as sewerage. Certainly, governments that try to increase, or to reduce, the size of the public sector *as an aim in itself* are highly unlikely to make a useful contribution to reducing stagflation.

Let us therefore assume that the levels of each of the forms of government outlay are being determined on an objective assessment of their relative costs and benefits. At any given level of activity there will then be various combinations of tax rates and monetary policy (in effect, the level of government borrowing from the non-bank public) with which the desired level of activity in the private sector can be brought about. We are interested in finding the combination of these instruments that will exert the least possible upward pressure on the price level.

Ways in which tax cuts *plus* bond sales can reduce stagflation

There are three broad channels through which tax cuts accompanied by an appropriate sale of bonds to the non-bank public can exert downward pressure on prices at any given level of employment.

In the first place, all nominal magnitudes are likely to be reduced under this mix by the relatively higher real interest rates after tax, coupled with the downward effects of tax cuts on wages and prices (at any given level of employment) – even without any change in the shares of profits or wages, or in productivity.

In the second place, high tax rates and low or negative real post-tax interest rates worsen the allocation of resources, and so reduce productivity; so that, for this reason also, tax cuts *plus* bond sales exert downward pressure on prices, at any given level of activity, and with any given wage and profit shares.

In the third place, tax cuts reduce real wage costs without reducing real post-tax wage incomes at any given level of activity, and this may facilitate a higher level of activity at any given level of prices and money wage rates. This is the case examined by Corden (1981) and Corden and Dixon (1980, reprinted in Corden, 1997), which is discussed in Chapter 11 in this volume.

Cost-increasing effects of high tax rates

One possible channel through which high tax rates may raise costs is that high marginal income tax rates may reduce incentives. (This possible effect is often stressed by politicians, especially in the USA and Britain.) We do not, however, have convincing evidence that any adverse effects of high tax rates on incentives generally exceed the ('income') effects of making people work harder when their disposable incomes are kept relatively low by high taxes.

Placing these possible disincentive effects of high tax rates on one side, however (as being dubious), there are other, more direct, cost-increasing effects of high tax rates. One of them is that high tax rates become (partly or wholly) built into the cost structure if the taxes are imposed on inputs of businesses or on payrolls, especially if prices are determined even partly on a cost-plus, 'mark-up', basis. Company taxes are also likely to become built into the cost structure – to some greater or smaller extent.

One of the most important ways in which high tax rates raise costs is through the various adverse effects they have on the allocation of resources. These include the social waste of all the effort devoted to administering them, paying them, trying to evade and avoid them and trying to close loopholes in the law relating to them. All this effort by many able people could otherwise have been devoted to raising the output of goods and services of inherent value to the consumer, and thereby holding down the price level. The slowing down of the rate of productivity increase throughout the OECD world in the 1970s may well be related in part to the generally high and rising tax rates.

Money wage rates and tax rates

If relatively high tax rates have any upward effect on money wage *demands* tax rates need to be cut as part of a package to stop stagflation. For if money wage demands are stimulated by relatively high tax rates, this means that the upward pressure on prices will be increased, at any given level of unemployment, by a mix with relatively high tax rates. Even if high tax rates did not give rise to higher wage demands, whenever company taxes are high a correspondingly greater proportion of any given wage increase is tax-deductible; and this presumably makes employers more likely to give way to wage demands than when company tax rates are correspondingly lower. A mix with low real post-tax interest rates (and high taxes) is therefore likely to give rise to rapid money wage increases. It is thus not surprising that the 1970s was a period of rapid increases in money wage rates (even with unemployment relatively high), in view of the high tax rates and low real post-tax interest rates that have prevailed during the past decade or so. (The possible effects on money wages are discussed in Chapter 11.)

Supply-side economics, American version

The so-called 'supply-side' effects that have been emphasised in recent discussions in the USA are among the most contentious arguments that may be raised for reducing tax rates. For they depend partly on the view that tax cuts increase the incentive to work harder and more effectively – which is debatable. They seem also to espouse the view that inequality of post-tax incomes will raise the propensity to save and make possible a higher ratio of productive investment to total output. Yet all the steps in that argument are also suspect.

The arguments for tax cuts upon which the policy proposals of this chapter are based do not rely on any such doubtful arguments. The policy prescriptions argued here are justified provided that taxes have some unfavourable effects on productivity (compared with higher real post-tax interest rates). Alternatively, they are also justified if taxes have some upward effect on money wage demands or on the readiness of employers to accede to wage demands (again, as compared with correspondingly higher real post-tax interest rates); or that high tax rates become built into the cost structure in a way (or to an extent) that is not true of monetary measures having the same effect in restraining the level of effective demand.

The mix and the level of activity

If a tax cut has little or no effect in stimulating the level of real demand, the cost-reducing effect of the tax cut become correspondingly more important. For in that case a tax cut could have little or no price-increasing effect. If it were true that tax cuts actually *increased* unemployment one ought therefore to cut tax rates hard in a situation of stagflation, until inflation disappeared – and give any desired stimulus by means of an easier monetary policy. Indeed, if tax cuts alone actually increased unemployment one could have lower tax rates and easier monetary policy or higher government spending and yet also have less unemployment and less inflation – obviously a politician's dream.

In the real world, however, where tax cuts certainly stimulate economic activity, lower tax rates would have to be accompanied by a lower ratio of government expenditure to total income or by a tighter monetary policy than would be appropriate at any given level of employment if tax rates were higher. But the adoption of this less inflationary mix, of lower tax rates and tighter monetary policy, would enable the economy to be operated with lower unemployment – or to avoid the temporarily high unemployment that policy makers often seem to believe to be necessary in order to check inflation. The overall setting of macroeconomic policy could and should therefore then be made more expansionary than if the more inflationary mix of higher tax rates (and easier monetary policy or higher government spending) had been adopted.

Real post-tax interest rates and the price level

The adoption of a mix with relatively low real post-tax interest rates on financial assets is likely to exert more upward effect on the price level (at any given level of employment) than a mix with higher real post-tax interest rates. An important reason for this is that low real returns on financial assets encourage people to try to hold more of their wealth in certain types of real assets – most obviously, real estate and gold bars – which are in inelastic supply.[1] If monetarists had spelt out this channel through which a mix with a relatively rapid expansion of the quantity of money can operate on the price level, their arguments would have carried more conviction. Moreover, the monetarist approach should not then have led policy makers to try to curb the rise in the quantity of money by higher tax rates. For if the taxes are being levied on interest income, that clearly makes the problem worse; and only if the reduction in the rise in the stock of money is achieved in a way that *raises* the real post-tax return on financial assets will this effect be reversed. It is, therefore, not appropriate simply to try to check the rise in the quantity of money. It is important to do so by reversing the policies that have been holding down real post-tax interest rates, and which have thus been a cause of the problem. For to choke off the rise in the quantity of money mainly by high taxes will simply make stagflation worse, as it has done during the later 1970s and early 1980s.

Pre-tax and post-tax interest rates

In public discussion the concept of real interest rates that is generally used is simply to adjust a nominal interest rate by some approximation to the prevailing (or expected) rate of inflation. But this is misleading and liable to lead to misguided policies when rates of inflation are high, and when taxes are levied on nominal interest, while nominal interest payments are tax-deductible – as they almost invariably are for businesses, and in some countries (such as the USA) also for consumers.

Real interest rates are often described as being 'high' simply because nominal *pre-tax* rates are well above the prevailing interest rates at the sort of levels that prevailed in the mid-1960s and earlier. When discussing these matters it is therefore important to make some reasonable allowance for tax rates – if only by some such crude approximation as assuming an average income tax and company tax rate of, say, a third or 40 per cent.

For example, if the pre-tax nominal rate of interest is 15 per cent, and the earner of this interest to being taxed at the rate of 40 per cent (or if a business borrowing at that interest rate in being taxed at a similar company tax rate) the *post-tax* nominal rate is only 9 per cent. With inflation rates in double digits this is clearly a negative real post-tax rate. It is thus of the utmost importance for those discussing policy to think and speak in terms of *real post-tax* rates in order to remove the psychological obstacle to raising real rates to the point at which they would do as much to check inflation as they were (for example) in the mid-1960s. (But merely making real post-tax interest rates positive will not necessarily be sufficient to solve the problem. They must also be reasonably attractive to lenders.)

Interest rates, tax rates and inflation

As the world reached higher rates of inflation in the 1970s this reduced real post-tax rates of interest (at each pre-tax real rate of interest).[2] Moreover, as tax rates rise, the pre-tax rate of interest must also rise *faster* than the rate of tax (at any given rate of inflation) in order to maintain any given real post-tax rate of interest. During the 1970s income tax (and in some countries also company tax) rates were generally rising. Indeed, high rates of inflation were themselves one factor tending to raise the effective level of tax rates, as the proportion of the population in higher tax brackets increased.

Yet over the past decade or so policy makers (and others) have failed to appreciate these points and their importance. There have also been other political obstacles to letting nominal pre-tax interest rates even keep up with the rate of inflation. All these factors have contributed to keeping real post-tax rates of interest down to levels that placed upward pressure on the price level (compared with the settings of monetary policy that had prevailed up to about the mid-1960s, or even the early 1970s).

The result was therefore a vicious circle: the higher the rate of inflation, the greater the risk of real post-tax interest rates being held down to low or negative levels. At the same time, each failure to ensure that real post-tax interest rates were at least maintained made the upward pressure on prices greater. The temptation to resort to tolerating high unemployment (in the hope of thereby checking inflation) was therefore also correspondingly greater.

Budget fetishes

The tendency to think of some figure for the budget deficit or surplus (or for the 'Public Sector Borrowing Requirement') as a target in its own right has become a serious obstacle to rational thought about macroeconomic policy making. Once one accepts such targets as aims of policy it becomes virtually impossible (apart from the merest chance) also to achieve the targets of full employment and of minimising inflation. There is, in any case, no logical basis for picking out of the air particular figures for the budget surplus or deficit, and especially not for making a target of the actual budget outcome rather than a 'cyclically adjusted' (or 'high employment') deficit or surplus. For to do so risks the adoption of policies that make a recession worse than it would otherwise have been. In any case, a given budget deficit or surplus can be achieved with many different combinations of revenue and outlay, some of which will reduce stagflation, whereas others will make it worse.

Moreover, the real level of budget deficits has been much smaller, and the level of real cyclically adjusted budget surpluses larger, than the nominal magnitudes that have been most often referred to in recent years. For the high rates of inflation have brought about a considerable reduction in the real value of the outstanding national debt – in effect a unilateral writing off of part of the debt, leading to a fall in the real value of the bonds held by the public.[3] This unrecorded dissaving by bond holders has led to a sharp rise in their (measured) propensity to save, as bond holders have tried to offset the downward effect on their real wealth of this (unrecorded) dissaving. It is true that this need not necessarily have resulted in reductions in the level of activity. But, if that was to be avoided, governments would have had to react symmetrically to the consequent reduction in their real liabilities by increasing their dissaving (or by reducing their net saving) – that is, by running larger (cyclically adjusted) deficits than they would otherwise have chosen.

Unfortunately, governments (and others) have generally been preoccupied with nominal budget deficits, which have often been swollen by the high level of nominal interest payments (even though these were often merely partial compensation for the fall in the real value of the bonds outstanding). This has even impelled governments to try to *reduce* their budget deficits. One should therefore always make due allowance for the real changes in net government borrowing – if one takes any notice at all of budget deficits and surpluses. But it is equally important to ensure that this leads to governments financing the budget deficit by offering appropriate amounts of the sort of interest-bearing obligations that the public wishes to hold, rather than by an excessive creation of money (in an effort to hold down rates of interest).

Part of the interest payments – sometimes all of them – made by a government in a period of inflation is thus not really a current budgetary outlay at all, but merely compensation for the decline in the real value of the financial assets on which they are being earned. In effect, therefore, this part of the interest payments is really a capital payment that merely holds the government's real obligations constant. So far as the rate of interest being paid is equal to the prevailing rate of inflation, these payments should not, therefore, be interpreted as adding to the real Public Sector Borrowing Requirement. For in real terms they are merely preventing, or alleviating, a fall in the real value of the national debt. If those interest payments that offset the fall in the real value of the debt resulting from inflation were equal to the nominal budget deficit, the real budget deficit would be zero.

Is government borrowing useless or even harmful?

Cuts in tax rates are likely to reduce tax revenue at any given level of employment unless favourable productivity effects are very large and the reduction in avoidance and evasion very great. But if the economy is being operated at a higher level of employment (as a consequence of using a more appropriate mix, instead of resorting to high unemployment in order to hold down inflation) total tax revenue might still rise. So far as a tax cut led to a higher level of government borrowing, however, the implications of this have to be considered.

Some extreme monetarists have suggested (or asserted) that 'government borrowing is the same as taxation'. It is difficult to see the rationale for such statements, or to find persuasive arguments to support them. But their view seems to be that if a government borrows now it will have to raise by taxes as much in future as it avoids raising by taxes now. Even if this were true, however, the effects are clearly not the same *in each period*. The future effects (as well as those in the present) of borrowing rather than raising taxes now will clearly be different from those of taxing now rather than undertaking the borrowing in question.

But only if there were no effects on total real output or economic welfare in the present and near future taken together (as a result of borrowing rather than taxing), would it be logical to start from the assumption that the choice between borrowing and taxation in the present merely redistributes the taxes over time. The essence of our present problem, however, is that concern about inflation in the present and near future is inhibiting governments from reducing taxes enough to reduce unemployment. This may be true even though they are also failing to borrow from the non-bank public on a scale that would keep real post-tax interest rates high enough to play the role that they could play in checking inflation.

Perhaps the monetarist counter-argument on this point is that tax cuts financed by bond sales now will not stimulate total demand. For they appear to assume that people will take (full) account of the extra taxes they may expect to have to pay in future. But the present writer (for one) would have to object that he has never met *anyone* who took *any* account in their spending decisions of the extent to which they felt responsible for those liabilities represented by the national debt. Yet, if no stimulus were to result from the tax cut, it would be necessary for *everyone* to take *full* account of any possible extra taxation in future associated with a given rise in the debt as tax rates were cut now.

Let us, however, for the sake of argument, grant this extraordinary argument that tax cuts offset by bond sales would exert no net stimulus. Such a policy could then have no demand-inflationary effect, so that it could (and should) be freely used for its cost-reducing effects – provided one concedes that tax cuts have some effect in the direction of reducing costs, or that higher real post-tax interest rates operate in that direction.

But we have still to consider whether tax cuts now will in fact lead to higher taxes in future, with consequent cost-increasing effects at that future time; and, if so, should this be an argument against adopting such a mix – in preference to tolerating high unemployment? If real output can consequently be higher now and in future, there will consequently be extra output of goods and services in future (as a result of the consequently larger stock of human and material capital). Part of any extra demand resulting from higher interest payments can thus be met without the need for tax increases. But even if tax rates are consequently higher in future *than they would otherwise have been*, this does not necessarily mean that they will at that future time be higher *than they are now*. Nor does it mean that even the present tax rates if they were imposed in future would cause as much cost inflation in future (when real incomes will presumably be higher than they are now). Nor can we assume that the main macro problem of posterity will be cost inflation at less than full employment. (Indeed, there is some presumption that the problem will be different in future: for the nature of the main macro problems has obviously changed dramatically and unexpectedly from decade to decade between the 1930s, the 1940s, the 1950s and 1960s, and then the 1970s and early 1980s.)[4]

The safest principle is to take the view that the best thing we can do for posterity is to stop stagflation. Even if that were not true, and if solving the problem would somehow inflict as much cost on posterity as it would bring benefit to us, we might still be reluctant to deny ourselves the benefits of adopting the policy that is best for us. ('What has posterity done for me that I should do so much for posterity?') But, in any event, we can be reasonably sure that posterity will also benefit if we solve the problem of stagflation.

Macroeconomic policy and resource allocation policy

Objection is sometimes made to the use of the sort of less inflationary mix that has been suggested above on the grounds that it might have some (usually unspecified) adverse effects on the allocation of resources.[5]

But such fears are dangerously wide of the mark. For the mix that does most to utilise resources to good effect, and so to maximise productivity at any given level of employment, is therefore likely to be the sort of mix that will do most to hold down the price level at any given level of activity. By contrast, the widely prevailing policies of tolerating high unemployment in the hope of thereby restraining inflation inevitably foster protectionism and so reduce productivity, and thus increase the price level; and the political obstacles to reducing excessive protection are obviously much greater when the general level of unemployment is high.

In any event, even if the mix that did most to stop stagflation was likely to have adverse resource allocation effects, this would not constitute a valid argument against adopting such macroeconomic policies. For the adverse resource allocation effects on economic welfare would not necessarily exceed the favourable effects of the adoption of the most appropriate macroeconomic policies.

One suspects that the main reason why some economists have reservations about such policies (of reducing tax rates and raising real post-tax interest rates) is that they have absorbed too uncritically over-simple macroeconomic models. In these models, low tax rates are generally supposed to stimulate consumption, and relatively high interest rates hold down something called 'investment'.

But in these models, 'investment' is – in effect – defined to mean simply 'those forms of spending that are sensitive to the rate of interest'. It is true that investment in additional productive capacity may reasonably be assumed to be among these categories of outlay. But other forms of outlay – most notably those on dwellings (especially when mortgage interest is not tax-deductible) and probably also those on consumer durables such as motor vehicles – are at least as likely to be sensitive to changes in the rate of interest as are outlays on fixed capital equipment. There is probably no presumption that a shift of mix towards one with relatively high (or at least positive) real post-tax interest rates will do more to restrain productive investment than to restrain dwelling construction and investment in consumer durables. Indeed, a decision to keep real rates of interest up may be expected to hold down both the volume, and still more the value, of outlays on new building construction (which is one of the most widespread alternatives to holding wealth in financial assets bearing interest). In any event, the tax cuts can be largely in forms that stimulate productive investment if this is thought desirable.

But suppose that the choice of a mix with rather higher real post-tax interest rates tends to reduce the ratio of productive investment, of types that we want to encourage, to total output. The purpose of adopting this less inflationary mix is to enable us to avoid tolerating higher unemployment than we would otherwise have chosen (in the hope of thereby checking inflation). If the adoption of the mix with higher real interest rates and lower tax rates makes it possible to avoid this waste of potential output it means that economic activity will be higher; and this is likely to be the most effective way of encouraging productive investment. The *absolute level* of investment is therefore likely to be higher with the mix that leads to less inflation and higher output – even if the *ratio* of investment to total output at a given (lower) level of activity might have been higher under the alternative policy. Furthermore, the tax cuts and the improvement in the working of the capital market (resulting from a return to a pattern of real post-tax interest rates that was a better reflection of the underlying real factors, especially the real social return on investment), should raise productivity. Productivity may then be higher at each level of employment, even if the ratio of investment to output were lower, provided that there were sufficiently favourable productivity effects

Interaction of macro policy and resource allocation policies

The relationship between macroeconomic policy and resource allocation policies is two-way. On the one hand, defective macro policies leading to unnecessarily high unemployment foster protectionism. But, on the other hand, unwise resource allocation policies tend to raise the price level at any given level of unemployment, and thus make governments more reluctant to adopt policies that will reduce unemployment, for fear that such a reduction may further increase the upward pressure on the price level.

At present virtually every government is misapplying both its macro policies and its resource allocation policies. For protectionist policies are being used to support many less economic industries, and so increasing the upward pressure on the price level by holding down productivity; while high unemployment is being tolerated, sometimes on the argument that this will help to squeeze resources out of uneconomic firms and industries.

What is in fact required, however, is exactly the opposite orientation of these two areas of policy. Macroeconomic policy should be directed towards minimising unemployment (by means of a mix of measures that does not exert upward pressure on prices), which will ensure that those people released from uneconomic industries where protection is reduced can readily find jobs elsewhere. At the same time, resource allocation policy should be directed towards exerting downward pressure on the least economic industries by reducing the various forms of assistance to them as quickly as possible – thus helping to increase productivity and reduce prices.

But either of these policies without the other is of doubtful value, and is, in any event, likely to be impracticable. It is therefore desirable that the recent orientation of the objectives of each of these two broad groups of policies should be reversed. In that case, the current interaction between them, which is at present setting up a vicious circle, could be replaced by a virtuous circle, in which the two groups of policies would facilitate and reinforce each other.

Incidentally, this proposition is quite independent of the arguments in the rest of this chapter – to the effect that different macroeconomic instruments have different effects on prices for a given effect on employment.

Open economy aspects

Those open economy aspects that operate through the current account may be inferred directly from what has been said about the closed economy. Mixes with relatively low tax rates and relatively high post-tax real interest rates make for a stronger current account (by holding down prices), and to that extent a stronger exchange rate, than does the opposite mix. (With a fixed exchange rate, a mix with low taxes and high real interest rates tends to strengthen the current account balance.) The exchange rate should be thought of as one of the channels through which an appropriate mix has its effects. But the exchange rate should not be thought of as an instrument in itself.[6]

But, in addition, there are effects of the policy mix that operate through the capital account. A mix with relatively high post-tax real interest rates attracts more capital from other countries. Such a mix strengthens the exchange rate (and to that extent reduces inflation) while the additional capital inflow is occurring. But in the longer run the consequently greater outflow of interest and dividends, and probably also of capital repayments, will operate in the opposite direction.

If the less inflationary mix is one with relatively lower tax rates, some would argue that if this involves a consequently greater budget deficit (at any given level of employment) such a policy might scare away some overseas capital. It is possible that some overseas investors might react in that manner. But unless this short-run effect exceeded the favourable short-run effects on capital inflow resulting from the rise in real post-tax interest rates, the net effect on the capital account (and so on the exchange rate) would still be favourable.

But whatever the net effect on capital inflow of the adoption of a mix with higher real post-tax interest rates, the net effect on the price level (if account is taken also of the closed economy considerations outlined above) seems certain to be downward, on any reasonable assumptions about its effects on the exchange rate. The greater the favourable effect on capital inflow and the upward effect on the exchange rate, the greater the immediate downward effect on inflation (through this channel) at any given level of activity. The greater, then, will be the net stimulus that can be applied to the economy, if employment would otherwise have been held down temporarily as a result of fears about inflation. But the government of a country operating such a policy must be ready and eager to cut tax rates hard enough and fast enough (as the least inflationary form of stimulus) to offset any downward effect on activity that would otherwise result from the appreciation.

The basic principles and recent experience

The *a priori* arguments outlined above suggest that a combination of high tax rates and low or negative real post-tax interest rates will exert more upward (or less downward) pressure on the price level at any given level of employment than would the opposite setting. For a shift towards a mix with lower tax rates and higher real returns on financial assets would have at least a once-for-all downward effect on the rise in the price level. It will thus have an effect such as governments are at present trying to achieve by tolerating temporarily high levels of unemployment. In either case – with the change of mix, as with the alternative of temporarily high unemployment – one can reasonably hope to achieve some more lasting effect on the observed rate of inflation. In addition, the use of a more appropriate mix, instead of under-utilisation of capacity, will leave the country at the end of the period in question with a higher stock of human and material capital, and thus a higher level of productivity. This will in itself help to reduce the price level in future.

The *a priori* arguments are consistent with the apparent effects of rising tax rates and lower real interest rates during the past decade of faster inflation and rising unemployment. These provide compelling evidence that something is badly wrong with the macroeconomic policy being followed and with the models on which the policy is presumably based. There has been a clear deterioration in the macroeconomic situation in the OECD over the past half-decade, unemployment having risen, and inflation having been higher, in 1980s than the average of the years 1974–6.

Tables 2.1 and 2.2 illustrate the way in which tax rates have risen and real interest rates fallen in the OECD countries over the period between the mid-1960s and the beginning of the 1980s – a period over which unemployment rates and inflation rates have increased dramatically. The indicator of tax rates shown in Table 2.1, namely, the ratio of government revenue to Gross Domestic Product (GDP), under-states the rise in tax rates in the sense that it would be desirable to quantify in support of the analysis given above. For part of the cost-increasing effect of high tax rates is the real social costs of avoidance and evasion. Obviously, these do not show up in the figures for the ratio of government receipts to GDP. Unless estimates of the extent of avoidance and

Table 2.1 Tax revenue as a ratio of GDP in OECD countries, 1965–80

1965	1966	1967	1968	1969	1970	1971	1972	1973	1974	1975	1976	1977	1978	1979	1980
27	28	29	29	30	31	31	31	32	33	33	34	35	34	35	35

Source: OECD, *Government Revenue in OECD Countries* (various years).

evasion in the OECD countries can be made, it is unlikely that this important element in the argument could be illustrated statistically. It is, at any rate, clear that tax rates, in the broadest sense, have risen consistently over the period even on the basis of this measure of the ratio of actual tax paid to GDP.

A statistical illustration of the fall in real interest rates is given in Table 2.2, where long-term government bond rates are used as an indicator. This is chosen as an indicator largely because an official (though unpublished) OECD estimate of the weighted average bond rate for the seven major OECD countries is available, as well as a weighted average for the rate of inflation, as measured by the consumer price indexes, in the same group of countries. Two average tax rates are used in Table 2.2 to estimate a real post-tax return on bonds; and it is clear how markedly this return fell over that period of increasing macroeconomic misery. But this measure under-states the fall in real post-tax interest rates, in that it assumes that constant tax rates were levied on nominal interest receipts over the period, whereas income-tax rates, and effective company tax rates, have in fact risen markedly.

It is apparent that the movement in tax rates and in real post-tax interest rates over the period is consistent with the *a priori* arguments given above, to the effect that a tendency towards mixes with high tax rates and low real post-tax interest rates makes stagflation worse.

If one aim of a government is to restrain the growth of the stock of money (an aim that was adopted widely during the 1970s), therefore, it is important that it should *not* be brought about mainly by increases in tax rates. For the greater the extent to which a given reduction in the stock of money is achieved by higher taxation, the greater will be the downward pressure on real demand, and so on employment. On the other hand, the more the restraint in monetary growth is achieved by bond sales, the less will be the downward effect on activity for a given reduction in the stock of money.

The onus of proof is thus clearly on those who are prepared to defend macroeconomic policy mixes such as those of recent years to provide some grounds for believing that the clear tendency towards such mixes has alleviated the problem. The presumption must clearly be that that such mixes have at least made the problem worse, and may have been largely responsible for it.

Why, then, have governments persisted in these misguided policies, and tried to stop the inflation merely, or mainly, by tolerating a level of unemployment that would have been unthinkably high in earlier post-war decades?

Table 2.2 Estimated real long-term bond rate, seven major OECD countries, 1965–80

	1965	1966	1967	1968	1969	1970	1971	1972	1973	1974	1975	1976	1977	1978	1979	1980
Pre-tax	3	3	3	2	3	2	2	2	0	−4	−2	1	0	2	0	−1
Post-tax:																
(Tax rate 40%)	0	0	1	0	0	−1	−1	0	−3	−7	−5	−3	−3	−2	−4	−5
(Tax rate 33%)	1	1	1	0	0	0	0	0	−3	−7	−4	−2	−2	−1	−3	−4

Source: Derived from (partly unpublished) OECD data, and rounded to nearest whole number. Figures for individual countries are published in OECD, *Historical Statistics* (various years).

Political obstacles to a saner mix

A major obstacle to a more appropriate mix is the political opposition to measures that seem likely to increase nominal interest rates. But on the effect of a tight monetary policy upon interest rates Robertson was, and Friedman is, much closer to the truth than the 'Keynesian' analysis.

> if Governments do not see fit to pay rather higher interest rates because capital is scarce they may easily find themselves having to pay much higher rates in a desperate attempt to keep pace with the foreseen depreciation of money. (Unpublished paper of D.H. Robertson, quoted in Wilson, 1980)

> Paradoxically, the monetary authority could assure low nominal rates of interest – but to do so it would have to start out in what seems like the opposite direction, by engaging in a deflationary monetary policy. Similarly, it could assure high nominal interest rates by engaging in an inflationary policy and accepting a temporary movement of interest rates in the opposite direction. (Friedman, 1968)

In short, both these writers are saying that efforts to hold down interest rates by monetary measures increase the rate of inflation, and with it, before long, nominal interest rates. The best way to hold down nominal interest rates (at any given level of employment) is thus to keep monetary policy tight and tax rates correspondingly low. In any case, provided that tax rates are cut at the same time as attractive (preferably indexed) bonds are offered to the public, there is no strong presumption about whether nominal interest rates will consequently rise or fall at any given level of employment. For the tax cuts increase disposable incomes, and to that extent the demand for bonds (at each rate of interest and each level of employment), and the cost-reducing effects of the tax cuts exert downward pressure on the price level (as do the bond sales) at any given level of employment, and so tend to reduce also the actual and expected rate of inflation in the period in question, and to that extent the nominal rate of interest. Part of the problem seems to be that those who assume that a shift to a mix with a tight monetary policy will raise interest rates are usually failing to take account of the effects of the simultaneous reduction in tax rates. The political gains in the long run may thus be reaped by a government that keeps monetary policy tight and taxes low.

Another obstacle is the opposition of treasuries everywhere to anything that looks likely to reduce revenue and to increase the national debt or the cost of financing it. The past decade has made life relatively easy for managers of the national debt, in the sense that they have been able to finance their borrowing at generally low, or even negative, real post-tax interest rates; while the inflation during the period has reduced the real value of the outstanding stock of bonds, and to that extent made people eager to rebuild the real value of their bond holdings. But the presumption that the national interest is served by high taxes and a low rate of increase in the real national debt (and a low rate of interest on it) is the very opposite to what is required if we are to stop stagflation.

Furthermore, there are political obstacles to reducing the rate of increase in those forms of government spending that do little or nothing directly to hold down inflation

The attitudes that constitute obstacles to the stopping of stagflation are not the monopoly of any particular political party. Parties of the right are more likely to favour the tax cuts and the tight monetary policy that would make possible less inflation, and they are likely to be tougher about restraining government spending, including some of the more inflationary forms of government outlay. But, unfortunately, they may be too inclined to hold down also those forms of government outlay (on better roads and railways, and in human capital, for example) that can help to raise productive efficiency. Moreover, they are likely to place excessive reliance on trying to solve the problem by high unemployment.

But a simple 'U-turn' is not likely to solve the problem. 'Wets' (in the UK sense of the term, apparently coined by Mrs Thatcher), and most parties on the left of politics are likely to make matters worse by adopting excessively easy monetary policies, over-rapid expansion of government spending, and perhaps also excessively high tax rates. One can thus see no presumption that one side of politics is more likely to adopt sensible macro policies than the other. But, by the same token, the way to power and success is open for policy makers on either side of politics if only they realise that the adoption of a more rational combination of measures of sufficiently lower taxes, and an adequate sale of bonds – of types that no longer exploit the lender – would enable them to stop both inflation and unemployment.

Conclusion

The principal implication of this analysis is that if governments wanting to stop stagflation try merely to apply the prescriptions of either 'Keynesians' or 'monetarists' they have a more or less equal chance of being either right or wrong – that is, of adopting policies that make the problem of stagflation either greater or less. For prescriptions that tell a government to exert a particular effect on aggregate demand or on the quantity of money (or on the budget balance) can be either helpful or the reverse according to the combination of instruments with which that intermediate objective is pursued. A policy that brings about a given rise in the nominal value of aggregate demand, or in the stock of money (or in the budget balance), can either increase or ameliorate stagflation according to the mix of measures with which it is achieved. Generally, the higher the level of taxes and the lower (or more negative) are real post-tax interest rates, the worse will be the stagflation; and every tax increase and every easing of monetary policy will make the problem of stagflation worse.

In other words, neither the typical 'Keynesian' nor the typical 'monetarist' approach contains enough dimensions to make it helpful for dealing with stagflation. After a decade or so of stagflation, macroeconomists should by now be focusing their attention on the most obviously relevant questions – rather than upon those that were appropriate to the problems of earlier decades. The principal questions that require answering, now and in the foreseeable future, are those that bear on the relative effects on prices (for a given effect on real output or employment) of each of the main alternative macroeconomic instruments. *A priori* arguments, and also recent experience, clearly imply that the relative effects on prices and on unemployment of each of the main instruments are likely to be in the directions suggested in this chapter. But only if there were compelling grounds for believing that the relative impacts on prices and on employment of each macroeconomic instrument were virtually identical with one another would there be any reasonable excuse for the wasteful and socially damaging policies that have been so widely pursued in most of the western world for the past half-decade or so.

Notes and references
1. I have found only one place in the literature where this effect seems to have been spelt out. (See Lindbeck, 1980, p. 17.) But even there insufficient stress is placed on the fact that the effect depends on the types of asset in question being in relatively inelastic supply, whereas this is the essential reason why the diversion of demand towards them raises the general level of real costs (at any given level of employment). Nor does Lindbeck mention the important fact that the essential reason why people try to hold more of these assets when the yield on financial assets is low is simply *because* the real assets in

question are in inelastic supply. This means that they hold their value well in the face of inflation and rising demand for them. See also Perkins (1981).
2. See Jump (1980) for a discussion of the basic theory of real post-tax interest rates.
3. See Taylor and Threadgold (1979), Siegel (1979), Jump (1980).
4. [Note added in 1998] They have changed again, very markedly, in the later 1990s; see Chapter 12 in this volume.
5. See, for example, Nevile (1980), p. 314.
6. The open economy aspects are discussed diagrammatically in Chapter 3, and more fully in Chapter 6 in this volume. See also Argy and Salop (1979); Bilson (1979); Perkins (1979a, 1979b, 1980, 1981); Jones and Perkins (1986); Argy (1981).

3
Macromiximisation (1980)*

The theory of macroeconomic policy that has dominated thought and policy making since the later 1930s is essentially one-dimensional in the closed economy (and two-dimensional in the open economy). That is to say, in a closed economy we have been taught to operate on the level of demand – with any or every macroeconomic instrument. When inflation is too rapid the aim has been to use (some or all of) our policy instruments to reduce demand; and when unemployment is too high we have learned to raise the level of demand.

This simplification of reality served reasonably well in the 1930s (when there was no appreciable inflation) and for a good deal of the post-war period up to about the late 1960s (when unemployment was never serious). But it has become unsatisfactory in a world when both unemployment and inflation are simultaneously too high ('stagflation').

If the only macroeconomic influence upon the price level (and so on inflation) were the level of employment, we would be confined of necessity to such a one-dimensional world: in other words, to choosing between inflation and unemployment, in deciding to use the single instrument of 'monetary-and-budgetary policy'. Governments and their advisers in most countries are still (apparently) framing their policies on the assumption that this is true. In the new situation of

---

* Originally published as 'Using the Macroeconomic Mix to Stop Stagflation', *Journal of Economic Studies*, 7 (1) (1980). The author acknowledges the constant stimulus of Ian McDonald to whom the diagrams are almost entirely due (though he may not agree with some of the uses to which I have put them, or with some of my modifications of them). John Black, Walter Eltis and anonymous referees made helpful comments on earlier drafts; as did participants in seminars at various British universities in 1979. None of these bears responsibility for remaining deficiencies.

stagflation this conventional approach therefore means that they concentrate their available instruments either on 'stopping inflation first' – which makes unemployment worse; or on reducing unemployment – which, if they are whole-hearted in pointing all their instruments in that direction, will make inflation worse.

But if two or more of the available macroeconomic instruments have different relative effects on the price level and on the level of unemployment (respectively) we are no longer confined to that one-dimensional world. For a wider range of policies is then available than that which orthodox macroeconomics has bequeathed to us. Our ability to deal with current problems will then depend on the readiness of policy makers, and of public opinion generally, to think in the slightly more complex framework of two (or more) dimensions; that is, of varying at least two instruments at a time, even in a closed economy.

The basic proposition underlying this view is that taxation, government spending and monetary policy can each reasonably be expected to have different relative effects on the level of employment (on the one hand) and the price level (on the other). If this view is accepted, therefore, they can be combined in appropriate ways in order to achieve a desired effect on the price level over a stated period, without accepting over that period a temporarily higher level of unemployment than would otherwise have been chosen.

The sort of approach to policy making in two (or more) dimensions that is being suggested here for a closed economy is familiar when dealing with the open economy. It has been widely employed in that context in discussions about the right choice of policy instruments for influencing both the level of activity and the balance of payments, but without differentiating between taxation and government spending.

The principles applied in the present analysis have much in common with these open economy approaches. But this analysis differs from them in two basic and essential respects. In the first place, (at least) two instruments with differential effects are normally needed to deal with stagflation in the closed economy; while three (or more) may be required in the open economy. Second, it will be stressed that the most marked contrast is not between monetary and fiscal policy, but between taxation and monetary policy, with government spending on goods and services being in less marked contrast with each of the other two in the relevant respects. In an open economy, this approach provides a superior alternative to devaluation for reducing an external deficit. For it largely operates not by raising the price level (in marked contrast to devaluation, import controls or high tariffs), but by holding it down.

In a stagflationary situation, if one combination of macroeconomic measures has a smaller upward (or a greater downward) effect on the price level at a given level of activity than some alternative, the former mix should be adopted. By changing the mix in this direction and also giving a net stimulus, it is also possible to increase output, exercise a downward pressure on the price level, and improve the current account of the balance of payments. It is therefore indefensible to accept a temporarily higher level of unemployment than would otherwise have been permitted merely in order to hold down the price level or to strengthen the current account of the balance of payments.

The effect of the switch upon prices may be once for all. If so it would be in that respect analogous to tolerating temporarily high unemployment with a view to bringing down the observed rate of inflation, and thus presumably the expected rate of inflation, and so the underlying rate of inflation over a longer period.

This chapter outlines the principal respects in which the choice of macroeconomic measures ought to be influenced by these considerations. It considers the relevance of some of the principal influences that determine the relative shift in the mix of measures that will be appropriate in particular situations. It also illustrates the argument diagrammatically. In these two latter respects it goes beyond earlier expositions (Perkins, 1979a/1980) by the present author of the same principles.

The aim of policy is assumed to be to stop stagflation. The guiding principle must be to keep in mind the dual objective of reducing unemployment without making inflation worse – and of changing more than one policy instrument in the proper directions so as to achieve this dual aim.

Closed economy

Let us first assume the level of government spending to be given. In other words, the suggestions made in this section do not have any inherent bias to left or right of the political spectrum. For a version of them could be found to satisfy either the proponents of a high level of government spending or those who prefer to keep it low. (But it is obviously helpful to base such decisions about the form and level of government spending on a careful comparison of alternatives, rather than on political prejudice.)

On what principles should we decide the most appropriate combination of tax rates (total taxes in relation to GDP) and of monetary policy to achieve a desired downward effect on the price-level at a given level of activity?

A given level of activity can be achieved (with a fixed level of government spending) either with high taxes and an easy monetary policy ('low bond sales'), or with relatively lower levels of taxation and a correspondingly tighter monetary policy ('higher bond sales') – provided that we accept the normal assumption that tax increases tend to hold down private expenditure, and that tighter monetary policies also operate in the same direction. We can therefore select any one of a number of combinations of tax rates and bond sales to achieve the desired level of employment. On these assumptions we must increase bond sales as we reduce tax rates – if activity is to remain constant.

Diagrammatically, we can show the various combinations of tax rates (on the horizontal axis) and monetary policy (on the vertical axis) that would achieve any desired level of employment – the $\bar{Q}$-bar line in Figure 3.1. (A move up the vertical axis signifies a tighter monetary policy.)

The nominal rate of interest is not a satisfactory indicator of the tightness of monetary policy. For example, a reduction in tax rates will tend to increase the net demand for bonds at a given level of employment. It may also reduce the expected rate of inflation, so that it is not certain that tax cuts plus an appropriate sale of bonds will raise nominal interest rates. If the level of activity (and government spending) is to be kept constant, however, a reduction in the ratio of taxes to total output will normally mean that real interest rates will have to be higher if the level of employment is not to rise. Nor is the level of the

Figure 3.1

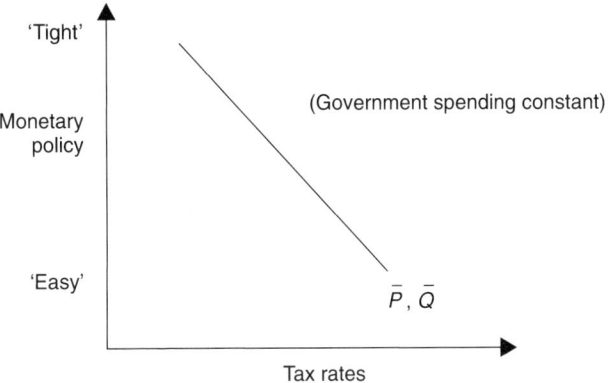

(real or nominal) money supply necessarily a good indicator of the setting of monetary policy – especially as we shall be assuming that tax cuts will have certain cost-reducing effects which would increase the real money supply (for any given nominal money supply). Any central bank must use its judgement, and all available indicators that can assist it, in deciding whether it is tightening or relaxing monetary policy. It therefore brings the analysis closest to its real world application to label the vertical axis as simply 'monetary policy' (a move up the axis signifying a tighter policy).

If the only way in which macroeconomic instruments can influence the price level is through the level of demand, the various combinations of tax rates and monetary policy that would establish the selected level of employment would (by definition) also have identical effects upon the price level over that period.

If $\bar{P}$ ('P-bar') is the line showing the combinations of monetary policy and tax policy that will have a given effect on prices over the relevant period), this line would then coincide with 'Q-bar' (as in Figure 3.1). This is the assumption that implicitly underlies the policies of any government that tolerates unemployment that is temporarily higher than it would otherwise have chosen merely in order to have a downward effect on the price level (or on the observed rate of inflation over the period in question).

Assume that tax cuts have a smaller upward effect on the price level than will an easing of monetary policy having the same effect on employment. It is then possible to keep activity constant while exerting a downward impact on prices by cutting tax rates (thus making it unnecessary to tolerate unemployment for that purpose) and simultaneously tightening monetary policy. Some or all taxes have cost-push effects. This is partly because of their possible impact on money wage rates. But it is also because of their direct effects on prices (so far as these are influenced by costs). Moreover, they also tend to increase costs through the diversion of resources to the collection, evasion and avoidance of taxation, and through other distortions in the pattern of production away from what people would have chosen in the absence of these taxes. Furthermore, if this leads people to try to raise their money incomes – in an attempt to increase their economic welfare above what is feasible with existing tax rates – this, too, is a cost-push effect.[1] Inflation and a progressive income tax structure have combined to raise effective income tax rates in many countries, so that a very sharp rise in pre-tax incomes has often become necessary in order to hold post-tax real incomes constant.

This underlines the importance of indexing the income tax structure if this problem is to be avoided.[2] These cost-push effects of high taxes are (normally) presumably only a partial offset to their downward effects on the price level through the level of demand.

A relatively tight monetary policy may also be expected to have some downward impact on the prices of real assets generally (most obviously real estate and non-perishable commodities), by making financial assets more attractive. By making money harder and dearer to borrow it also shifts the aggregate supply curve downwards (meaning that prices and wages at any given output will be lower than if money had been easier and cheaper to borrow). Moreover, a slower growth of the money supply (as would occur with a relatively tight monetary policy) may in itself make people expect less upward pressure on the price level, and to that extent help to restrain the rise in prices. All these considerations increase the force of the contention that a shift from high tax rates to a tighter monetary policy will – at any given level of employment – exercise some downward impact on the price level. Even if a tighter monetary policy had net cost-push effects – which seems inconceivable – provided that this effect was less than the cost-push effects of the taxes having the same effect in holding down the level of employment, the appropriate mix would still be to cut taxes and tighten monetary policy.

On these assumptions, therefore, as in Figure 3.2, the P-bar line and the Q-bar line diverge, the P-bar line having a more nearly horizontal slope than the Q-bar line. Generally, however, they would slope the same way (the anti-inflationary effects of high taxes through curbing demand normally exceeding their cost-push effects). 'Stagflation'

Figure 3.2

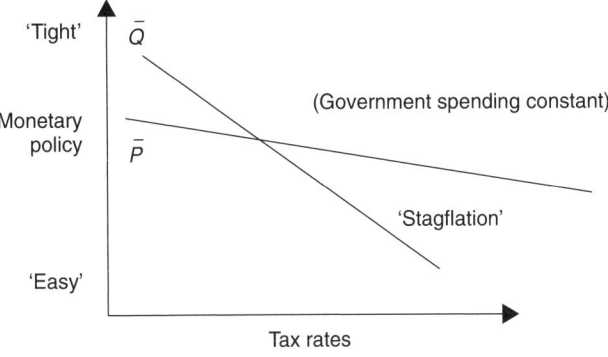

Figure 3.3

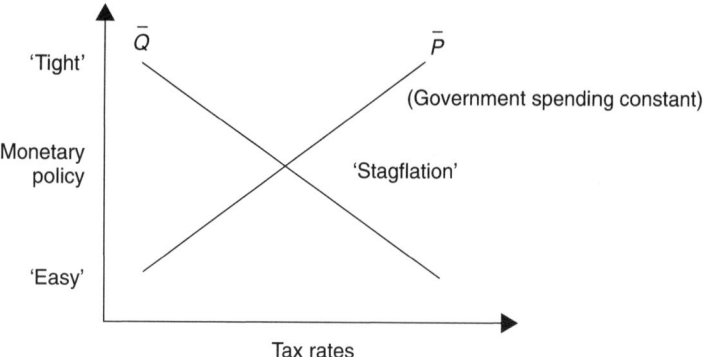

prevails in the indicated sector, for in that sector unemployment is too high while there is also a need to restrain upward pressure on prices. In that situation taxes should be cut and bonds sold until the desired level of activity is established with the desired degree of downward pressure on the price level. It is therefore not necessary to accept temporarily high unemployment in order to achieve a once-for-all downward effect on the price level, unless we are prepared to argue that these lines do not diverge from one another. (If the P-bar line had cut the Q-bar line from above, the right mix would have been the opposite one.) If taxes are so cost-push inflationary that a cut in them (alone) actually exerts a downward effect on prices even without a tightening of monetary policy the lines slope in opposite directions to one another. For tax cuts would then both stimulate employment and exert a downward impact on the price level, as in Figure 3.3. (This might be true for a limited period, though it would be highly unlikely to be true for long.) To cure stagflation, tax rates should then be cut, but monetary policy might need to be eased, tightened, or kept constant.

Varying government spending and taxation

If one holds monetary policy constant (on the basis of all the relevant available indicators) it is possible to vary tax rates and government spending in such a way as to have some effect in restraining price increases without changing the level of activity. This would be true provided only that the taxes that are cut are ones that were having some degree of cost-push inflationary effect. Some forms of government spending on goods and services (and certainly cost-reducing subsidies – which are equivalent to tax cuts) may also have effects in reducing costs. Government outlays that assist research in industry, or for the construction of a bridge that reduced the costs of taking manufactured goods to the consumer, might be examples. But the typical form of government spending is certainly not likely to be cost-reducing (especially in the short run), whereas tax cuts do usually reduce costs.

If one draws a line linking all the possible combinations of government spending and taxation that will bring about a certain level of employment or real output (with monetary policy constant), it slopes upwards. For higher tax rates will have to be accompanied by higher levels of government spending in order to maintain a given level of employment. The $\bar{P}$-bar line showing combinations of these two instruments that will have a given effect on the price level could normally also be expected to slope upwards. But if taxes have a cost-push effect, the slope of the $\bar{P}$-bar line is nearer to the horizontal than is the $\bar{Q}$-bar line. For if the effect on the price level were to remain constant as tax rates rose it would be necessary for government spending to rise less rapidly than would be appropriate if the aim were to hold activity constant. The $\bar{P}$-bar line, showing the various combinations of these instruments that would have the same effect on the price level, will thus (like the $\bar{Q}$-bar line) normally slope upwards (as in Figure 3.4). But as the degree of cost-pushfulness of taxes increases, the $\bar{P}$-bar line rotates in a clockwise direction, and if taxes were very cost-increasing it could slope in the opposite direction to the $\bar{Q}$-bar line. It would then be appropriate to raise government spending as taxes were reduced – if the aim were to hold constant the effect on the price level

Figure 3.4

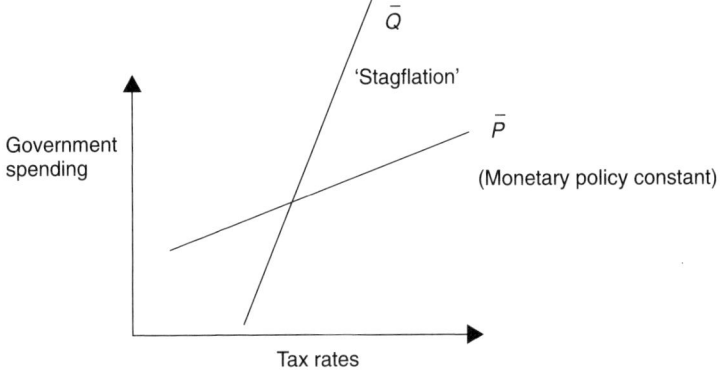

36   *The Reform of Macroeconomic Policy*

Figure 3.5

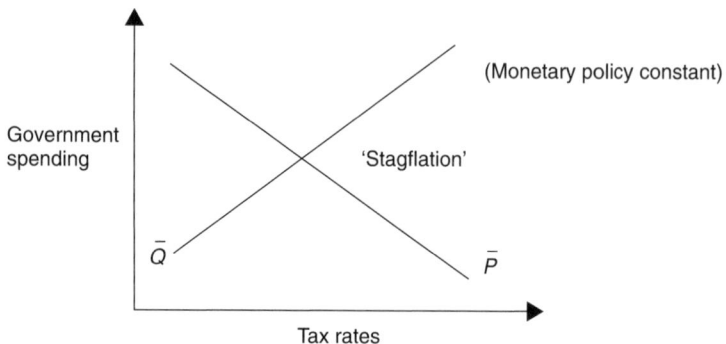

(as in Figure 3.5). A tax cut might then help to reduce both unemployment and the upward pressure on the price level, and it might need to be accompanied by constant, rising or falling government spending, according to circumstances.

Varying government spending and monetary policy

If tax rates are kept constant, it is possible for a given level of activity to be established with varying combinations of government spending and monetary policy. Under the normal assumption that a tightening of monetary policy has some downward effect on private expenditure, if the level of activity is to be held constant a relatively tighter monetary policy will thus be required to accompany a relatively high level of government spending. The Q-bar line showing the various appropriate combinations of increasing government spending and (increasingly tight) monetary policy will therefore slope upwards (as in Figure 3.6).

A tighter monetary policy presumably has some direct downward effect on the price level. This is partly because people associate a relatively low level of the money supply with relatively low prices, and partly because relatively tighter and more costly money leads to the fixing of lower prices and lower money incomes (at any given real level of activity) than when money is easier. If so, the choice of a mix with relatively tight money will be accompanied by some downward effect on the price level (by comparison with a mix that includes an easier monetary policy). In other words, in order to have a constant effect on the price-level as monetary policy became tighter, a higher level of government spending would be appropriate than would be necessary in order to maintain a constant level of activity. That is to say, the

Figure 3.6

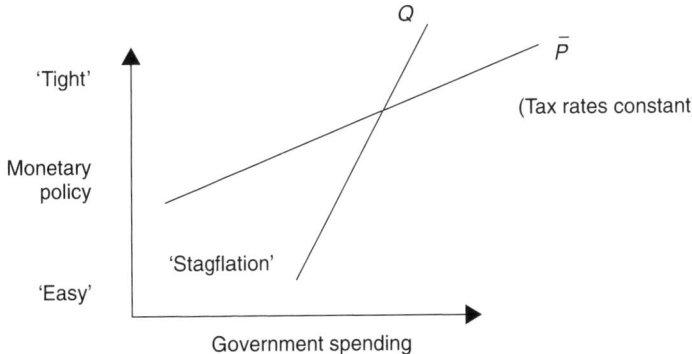

$\bar{P}$-bar line – showing various combinations of government spending and monetary policy that will all have the same effect on the price level – will have a slope nearer to the horizontal than will the $\bar{Q}$-bar line. If a tight money mix had a very large direct price-reducing effect, the $\bar{P}$-bar line could even slope below the horizontal (as Figure 3.7). In that case a rise in government spending might need to be accompanied by an easing, or a tightening, of monetary policy, or by holding it constant (according to the circumstances) in order to achieve a given effect on the price level.

With constant tax rates, therefore, in a stagflationary situation the appropriate policy is to raise government spending and sell bonds. A government that does the opposite – curtailing government spending,

Figure 3.7

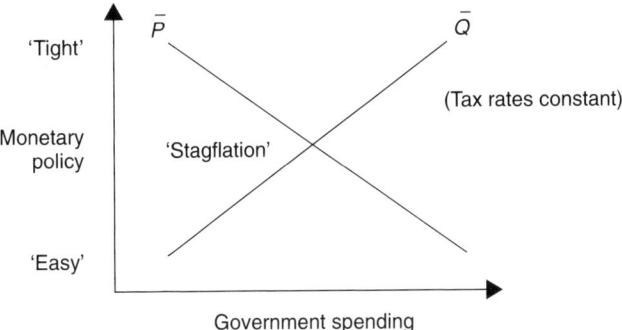

or trying to force interest rates down by monetary measures, or both – can expect to make stagflation worse (increasing unemployment for a given price level, or raising prices at a given level of unemployment).

Varying all instruments simultaneously

It may be seen from the foregoing analysis that tax cuts or a tighter monetary policy (individually, or preferably in harness) will generally constitute an essential part of the remedy for stagflation. This will be true provided only that taxes have cost-push effects, or that tight monetary measures have some direct downward effect on the price level (at any given level of activity), or both. Government spending is essentially neutral in the sense that if reductions in it are accompanied by tax cuts (on an appropriate scale) these cuts in government spending can be used to overcome stagflation. If, on the other hand, increases in government spending are accompanied by bond sales (on an appropriate scale) the increases in government spending financed in this way can have at least a once-for-all downward impact on the price level. If, however, a government combines cuts in its own spending with easier money and also with higher taxes it must expect this policy to make stagflation worse.

Combining the change of mix with a stimulus

Instead of tolerating (temporarily) relatively high unemployment in the hope of checking the tendency for the price level to rise, a government can achieve the same effect by a sufficient twist of the mix in the appropriate direction. Moreover, provided either that taxes have some cost-push effect or that a tightening of monetary policy has some direct downward effect on prices – or both – a government can always raise employment and have a downward impact on the price level by combining an appropriate change of mix with a net stimulus. The greater the desired stimulus, the greater should be the tax cut (for any given sale of bonds). At the same time, the greater the desired downward impact on prices, the larger the scale of both the tax cut and the bond sale that will be appropriate. The more it is feared that a given real stimulus will exert upward pressure on prices, therefore, the greater the 'twist' of the macroeconomic mix towards lower taxes and tighter monetary policy that should accompany the provision of that real stimulus.

Effects of tax cuts on productivity

If the policy mix is changed in such a way that tax rates are lower, it is quite likely that there will be favourable effects upon real output at each level of employment, as a result of a consequently better allocation of resources and increased effort. This will tend to hold down the price level at any given level of money incomes or employment.

So far as this is true, the available supply of goods and services at any level of employment will consequently be greater. Correspondingly less by way of tightening of monetary policy will then be required in order to offset the upward effects of a tax cut upon employment or the price level. Clearly, the greater the extent to which tax cuts result in higher real output *at any given level of employment*, the less the extent to which monetary policy would need to be tightened in order to ensure that the tax cuts do not raise prices or employment.[3]

The slopes of the lines

If a small change in tax rates has a relatively large effect in stimulating demand, it will require a relatively large change in monetary policy to achieve the same effect on employment as a given tax cut. In other words, if a given change in monetary policy has a relatively small effect in changing employment, a relatively large purchase or sale of bonds would be required to offset the effect on demand of any given change in tax rates. In these circumstances, therefore, the Q-bar line showing combinations of (increasing) tax rates and (tightening) monetary policy would slope sharply upwards – indicating that a relatively small rise in tax rates would be equal in its effects on employment to a relatively severe tightening of monetary policy.

This also means that if the aim was to give a net stimulus to employment, a given reduction in tax rates should, on the assumptions stated in the previous paragraph, be accompanied by a tighter setting of monetary policy than would be appropriate if this assumptions were reversed.

If, on the other hand, demand were very sensitive to changes in monetary policy but relatively unresponsive to tax cuts, these conditions would make the Q-bar line approximate to the horizontal position. The P-bar line generally diverges from the Q-bar line as a result of the cost-push effects of high taxes, or because of direct effects on the price level of a change in monetary policy (or both). This makes the P-bar line approach the horizontal. The closer it was to that position, the greater would be the possibility that it would swing to the other side of the horizontal (that is, slope positively – as in Figure 3.3). This is important, for a P-bar line sloping in that direction signifies that a tax cut will both tend to reduce the price level and to stimulate employment, and so be a perfect cure for stagflation, even without any change in monetary policy.

The slope of the *P*-bar line depends upon the relative effects on the price level of a given change in tax rates and of a given change in the setting of monetary policy. The greater the extent to which taxes are cost-increasing, the greater the extent to which the *P*-bar line will diverge from the *Q*-bar line. If a tightening of monetary policy also has a considerable direct downward effect on the price level (at each level of activity) the *P*-bar line will diverge to a still greater extent from the *Q*-bar line. The chances of this line sloping (positively) the other side of the horizontal from the *Q*-bar line will thus be greatest if taxes have large cost-push effects and if a tightening of monetary policy has considerable direct downward effects on the price level.

This means that such a (positive) slope of the *P*-bar line will be most likely when the conditions outlined in the preceding paragraph are combined with a situation where demand rises little in response to tax cuts and where it reacts very sharply to changes in monetary policy. But it should be emphasised that the feasibility of the suggested mix does not depend upon the likelihood of the *P*-bar line sloping (positively) the other side of the horizontal, or upon how close it is to that position. The feasibility of this mix depends only on there being some divergence of the *P*-bar line from the *Q*-bar line – that is, on taxes having some cost-push effects, or on a tightening of monetary policy having some direct downward effect on prices, or both. (Even if tighter monetary policy had some upward effect on prices, the proposed mix would still work provided that this effect was less than the cost-push effect of a tax increase having the same effect on employment.) If the divergence of the *P*-bar line from the *Q*-bar line is slight, it will be necessary to make correspondingly larger tax cuts and larger bond sales in order to achieve a given effect on prices.

If private spending is very responsive to changes in monetary policy, but tax cuts have relatively little effect in stimulating activity, this will then make the *P*-bar and the *Q*-bar lines in Figures 3.2 and 3.3 near to the horizontal. If tax cuts had no direct upward (or a *fortiori* if they had a downward) effect on employment, this would mean that they could have no demand-inflationary effect. All the stimulus would then come from the fall in prices and from the consequent rise in the real money supply, as cost-push taxes were cut. This would then be an ideal way to stop stagflation, as it would bring about a rise in the real money supply as a result of a fall in the price level with a constant (or even falling) nominal money supply. That would then (obviously) be a form of stimulus that would operate without any increase in the price level.[4]

Naturally, one cannot really believe that a tax cut would ever have no upward effect on activity. But if tax cuts have relatively little upward effect on employment, this constitutes an argument for cutting them correspondingly more.

In summary, then, the scope for stopping stagflation by cutting taxes and selling bonds is greatest (a) if taxes have strong cost-push effects; and (b) if monetary measures have considerable direct effects on prices – a tightening of monetary policy having direct downward effects on the price level. If either of these effects is present there is a change of mix that will hold down prices without the need to tolerate unemployment.

What bearing have 'budget deficits' on the analysis?

One of the main political obstacles to achieving the appropriate mixes to stop stagflation seems to be the pseudo-objective of keeping down the 'budget deficit' (or what is called in Britain the 'Public Sector Borrowing Requirement') below some particular level. Recessions tend to raise the actual budget deficit (as a result of tax revenue being cyclically low and unemployment benefit payments cyclically high). It is therefore obvious that if a government reacts to that situation by raising tax rates further, or by cutting government spending, in an effort to reduce the budget deficit, it will make unemployment higher. Moreover, if it raises taxes it will push up the price level (at any given level of employment) – as well as probably also bringing about a further rise in the budget deficit in the not too distant future as unemployment rises.

But it cannot be denied that if businessmen – sometimes prompted (inexcusably and incredibly) by the statements of some governments – believe that a budget deficit is a sign of an irresponsible policy, a rise in the deficit caused in that way might have the effect of restraining business expenditure. If this is true, it would mean that the expansionary effect of any given budget deficit would be less than that which could normally be expected to result from the upward effect of either tax cuts or increases in government spending upon consumption and investment. It is, however, virtually inconceivable, especially in a situation of considerable unemployment and under-utilisation of capacity, that this adverse effect upon business expectations and investment could offset more than a part of the upward effect on demand of the improvement in the prospects of business profits that could be expected to result from tax cuts or higher government spending.

It should be observed that possible adverse effects on business confidence, even though they may be 'real' enough in certain circumstances, are at a different level of reality from the other effects of macroeconomic policy. For effects of this sort are inherently remediable so far as they spring from fallacious reasoning: a government that explains and analyses its policy decisions properly should be able to minimise or even prevent such irrational reactions. At the very least, it ought to do nothing to perpetuate or intensify them; and if it is so misguided as to do so it will increase its own macroeconomic difficulties unnecessarily.

But let us consider the possible implications for the policy mix that may result from such psychological repercussions caused by a relatively high budget deficit. Two of the mixes that have been suggested above tend to increase the planned budget deficit on the definition of 'government outlays *less* tax revenue' – at any given level of activity- and the third (cutting both taxes and government spending) *may* do so.

Suppose the existence, or announcement, of a large budget deficit has some adverse effects on private demand – perhaps by making businesses less ready to invest. If this effect were really so large as to exceed the orthodox upward effect on total demand of the stimulus given to consumption and investment by a relatively expansionary budget, 'orthodox' analysis might lead us to suggest that the right policy would be a simple reversal of the basic principles of sound macroeconomic policy (as normally understood): that the budget should instead, be made more 'contractionary' (a smaller deficit) in a recession and correspondingly more 'expansionary' (a larger deficit) in a time of excess demand. But this is not the appropriate policy prescription if taxes have cost-increasing effects.

Let us first suppose that any adverse effects on private demand of a move in the direction of a more expansionary budget offset only part of the direct expansionary effects of that change of policy. The implication would then be that the budget should be made more expansionary still. For a given tax cut (or a rise in government spending) will then have only a small upward effect on employment – and so have little by way of demand-inflationary effects. It would also mean that a relatively large rise in the budget deficit (or PSBR) would be required in order to bring about a given fall in unemployment. If, therefore, the aim was to achieve a given fall in unemployment in the least inflationary way possible, cost-push taxes should still be cut. It would be both possible and desirable to do this on a relatively large scale (accompanying it by an appropriately larger sale of bonds to the public). This assumption therefore turns out to be especially propitious to the operation of the preferred mix (tax cuts and bond sales) that has been suggested for reducing unemployment without reviving inflation.

If, however, a rise in the budget deficit actually reduced employment (by having very serious adverse 'confidence' effects on private investment), a tax cut would have no demand-inflationary effect. It could therefore be carried to the point when inflation was stopped, monetary measures being used to stimulate employment. A politician who really believed that a higher budget deficit would reduce employment would thus be able to adopt the politician's 'dream' policy of reducing both unemployment and inflation through tax cuts and relatively easy money. (But one would require very convincing evidence to take this possibility seriously; and the only reason for mentioning it is that some politicians and economic advisers actually seem to believe it.)

'Rational expectations', the national debt and tax-push inflation

There is a literature that considers the effect on demand of the assumption that taxpayers take account in their expenditure plans of the future tax liabilities to which they will be subject in order to service and repay any addition to the government's borrowing.[5] This literature does not, however, appear to be interested in the practical issue of whether this is a reasonable description of the way people actually think and act. Its relevance for current macroeconomic policy decisions is, therefore, by no means obvious.

But if taxpayers take account of the future tax liabilities to which they may be subject when taxes are cut and extra bond sales made at the same time, one should ask whether such considerations would also affect the price level at any given level of employment.

The most reasonable assumption would be that if taxpayers take account of the prospective rise in their future tax liabilities when making their expenditure plans, they will also do so when making their wage demands; and that producers will act in a similar manner when determining their prices.

But there are two mutually offsetting forces at work. If taxpayers do take considerable account of this addition to their future tax liabilities when deciding on their expenditure plans, a given tax cut will need to be accompanied by only a relatively small bond sale in order to keep activity constant. (In our analysis the combinations of the two instruments is chosen in such a way as to hold activity constant; whereas in most of the literature on this subject the approach seems to be to hold the nominal money supply constant. In that case, a fall in tax revenue is accompanied by an equal sale of bonds.)

By the same token, therefore, as a result of the required bond sale consequently being relatively small, there would be a correspondingly small increase in the future tax liabilities that wage-earners and producers would (if they were rational) need to take into account in determining money wage rates and prices. One can, then, make what assumption one likes about how far (if at all) taxpayers take account of the extra future tax liabilities that result from a sale of bonds by the government. But provided that people are rational enough for such considerations to influence their expenditure plans to about the same extent as their wage and price-setting behaviour, the policy prescriptions are not affected. If, however, people took account of such considerations mainly in their spending decisions, this would mean that only a small bond sale would be needed to offset the expansionary effects of a tax cut. (The Q-bar lines in Figures 3.1, 3.2 and 3.3 would then have a slope near to the horizontal, and the likelihood that a tax cut would reduce both inflation and unemployment – the P-bar in Figure 3.3 sloping below the horizontal – would thus be increased.) If such considerations were taken into account mainly in wage demands and price-setting behaviour (but only to a lesser extent in deciding levels of expenditure), the opposite conclusion would naturally follow.

It is worth stressing the literature on this subject does not yet appear to have caught up with the real world of the 1970s, in which governments have very often (perhaps more often than not) been borrowing at negative real post-tax interest rates. This means that when taxes are cut and bonds simultaneously sold, a rational taxpayer would not be reducing spending very much. For the taxpayer would then have correspondingly less by way of extra future tax liabilities than if a positive real interest were being paid to lenders. If, then, taxpayers really were rational, so long as bonds are being sold at low or negative post-tax interest rates, a tax cut accompanied by a bond sale would require a greater tightening of monetary policy (that is, a larger sale of bonds) in order to hold activity constant than would have been required with positive (or higher) real post-tax interest rates. It is true that if taxes were cut considerably and real interest rates after tax once more became reliably positive, this situation would not continue. But excessively high tax rates coupled with low or negative real post-tax interest rates have probably been largely responsible for the stagflation of the later 1970s; so that a switch back to lower tax rates and tighter monetary policy would go far towards solving the problem of stagflation.[6]

The open economy

The combination of measures that does most to hold down the price level (at any given level of activity) in a closed economy will also consequently be the one that will do most to strengthen the current account in an open economy.

For example, assume that a $\bar{B}$-bar line is one that shows all the combinations of tax rates and monetary policy that will bring about a particular state of the current account (as in Figure 3.8). Such a line has a slope closer to the horizontal than the $\bar{Q}$-bar line (showing the various combinations of tax rates and monetary policy that give the desired level of activity). The intersection of these two lines shows the combinations of the two instruments that combine the desired level of employment with the desired state of the balance of payments. So long as tax rates have any cost-push effects, or monetary policy has any direct effect on the price level (or both), the two lines have different slopes. It is therefore not necessary to accept a lower level of activity than would otherwise have been chosen merely in order to avoid too great a current account deficit. Provided that the country is willing to cut tax rates and sell bonds to a sufficient extent, there is a combination of these measures (together with any given level of government spending) that will achieve the desired level of the current account and of employment. Furthermore, if the current account is at all sensitive to a change in the net demand for money balances an expansionary budgetary policy accompanied by a tight monetary policy will lead people to export more and import less, and so improve the current

Figure 3.8

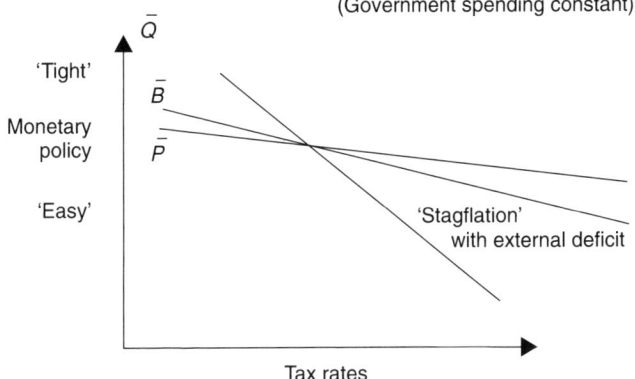

account while they are building their cash balances up to a more satisfactory level.

The B-bar line (defined as including only current account transactions) does not diverge from the Q-bar line as far as does the P-bar line. In other words, it stands between the Q-bar line and the P-bar line (as shown in Figure 3.8).

This is because, as one moves along the Q-bar line towards the level where tax rates are relatively low, the tightening of monetary policy that will be needed to keep the current account constant will be less than that which would be needed to hold output constant. But it will normally be more than that which will be required to keep prices constant.

Capital account transactions

In an open economy part of the case for adopting a policy mix that combines tight money and low tax rates is that it will have favourable effects upon capital inflow. If we define the balance of payments objective as including these effects, a move up the Q-bar line in the direction of tighter money and lower tax rates will have a more favourable effect on the overall state of the balance of payments than that upon the current account alone. For, in addition to the favourable effect on the country's competitive position of achieving the desired level of employment (Q-bar) with lower tax rates and tighter money, such a mix will make the country more attractive to lenders. It will also make it less attractive as a place in which to borrow, so that the capital account will improve. In other words, the B-bar line defined to include both current and capital account transactions will diverge (towards the horizontal) to a greater extent from the Q-bar than does the B-bar line defined as current account transactions alone. The more responsive are capital flows to interest rate changes and to tax cuts, the greater will be the divergence of the B-bar line from the Q-bar line.

If the country's external reserves are kept constant, a mix with relatively tight money and low tax rates will thus make it possible for the exchange rate to appreciate by more (or depreciate by less) at any given stimulus to employment, with a consequently helpful effect in holding down domestic prices. In other words, with a fully flexible exchange rate the mix operates essentially as in a closed economy, with part of the effect of the mix operating through variations in the exchange rate.

The B-bar line defined to include effects on capital flows could even diverge from the Q-bar to a greater extent than does the P-bar

Figure 3.9

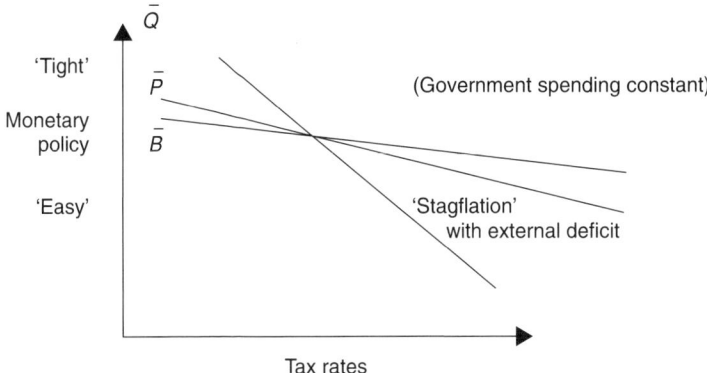

(as in Figure 3.9). That would mean that as taxes were cut and monetary policy tightened the favourable effect on the capital account would be so great that, for any given tax cut, a smaller tightening of monetary policy would be needed to hold the balance of payments constant than would be needed to hold the price level constant in the face of the same tax cuts.

It might be argued that in an open economy, an actual or projected rise in the budget deficit (as such) may tend to increase capital outflow (or reduce capital inflow). So far as that occurred, it would tend to reduce the level of liquidity in the economy and to make the reserves lower (if the exchange rate were kept fixed) or to cause a depreciation (if the exchange rate were allowed to vary). But any unfavourable effect on net capital inflow would probably be less than the favourable effect on it resulting from tight money and lower tax rates (and so a high post-tax return to capital). It is true, however, that this consideration weakens the case for using monetary policy together with tax cuts for the purpose of raising the reserves, or that of strengthening the exchange rate and so holding down inflation. It thus makes it less likely that the *B*-bar line will slope, 'outside' the *P*-bar line, and brings it closer to the *Q*-bar line. The use of a tight monetary policy and an expansionary budgetary policy (preferably tax cuts) will raise the demand for money relative to the supply of it. Provided that the consequent rise in the net demand for money affects expenditure and borrowing decisions, it will tend to improve both the current and the capital account (at each level of activity) until actual money balances have risen to meet the desired level for new balances.

If a country were to vary only two of the three basic macroeconomic instruments it would not generally find that it had had the desired effects on the level of employment, the price level and the state of the balance of payments simultaneously. But if it varies all three of them in appropriate directions it could in principle find an appropriate combination. If, however, it is willing to let the exchange rate vary in such a way as to keep the reserves constant in the light of the variations in the other instruments, the problem is essentially the same as in a closed economy. There are in effect three possible budgetary and monetary instruments, and two real internal macroeconomic objectives.

There will, however, be a constraint imposed by forces in the outside world, in the shape of the rate of interest at which capital can be imported – or the return on it if it is exported. This determines the real rate of interest that will need to be established, at least in a small country that has a negligible effect on interest rates in the world as a whole.

This will determine whether it ought to undertake more or less by way of particular government projects. For it should not undertake ones that do not yield a social return sufficient to justify themselves at the rate of interest that the country is having to pay on capital inflow (or which it could earn on capital outflow) at the margin. This is what should determine the scale and form of government (and private) spending. It should then vary its other measures in such a way as to achieve full employment without inflation. Those private projects (also) which are expected to be justified at the prevailing level of world interest rates will then take place, but not those expected to yield a return less than that. If there is stagflation the best mix will be to cut taxes and sell bonds. This will not change the rate of interest appreciably in a small country, but it will affect the flow of capital and so the exchange rate, the rate of inflation, and the level of activity.

Tariffs and quotas

Governments frequently use tariffs and other restrictions on imports – despite their adverse effects on the allocation of resources – in the hope of thereby reducing unemployment. These measures are certain to raise the prices of the imported goods in question. They may sustain employment in protected industries, but there is no reason to suppose that they reduce unemployment generally; and, indeed, they are more likely to increase it. For their adverse effect on the allocation of resources tends to raise the price level at any given level of demand or unemployment (just like any other tax having adverse effects on productivity): and even if they had no other cost-push effects, this would mean that an elimination of those tariffs (like a reduction in any tax adversely affecting productivity) would make possible a higher level of employment for any given effect on prices, and would have a downward effect on prices at any given level of employment. Tariff increases and import quotas thus make stagflation worse; and their removal reduces stagflation, if accompanied by the appropriate adjustment of other (macroeconomic) measures.

Controls over capital inflow and outflow

Measures that involve limiting, or even merely vetting, proposed projects financed from overseas tend to inhibit capital inflow. If a country is trying to maintain a strong balance of payments (inclusive of capital inflow), therefore, the existence of any such controls makes it necessary to tolerate higher unemployment in order to achieve a given effect on the price level or the balance of payments with a given setting of macroeconomic measures. Removing such limitations on capital inflow is thus a contribution to correcting a situation of stagflation and external deficit. Removing restrictions on capital outflow may cause devaluation, and to that extent tend to raise the price level. But if it results in a more economic use of the country's resources, that is likely to make it easier to restrain the upward pressure on the price level in the longer run.

The macro mix in an open economy: conclusion

Provided that the exchange rate is allowed to vary freely, the three macroeconomic instruments of taxation, government spending and monetary policy can in principle be varied in such a way as to achieve a desired effect on the price level and the level of activity.

It will not necessarily also be possible to establish any desired level of government spending or of capital inflow. But a country should in any event carry out only those projects – whether officially or privately financed – that it believes to be economic in the sense of yielding a social return greater than the prevailing level of world interest rates. If it implements projects with a return lower than that, it will bring about some inflows of capital on which it will be paying higher returns than are in its interests.

In general, therefore, it should fix government spending at that level where the social return to the country equals the real cost of importing (or the yield from exporting) capital. It should then choose the mix of taxation and monetary policy that will achieve the desired effect on employment and the price level, letting the exchange rate vary in such a way as to make this consistent with the prevailing (or desired) level of the reserves.

Real objectives and pseudo-objectives

The real objectives that a government should aim to achieve are as high a level of activity as is necessary to provide jobs for those who want them, without an undesirably high rate of inflation. (The external objective can ultimately be subsumed in these objectives.) But it cannot, except by the most extraordinary accident, expect to achieve these real objectives if it simultaneously saddles itself and its policy instruments with pseudo-targets such as a particular exchange rate, a particular level of the rate of interest, or a particular level of the budget deficit (or PSBR). The first step towards a rational macroeconomic policy is to concentrate whole-heartedly on the real objectives and to cease trying to achieve ones that cannot on any reasonable expectation be attained at the same time as minimising stagflation and maintaining a sound balance of payments.

Conclusion: the mix and the level of activity

It has not been argued in this chapter that the level of unemployment, or changes in it, have no effect on the price level of the rate of inflation. It has merely been argued that the combination of measures with which any given level of unemployment (or economic activity) is established may (also) be expected to affect the price level (and so, at least over some period, the observed rate of inflation that will be experienced). Questions relating to the mix of macroeconomic measures probably cannot properly be separated from ones about the level of employment. For to do so involves asking what effect there will be on prices if we raise the level of activity while keeping the mix constant. But it is not certain that one can give an unambiguous definition of what that means. For, although one might speak of keeping tax rates and government spending each at constant percentages of GNP, it is doubtful whether an unambiguous meaning can be given to a definition of monetary policy according to which it would remain 'constant' when the level of activity is changed. But if one believes in some sort of 'Phillips curve' one can consider the issues discussed above as being ways of 'shifting the Phillips curve', at least temporarily – whether by shifting expectations or in some more fundamental sense.

If we are among those who sympathise with the hypothesis of a natural' (or, if you prefer, 'sustainable') level of unemployment, we shall be concerned about the danger of letting 'Keynesian' unemployment fall below this level – at which inflation may (on this theory) be expected to rise cumulatively. But the combination of macroeconomic measures employed may itself play a part in determining what that (sustainable) level of unemployment will be; and it will certainly play a part in deciding what rate of inflation to expect when and if unemployment falls to that point. Once full employment is restored it is equally important to maintain a mix with low taxes and positive real post-tax interest rates, if the upward pressure on the price level is to be minimised.

The sort of measures discussed above are not intended to deal with 'structural' unemployment: but it is impossible to say how much of any existing level of unemployment is 'structural'. For the prevailing level of unemployment and spare capacity may be so great that it is not worth while for people to retrain and resettle in new jobs, or for businesses to establish new and more appropriate levels of capacity. Moreover, in such situations latter-day Luddism thrives: people become afraid of technological developments, and 'make-work' remedies for unemployment are bandied about. If we could really meet everyone's demand for real income while willingly working for a shorter period in the week, or in a life-time, it would be a sensible policy to reduce the amount of work. But so long as there are people with so many unsatisfied needs, and at the same time many people looking for work, it should not be impossible to bring them together – especially as it is to a large extent high tax rates that keep the two apart. The first step towards doing so is to overturn what appears to be the disastrous and widely prevailing fallacy that the only way to prevent unduly high inflation is to tolerate, at least temporarily, unduly high unemployment.

Notes and references

1. For a more detailed discussion of the reasons why different instruments may have different effects, see Chapter 2 in this volume.
2. Moreover, high tax rates may cause inflation by giving rise to inconsistent wage and profit claims. See Pitchford and Turnovsky (1975, 1976) and Rowthorn (1977).
3. An extreme form of this hypothesis is the view that this effect might even be so great that a reduction in tax rates actually led to a rise in tax revenue – even at a given level of employment. No such extreme assumption is being made here, but only that tax cuts may have some positive effect on real output at each level of employment.

4. If it should happen that an interest rate increase *stimulates* activity – by reducing the propensity to save (which might occur if people feel that the real return on their financial assets has consequently become more adequate for yielding them a sufficient income when they retire or when they become unemployed) – tighter monetary policy alone would become the ideal cure for inflation, provided that a tightening of monetary policy had some downward effect on the price level. An easier monetary policy would then make stagflation worse in both its aspects.
5. See, for example, Barro (1974, pp. 1095–117).
6. It is true that a mix that involved lower tax rates and higher real interest rates might have the effect of causing an unwanted fall in the ratio of investment to total output. But the effect on the relative proportions of consumption and investment would depend largely upon which taxes were cut most, and upon the effects on each of a rise in real interest rates. The net effect of the change of mix could be to *reduce* the ratio of consumption to total output, especially if a rise in real post-tax interest rates raises the propensity to save considerably. This seems to have been the direction of the relationship in the USA (see Boskin, 1978), and might be especially likely in an economy where a good deal of consumption is financed by borrowing. In any case, if the ratio of investment to total output is altered in a way that is thought undesirable, a change in the tax structure could offset this effect, for only two taxes (or a tax and a subsidy) that had differential effects on this ratio would be needed to change it. This could be done at the same time as total taxes were being reduced. But the optimal tax structure from this point of view need not be the one that would do most to reduce cost-push inflation.

4
Towards the Formulation and Testing of a More General Theory of Macroeconomic Policy (1987)*

J.O.N. Perkins and Tran Van Hoa

Introduction

Virtually all the macroeconomic policy discussion in the literature is based on a very limited number of the possible alternative combinations of assumptions about the effects of changes in particular policy instruments on the principal macroeconomic objectives. At the monetarist extreme, budgetary instruments are taken to have no impact on the real variable of unemployment (or real output), whereas monetary policy is taken to influence the price level, with no more than a short-run influence on unemployment. At the other ('Keynesian') extreme, all the instruments are taken to have similar effects to one another in reducing unemployment, for any given effect on nominal aggregate demand, an effect that is transferred to the price level as full employment is approached. The possibility of different macroeconomic instruments having different relative effects from one another on the price level and on unemployment respectively has been relatively little discussed. Nor has the possibility that one or more of those instruments may have no effect on one of those objectives, whereas another instrument may affect both objectives. Where these possibilities have been discussed, the approach has still been in terms of a relatively small number of the logically possible alternative combinations of the possible effects of the main macroeconomic instruments on the two principal macroeconomic objectives. A very limited number of special

---

* Originally published in *Weltwirtshaftliches Archiv (Review of World Economics)*, 123(2) (1987). The authors gratefully acknowledge the comments from Duncan Ironmonger, Bob Jones, Ian McDonald and Kirker Stephens. The usual caveat applies.

theories about the appropriate set of assumptions – rather than a really general theory – has therefore constituted the basis for discussion of macroeconomic policy.

The purpose of the present chapter is to consider in general terms the range of alternative possible combinations of assumptions about the effects on unemployment and inflation of changes in each of the three main macroeconomic instruments. The evidence considered here about this takes the form indicated by the general level of tax rates, the general level of government outlays, and monetary growth. We report the results of tests of the apparent effects (over a three-year period) of year-to-year changes in the setting of these macroeconomic instruments as evidenced by changes in a monetary aggregate, and by changes in the ratio to Gross Domestic Product (GDP) both of government outlays and of government receipts. The two sides of the budget clearly need to be considered separately as indicators of changes in the setting of fiscal policy. For focusing on some measure of changes in the budget deficit or surplus is inappropriate if the two sides of the budget have different relative effects on inflation and unemployment, respectively.

The second section outlines the various logically possible combinations of assumptions about the effects of each of these three broad macroeconomic instruments on the two principal macroeconomic objectives. The third section sets out the empirical tests that have been used to assess the apparent effects on the consumer price index (the CPI) and on the rate of unemployment in a given year of year-to-year changes in certain indicators of the setting of the main macroeconomic instruments in fifteen OECD countries (over the preceding three-year period) from 1967 to 1984. The fourth section summarises the implications of these results for policy. The fifth section presents a brief summary.

Set of logically possible combinations of assumptions about the effects of instruments on objectives

There are three logically possible assumptions to make about the broad effect (or lack of effect) that a policy instrument may have upon a macroeconomic objective over the period that one is considering. It may increase it; or it may reduce it; or it may have no appreciable effect upon it. Consider first only two instruments – say, a tax cut, on the one hand, and an easing of monetary policy (by an open-market purchase of bonds by the central bank) – on the other. There are therefore no less than 81 ($3 \times 3 \times 3 \times 3$) logically possible combinations of assumptions (positive, zero or negative) about the direction of the effects of each of these two instruments on each of the two objectives of reducing inflation and unemployment. Each of these sets of assumptions may be expected to have somewhat different implications for policy. Each of these possibilities may also be combined with the possibility of varying another instrument – the ratio to GDP of government outlays. Each of the 81 logically possible sets of assumptions about the effects of two instruments can then be combined with each of the nine possible combinations of the possible effects (positive, zero or negative) of government outlays upon each of the two macro objectives. (These are the three alternative effects on unemployment, each combined with the three possible alternative effects on prices.) That makes no less than 729 logically possible combinations of assumptions in all.

The standard literature, however, focuses on only four of these. The typical Keynesian approach suggests that fiscal measures (whether tax cuts or government outlays) and monetary policy are all equally likely, at least by implication, to affect unemployment (rather than the price level) up to full employment. Then, as full employment is more closely approached the three types of policy measures will thereafter affect (mainly, and eventually solely) the rate of inflation or the price level. The typical monetarist approach, by contrast, suggests that monetary policy affects only the price level, except in the short run – when it may affect unemployment – and that fiscal measures alone do not affect either the price level or unemployment.

All these familiar sets of assumptions have one unfortunate characteristic in common: they direct attention towards very special cases in which it is not possible to find combinations of measures that will tend to reduce both unemployment and inflation at the same time. Presumably largely as a result of the dominant position of these special cases in macroeconomic thought, it has come to be widely accepted in practice, and largely in principle, that in situations of stagflation governments are likely to have to choose between reducing unemployment and reducing inflation.

Yet there are many other (*prima facie* reasonable) sets of assumptions about the effects of the available macroeconomic instruments upon the two main macroeconomic objectives that afford the possibility of changing policy in ways that tend to reduce both inflation and unemployment at the same time. Indeed, many of these possibilities are in some sense or another intermediate between those combinations of assumptions that are widely discussed or accepted.

A priori arguments for alternative sets of assumptions

It is possible to provide some reasonable *a priori* justification for considering as potentially valid the vast majority (conceivably, all) of the various logically possible alternative combinations of assumptions about the nature of the effects of the instruments on the two objectives.[1]

As to tax cuts, one might argue either that their cost-reducing effects exceed or, alternatively, that they fall short of, their effects in tending to raise the price level (through raising nominal aggregate demand); or, of course, that those two effects approximately offset one another. (High tax rates may have cost-inflationary effects by encouraging wage demands, by reducing productivity growth and by becoming built into business costs.) One might argue either that their demand-creating effects on employment may exceed or fall short of the 'crowding out' effects that a bond-financed tax cut can have upon private spending or, of course, that these two effects more or less offset one another.

A bond-financed rise in government outlays may tend to raise prices by adding to demand. Alternatively, it may tend to hold down costs and prices (for example, by subsidising business costs, or providing better roads, which could bring the goods to consumers at lower cost). Or, of course, these conflicting effects might approximately offset one another. Similarly, the employment-creating effects of a government outlay (financed by bond sales) might (alternatively) be more, or less, or about the same, as any 'crowding out' effects that it might have on private outlays.

As to monetary policy, it is generally assumed that monetary expansion tends to raise the price level.[2] But if it also raises real output, especially if the economy is initially operating at far below capacity, so that it is subject to increasing returns as employment rises, monetary expansion could raise real output sufficiently to reduce the upward pressure on prices. It is, however, unlikely that an easing of monetary policy could have a downward effect on inflation unless it does stimulate productivity, and so real output, in this way. Combinations of assumptions that include that supposition that monetary expansion could reduce prices without stimulating output will therefore here be labelled 'unrealistic'.

Policy prescriptions with two instruments

There are four basic groups of assumptions on the basis of which a mix of instruments is available that will make it possible to reduce unemployment and inflation simultaneously. For simplicity, we shall illustrate these principles for the case of two instruments, which is sufficient to explain the basic argument. With three instruments a much wider range of possibilities is available, and these will be summarised briefly at a later stage; but the basic principles are the same.

The first such group of assumptions is where there is an instrument (or, of course, more than one such instrument) that will have a helpful effect on both objectives. If tax cuts stimulate employment whilst also reducing the upward pressure on the price level (their cost-reducing effects exceeding any demand-inflationary effects), tax cuts would be such an instrument, and tax increases would worsen the macroeconomic situation on both counts.

Secondly, if there is an instrument that affects only one objective, whereas another instrument affects only the other objective, it is clearly possible to further both objectives by appropriate changes in each instrument to deal with the objective on which it has an effect. For example, tax cuts may promote employment (without having a significant effect on the price level), and a tighter monetary policy may reduce the upward pressure on the price level (without affecting employment).

Thirdly, there may be one instrument that affects both objectives – one of them in the desired direction, the other not – whereas there is another instrument that affects only one of the two objectives. If so, the latter can and should be used to deal with the objective that it can affect, and an appropriate adjustment of the other instrument can be employed to deal with the other objective. Finally, if two instruments each affect the two objectives in the same direction – each increasing inflation while reducing unemployment – but to different relative extents, there is a change of mix that will promote both objectives. The more inflationary of the two instruments should be moved in a contractionary direction and the less inflationary one in an expansionary direction (to an appropriate extent in each case). A simple application of the principle of comparative advantage shows that appropriate changes of the two will further both objectives.[3]

In other words, it will in such cases be possible to deal with inflation by moving in a contractionary direction the instrument that has the larger effect on the price level for a given effect on employment, and simultaneously moving the less inflationary instrument in an expansionary direction. (There are four such cases.)

One way to illustrate this is to depict it as a shift of the aggregate supply curve resulting from the use of one of the instruments (though not to the same extent as that which would result from the use of the other) when each of them is used to shift the aggregate demand curve to a given extent. (See Jones and Perkins, 1986, pp. 387–91.)

If, for example, an easing of monetary policy has a greater upward effect on the price level than a tax cut having the same effect in reducing unemployment, there is a combination of tax cuts and tighter monetary policy that will reduce both inflation and unemployment.[4] If there is even one macroeconomic instrument that has a smaller upward effect on the price level than some other instrument for a given effect in reducing unemployment it is therefore pointless to try to check inflation by holding unemployment at a temporarily high level. For, if so, even assuming that that would succeed in reducing inflation, the same aim can, on those assumptions, be achieved by a suitable change of the policy mix without the need to tolerate the temporarily high unemployment.

In the twenty-one remaining logically possible cases no mix is available that can deal simultaneously with both inflation and unemployment. In some of these cases, (at least) one of the instruments does not affect either objective. In others neither instrument affects one of the objectives; and in still others both instruments affect the two objectives to the same relative extent (that is, each increases inflation to the same extent for a given effect on unemployment).

Three instruments

With three macroeconomic instruments – say, government outlays in addition to tax rates and monetary policy – the number of possible combinations of assumptions is obviously much larger – 729 ($3 \times 3 \times 3 \times 3 \times 3 \times 3$). For there can be a plus, a minus or a zero in each cell of a matrix relating each instrument to each of the two objectives. Moreover, there is a much smaller proportion of these (59 of them) than there was with only two instruments on the basis of which there is no change of one or more macroeconomic instruments available with which to tackle both inflation and unemployment at the same time (see Table 4.1).

There are a large number of cases in which there is at least one instrument of the three that has a negligible effect on one objective and a helpful effect on the other, while there is at least one other instrument that affects both objectives. In these cases there is a change of mix that can be used to tackle stagflation. The vast majority of the logically possible combinations of assumptions about three instruments fall into this category. One requires, therefore, to have reasonable evidence about the

Table 4.1 Analysis of possible combinations of assumptions with three instruments

	'Unrealistic'[a]	Potentially realistic	Total
Comparative advantage only required	4	8	12
Change of mix available	151	507	658[b]
No useful change available	7	52	59
Total	162	567	729

Notes:
[a] The cases described as 'unrealistic' are those where an expansionary monetary policy would be assumed to reduce inflation without also stimulating output.
[b] 414 of these are single-instrument cases.

sign (and, in certain cases, also about the existence of a comparative advantage) of the effects of two or more instruments upon each of the two macro objectives. It will then be possible to find any available combinations of changes in instruments (and in some cases, single instrument changes) that will help to solve the problem of stagflation. The tests reported in the next section are addressed to the question of what combinations of assumptions about the effects of changes in the main macroeconomic policy instruments appear to be most consistent with the evidence of OECD countries during the period 1967–84.

Empirical analysis

The hypothesis to be tested is that the rise in the CPI and the level of unemployment in a given country in a particular year is significantly related to different combinations of monetary growth and of changes in the ratios to GDP of government outlays and of government current receipts in that country over the immediately preceding three years. It is true that these measures of the changes in the setting of macroeconomic instruments are themselves to some extent endogenous variables (at least if the raw data for the fiscal variables, without cyclical adjustment, are employed). But this may also be said of such indicators of the setting of policy as budget deficits, as well as of the various measures of monetary growth rates, which are very widely used as indicators of policy. Clearly, however, if a given change in taxes has different effects on the CPI or unemployment from those of a change in government outlays of the same magnitude, the use of changes in budget deficits will be misleading as a guide to policy. The use of these budgetary indicators (one of outlays and one of receipts) to indicate the setting of policy is thus what will be required.

It is desirable to minimise the problem arising from the use of indicators of policy that may be considered to some extent endogenous. In addition to the results of tests using unadjusted data throughout, we therefore also report the results of tests using cyclically adjusted ('structural') budgetary figures produced by OECD economists (see Muller and Price, 1984) for the period since 1971. These results can be considered in combination with unadjusted data for earlier years, when unemployment was much lower than it has been since 1971. The unadjusted data were therefore in those earlier years presumably much better indicators of changes in the setting of policy than they became in later years of much higher unemployment. The countries selected are all those for which complete sets of the relevant data are available from the OECD or the IMF for the relevant years (1967–84) for the CPI and unemployment, and from 1964 onwards for explanatory variables.

The use of monetary growth alone as any sort of target or indicator of the setting of policy is clearly highly misleading. For the effects on the CPI or employment (or both) of a given monetary change brought about by measures of monetary policy alone are different from those that occur when the same change in monetary growth is accompanied by a change in tax receipts or in government outlays. Our tests are therefore intended to identify separately the apparent effects of each of the constituent items in such combined packages.[5]

A general statement of the underlying model is that there is a set of M objectives (two – the unemployment rate, and inflation as indicated by changes in the CPI) and N instruments (three – monetary policy, tax rates and government outlays) in our tests (see Tables 4.2 and 4.3). If policy is able to deal with both problems simultaneously N must be at least equal to M – unless there is a single change in one instrument that affects both objectives in the desired directions. (Our approach considers all these possibilities.) The set of M objectives is denoted by Y and the set of N policy variables is denoted by X. We assume that there exists a certain relationship between combinations of Y and X, and that this relationship is complete and denoted by an implicit function. That is to say (in mathematical terms)

$$F(Y, X, A, B) = 0 \tag{4.1}$$

where F is an arbitrary function, A and B are the parameters or reaction weights associated with Y and X, respectively. When F is linear (that is when the reaction between the instruments and the targets is assumed to be linear) we then have from (4.1)

$$AY + BX = 0 \tag{4.2}$$

which is a policy impact function in the structural form. If, in addition, $\det(A) \neq 0$, we have from (4.2)

$$Y = -A^{-1}BX = CX \tag{4.3}$$

This is a policy impact function in the reduced form.

As is well known (see, for example, Turnovsky, 1977), (4.3) forms the basis of Tinbergen's static controllability theory if C is constant. Also, with the addition of a random component, (4.3) forms the basis of Theil's (1958) optimal stabilisation policy. In both cases, (4.3) is used as a set of constraints, subject to which an objective utility function may be maximised to derive optimal policy. Equation (4.3) is thus crucial in determining the condition under which an optimal stabilisation programme or a macroeconomic policy mix may be formulated. With the addition of an autoregressive vector component, (4.3) provides the basis for a dynamic stabilisation programme or policy mix (Turnovsky, 1977). Earlier empirical work on macro policy mixes includes a study by Ironmonger *et al.* (1984) using OECD data, in which a reduced form model with an *a priori* lag structure was estimated by single-equation methods. Tentative results on causality in a macro policy model in the reduced form using US data were also reported by Stephens (1984). In the tests below, we adopt a generalised framework of autoregressive distributed lags (AD) or dynamic regressions. (See Hendry *et al.*, 1983, for a macro policy model in the structural form for system estimation and analysis.) In this framework, both the dynamics of the instrument transmission mechanism and the simultaneity of the targets are integrated for policy study.

In our tests, a minimal macroeconomic policy model is constructed for OECD countries over the period 1967–84, which consists of two objectives, namely, reducing inflation (CR) and unemployment (U), and three policy variables, namely changes in the ratio to GDP of taxes (TAR) and of government outlays (LAR), and the rate of growth of a monetary aggregate ($M2$). In addition, the model includes the lagged values of unemployment, the change in the CPI, the real price of oil ($ROIL$) and a time trend ($TIME$). All the data are annual series, obtained from the OECD publication *Economic Outlook* (up to the June 1985 issue); and for '$M2$', the series for $M1$ *plus* quasi-money published by

Table 4.2 Estimated macro policy effects, 15 OECD countries, 1967–84 (cyclically adjusted fiscal data, 1971–84; Full Information Maximum Likelihood)

	Effects of policy variables on target variables:			
	Inflation (CR)		Unemployment (U)	
	Weighted mean of effects[a]	% weight[b] of each year in total	Weighted mean of effects	% weight of each year in total
$\overline{TAR}$	−0.161 (1.6)		−0.062 (2.8)	
TAR_{t-1}		0.340 (0.8)		1.040 (3.8)
TAR_{t-2}		0.660		−0.040
$\overline{LAR}$	0.252 (2.6)		−0.007 (0.3)	
LAR_{t-1}		0.708 (3.5)		1.376 (0.4)
LAR_{t-2}				−0.346
$\overline{M2}$	0.291 (5.5)		−0.027 (1.5)	
$M2_{t-1}$		0.488 (2.8)		1.624 (1.6)
$M2_{t-2}$		0.512		−0.624
	Effects of autoregressive and other variables:			
$\overline{U}$			0.969 (21.3)	
U_t	−0.281 (2.4)			
U_{t-1}		2.020 (1.5)		1.346 (14.8)
U_{t-2}		−1.020		−0.346
$\overline{CR}$	0.477 (8.7)			
CR_{t-1}		1.448 (9.3)		
CR_{t-2}		−0.448		

Table 4.2 *continued*

Effects of autoregressive and other variables:

	Inflation (*CR*)		Unemployment (*U*)	
	Weighted mean of effects[a]	% weight[b] of each year in total	Weighted mean of effects	% weight of each year in total
$\overline{ROIL}$			0.004 (3.3)	
$ROIL_{t-1}$				0.950 (5.1)
$ROIL_{t-2}$				0.050
$\overline{TIME}$	0.245 (3.9)		0.920 (2.0)	
R^2	0.751		0.961	
DW	1.944		1.806	
LF		−802.69		

Notes:
[a] Coefficients in the columns headed 'weighted mean of effects' indicate the percentage change in the CPI or in the unemployment rate associated with a 1 per cent change (e.g. from 30.0 to +30.3% of GDP) for *TAR* or *LAR* in the weighted average of explanatory variables.
[b] Relevant weights are figures given in the column headed 'percentage weight of each year in total', indicating year-to-year proportionate contribution of an instrument to weighted mean of its effect on a target, the sum of these contributions for each instrument adding to one.
CR = percentage change in the CPI.
U = level of unemployment as a percentage of labour force as standardised by the OECD. *TAR* = percentage change in ratio to GDP of current government receipts (over 90% of which consists of tax receipts). *LAR* = percentage change in ratio to GDP of government outlays. *M2* = percentage change in M1 *plus* quasi-money (as defined by the IMF in *International Financial Statistics*). *ROIL* = percentage change in weighted official/contract price of crude oil exports (fob) deflated by percentage change in CPI. *TIME* = linear time trend.
Barred variables denote the composite variables whose components are their weighted lagged observations; weights are the estimated α_{ji}s and β_{ji}s as formulated in (4.5).
Barred *U1* and *U2* are the composite variables for *U* in the *CR* and *U* equations, respectively.
R^2 = explained sum of squares/total sum of squares.
DW = Durbin–Watson statistic.
LF = system log likelihood function.
Estimated *t*-values in parentheses.

Table 4.3 Sensitivity analysis of estimated macro policy effects, 15 OECD countries, 1967–84 (Full Information Maximum Likelihood)

Effects on target variables:

	Cyclically adjusted data		Unadjusted data			
	CR*	U*	CR	U	CR*	U*
$\overline{TAR}$	0.108 (1.1)	0.061 (2.8)	0.116 (1.1)	0.080 (3.3)	0.209 (2.2)	0.047 (2.1)
$\overline{LAR}$	0.149 (1.6)	−0.030 (7.4)	0.078 (0.9)	−0.012 (0.5)	0.004 (0.1)	0.074 (3.6)
$M2$	0.299 (6.0)	−0.030 (1.7)	0.312 (6.3)	−0.025 (1.4)	0.308 (6.5)	−0.033 (1.9)

Effects of autoregressive and other variables:

	CR*	U*	CR	U	CR*	U*
$\overline{U}$	−0.257 (2.4)	0.969 (20.8)	−0.329 (2.8)	0.980 (19.3)	0.255 (2.4)	0.969 (19.3)
$\overline{CR}$	0.466 (8.7)	0.486 (8.3)			0.483 (8.9)	
ROIL		0.004 (3.1)		0.004 (3.1)		0.002 (1.7)
TIME	0.257 (4.4)	0.049 (3.0)	0.224 (3.3)	0.046 (2.7)	0.241 (3.9)	0.048 (3.0)
R^2	0.749	0.962	0.744	0.961	0.750	0.967
D	1.96	1.82	1.94	1.81	1.97	1.79
LF	−800.12		−806.09		−780.96	

Notes: The lag structure for all variables is as in Table 4.2, except that:
(i) In the CR* equations the first component of barred TAR is the current observation, TAR_t, and the other component is TAR_{t-1}.
(ii) In the U* equation the first component of LAR is the current observation, LAR_t, and the other component is LAR_{t-1}. See also notes to Table 4.2.

the IMF in *International Financial Statistics*. The cyclically adjusted data are taken from Muller and Price (1984). Finally, as our model uses both cross-country and time-series data, each of the two equations (that is, CR and U) is in fact an unweighted stacked equation (Zellner, 1962) over 15 OECD countries with 15 country binary dummy variables (D_i, $i = 1 \ldots 15$).

As mentioned above, each of the equations is a generalisation of the AD scheme. This means that the model is flexible in terms of dynamic characteristics. Further, the equations are formulated in such a way that they are identified. There therefore exists a correspondence between the structural and reduced form parameter estimates. (See Malinvaud, 1980.) As a consequence, either the structural or the reduced form parameter estimates may be used for analysis. In their structural form, the CR and U equations can be written in full (excluding TIME and D_i) as

$$CR_t = \alpha_0 + \alpha_1 CR_t + \alpha_2 TAR_t + \alpha_3 LAR + \alpha_4 M2_t + \alpha_5 U1_{t+e_t}$$
$$U2_t = \beta_0 + \beta_1 U2_t + \beta_2 TAR_t + \beta_3 LAR + \beta_4 M2_t + \beta_5 ROIL_t + u_t \quad (4.4)$$

where e_t and u_t are the equation disturbances with classical properties and, for an arbitrary lag order m,

$$\overline{U1}_t = \sum_{i=0}^{m} \alpha_{5i} U_{t-i} \text{ with } \sum_{i=0}^{m} \alpha_{5i} = 1$$

$$\overline{CR}_t = \sum_{i=0}^{m} \alpha_{1i} CR_{t-i} \text{ with } \sum_{i=1}^{m} \alpha_{1i} = 1$$

$$\overline{TAR}_t = \sum_{i=1}^{m} \alpha_{2i} TAR_{t-i} \text{ with } \sum_{i=1}^{m} \alpha_{2i} = 1$$

$$\overline{U2}_t = \sum_{i=1}^{m} \beta_{1i} U_{t-i} \text{ with } \sum_{i=1}^{m} \beta_{1i} = 1$$

and similarly for the other variables specified in (4.4).

In the above equations, the αs and βs denote the long-run effects and the α_{ji}s and β_{ji}s may be regarded as the short-run reactions and, to emphasise the importance of data-based evidence, the signs of these parameters are not restricted *a priori*.

In (4.4) and (4.5), we formulate the basic structure of our testing model to determine empirically the relevance of the policy mix. The model is dynamic in that it assumes that all instruments have a delayed impact on inflation and unemployment. It is also simultaneous, in that it contains jointly dependent variables. The model is also functionally flexible in the sense that all well known models used in empirical econometrics can be derived from it as simply subsets with specific assumptions. (See Hendry *et al.*, 1983, for an illustration of a simple linear first-order or $m = 1$ case.) As it stands, the model is not neoclassical but represents a solution to the Hotelling canonical problem of finding the best predictor of the objectives or targets from an optimal combination of the available instruments. (See Hotelling, 1936; Van Hoa, 1985). It can also be seen that the model contains over-identified equations according to the order condition for identifiability. In this case, we have estimated the model by the full-information maximum-likelihood (FIML) method, and the results are reported in detail in Table 4.2 (pp. 61–2).

In the estimation we used a lag order of two (rather than three or more), both because we have found that the estimates are robust to a longer order and also because this is appropriate for preserving enough degrees of freedom to ensure reasonable accuracy in a sample of this size.

The results, given in Table 4.2, show that the modelling performance of both the CR and U equations satisfies the usual statistical tests, as indicated by the explained sum of squares, adjusted for the degrees of freedom (R^2). First-order serial correlation is also absent among the residuals of CR and U. The results are thus consistent and efficient. At the conventional 5 per cent critical level, these results indicate that the two policy variables, government outlays (LAR) and the monetary aggregate ($M2$), each appear to have a significant effect upon inflation. On the other hand, only taxes (TAR) and the real price of oil ($ROIL$) among the explanatory variables appear to have a significant effect upon unemployment. In addition, unemployment has a significant effect on inflation, and this establishes the one-way instantaneous causation from unemployment to inflation. As Table 4.3 shows (p. 63), the conclusions are also statistically robust, both with respect to a temporal shift of the autoregressive scheme and the distributed lags, and also with respect to the incorporation of contemporaneous taxes and government outlays in the CR and U equations. They are also robust to the use of both unadjusted and cyclically adjusted data (from 1971 onwards) in the same model. (A qualification of this statement is that we find that in the cyclically adjusted formulations government outlays do not appear to have a statistically significant upward effect on inflation.)

Policy implications

The principal conclusions to be drawn from these results are as follows (Table 4.4):

(1) A rise in the ratio of taxes to GDP tends to be followed by a rise in the level of unemployment in the following year. Tax increases do not appear to have a statistically significant (downward) effect on inflation. (The cyclically unadjusted figures suggest that relatively large tax increases may tend to be followed by higher rates of inflation.)
(2) A rise in the rate of monetary growth tends to be followed by a faster rise in the CPI over the following two years, but monetary growth does not appear to have any significant lasting effect on unemployment.
(3) A rise in the ratio of government outlays to GDP appears (on the evidence of the cyclically unadjusted data only) to be followed by a faster rate of increase in the CPI. But there is no evidence that it tends to have a significant downward effect on unemployment, either immediately or over the course of the three-year period.

Table 4.4 Combinations of assumptions closest to those implied by the test results

	Effect on		Effect on	
	Inflation	unemployment	Inflation	unemployment
Instrument:				
Tax cuts	0	−	0	−
Easier monetary policy	+	0	+	0
Government outlays	+	0	0	0

Notes:
A plus sign indicates 'has an upward effect on'.
A minus sign indicates 'has a downward effect on'.
A zero indicates 'has a negligible effect on'.

(4) The results are consistent with the view that a relatively high level of unemployment tends to have some effect in reducing inflation. But as the mix of macroeconomic measures with which any given level of unemployment is achieved itself affects the extent of inflation in that year, it is not necessary to tolerate a temporarily higher level of unemployment than would otherwise have been chosen, merely with the aim of checking inflation.

Table 4.4 illustrates the combinations of assumptions about the effects of the three instruments on the two objectives that most closely approximate to the results of these tests. The policy conclusions to be drawn from these results are as follows:

(1) As tax increases tend to increase unemployment a year or so later, tax rates clearly ought not to be increased, and should be reduced. This should be done so long as there is a situation of stagflation (or so long as there is any reluctance to adopt measures to reduce unemployment merely in the fear that such measures might tend to increase the upward pressure on the price level); whereas other instruments can be used to tackle inflation. (As such a policy would make it possible to operate the economy closer to full employment, a reduction in the ratio of government outlays to GDP would not necessarily involve a reduction in the actual level of government outlays – apart, of course, from those types of outlay, such as unemployment benefit payments, associated with a high level of unemployment – as real output would then be higher.)

(2) In short, these results are consistent with sets of assumptions about the effects of the macroeconomic instruments upon the principal macroeconomic objectives (over a period of three years) that make it possible to employ appropriate changes in the mix of instruments in such a way as to deal simultaneously with both inflation and unemployment. They are consistent with particular elements in the monetarist approach (namely, that monetary expansion tends to increase inflation and to have no more than a temporary effect in reducing unemployment). They are also consistent with some elements in the Keynesian approach; in particular, that tax cuts reduce unemployment when the economy is less than fully employed. But they provide no support whatever for either of the combinations of assumptions that may be characterised as typically 'monetarist' or typically 'Keynesian'. Finally,

the results suggest that any policy prescription couched in such terms as 'ease fiscal policy and tighten monetary policy' is likely to be a misleading guideline. On the one hand, it is true that one of the combinations of measures most likely to stop stagflation – tax cuts and reasonably tight monetary policy – is, indeed, a form of fiscal expansion and monetary tightness. But, on the other hand, another form of fiscal expansion – a rise in the typical form of government outlays – is unlikely to reduce unemployment, and may be expected to increase the upward pressure on prices. Furthermore, an alternative combination of measures – a reduction in the ratio of both government outlays and taxation to GDP – is likely to reduce both unemployment and inflation, and there is therefore no reason to fear that a budgetary stimulus can be provided only by increasing the budget deficit. By the same token, therefore, the results also imply that changes in the budget deficit (even after cyclical adjustment) are no indicator of the extent, or even the direction, of any fiscal stimulus: and that a balanced budget 'expansion' is likely to be contractionary.

In short, the fiscal-monetary policy dichotomy is both inadequate and potentially misleading as a guide to policy. At the very least we require a trichotomy of government outlays, tax rates and monetary policy measures if we are to frame appropriate policy prescriptions for dealing at one and the same time with both inflation and unemployment.

Conclusions

Of the many assumptions that one might make about the effects of different macroeconomic instruments on different objectives, only a very limited number leave no scope for varying the combination of macroeconomic instruments in such a way as to tackle inflation and unemployment simultaneously. But both the typical Keynesian and typical monetarist sets of assumptions share the characteristic of directing attention to cases where such a simultaneous tackling of inflation and unemployment is not possible. By contrast, the tests reported here relating to 15 OECD countries between 1967 and 1984 afford strong evidence for the view that monetary expansion affects inflation but not unemployment, and that tax cuts have a substantial effect in reducing unemployment. But government outlays (in general, and in the forms that were typical for those countries during the years in question) do not appear to affect unemployment, and probably tend to make inflation worse. This means that tax cuts plus tight money could be expected to reduce stagflation, and that restraint in the typical form of government outlays would not worsen unemployment, and might well reduce the upward pressure on the price level.

Notes and references

1. *A priori* arguments relating to their different relative effects on inflation are analysed in Perkins (1979a, 1979b, 1982, 1985). See also Chapter 2 in this volume.
2. For reasons why an easing of monetary policy might tend to raise the price level through its effects on real interest rates (apart from its effects on aggregate demand), see Lindbeck (1980), p. 171; Perkins (1982), pp. 30–40, (1985), p. 101. See also Chapter 2 in this volume, pp. 4–27.
3. These cases, and only these, out of the sixty cases where a helpful change of mix is available – may be seen as an application to the closed economy of something like the principles (associated especially with the name of Mundell) for the open economy where two instruments have a different effect on external balance for a given effect on internal balance, but where the direction of their respective effects on each objective is the same.
4. This case has been considered in Dernburg (1974, 1975); Perkins (1979a, 1980, 1982, 1985); Jones and Perkins (1986); Stephens (1980, 1984).
5. [Note added in 1998] The model we used in this paper is based on a multi-equation system, and the econometric tests applied are essentially a version of dynamic regressions with a three-year weighted distributed lag structure. These tests were suitable (rather than the full estimable parameter autoregressive dynamic specification) in view of the limitations of the data series available, and also of the short-term nature of the model. The same model has been adopted more recently to investigate the causes and the long-term impact of the 1997–8 Asian economic and financial crisis in Van Hoa and Harvie (1998), Chapter 3.

5
Some Empirical Evidence about the Macroeconomic Mix (1990)*

Introduction

In Chapter 4, the present writer, with Van Hoa (1987), discussed evidence that different forms of macroeconomic stimulus have different effects on the price level for a given effect on unemployment. The conclusion of that study was that measures of monetary expansion have been by far the most inflationary, and the least likely to have an appreciable downward effect on unemployment of the three forms of stimulus tested. Tax cuts appeared to be followed by a significant fall in unemployment over the immediately ensuing years, but without significant apparent upward effects on inflation. Rises in government outlays were intermediate between these two extremes in appearing not to be followed by significant downward effects on unemployment and by only a fairly small upward effect on inflation.

A limitation of the approach there adopted is that the observed lack of a statistically significant relationship between changes in government outlays and changes in unemployment could be because governments may often foresee an increase in unemployment, and then increase their outlays in order to alleviate it. Governments may successfully foresee rises in unemployment, and then increase their outlays on a scale that reduces the extent of the ensuing rise in unemployment, without entirely preventing it. If so, some of the fall in unemployment that might otherwise have resulted from the rise in government outlays is obscured by the rise in unemployment that still occurs. This could account for the absence of a statistically significant

---

* Originally published in *Weltwirtschaftliches Archiv (Review of World Economics)*, 126,(2) (1990).

relationship between changes in government outlays and changes in unemployment in the immediately succeeding years. It is, however, difficult to see why a similar argument should not apply also to tax cuts – whereas the latter do appear to have a statistically significant relationship with unemployment in the expected direction over the years immediately following the tax changes.

It is therefore important to compare the results of such empirical tests with those of simulations from large macroeconomic models, so far as these can throw any light on the relative effects on prices and real targets (such as real GDP/GNP or employment) of alternative forms of macroeconomic stimulus. The results of a number of such simulations are now available, and the present work compares the conclusions that can be derived from those results with those of the earlier article.

Until fairly recently the predominant macroeconomic problem facing policy makers in most countries was to reduce unemployment and also to reduce inflation. Over the last few years this problem has changed slightly, in that although unemployment still generally needs to be reduced in most countries, with inflation now at a tolerable level (in most industrialised countries, at any rate) the problem has become that of reducing unemployment without substantially increasing inflation.

But the basic problem continues to be that policy makers are often reluctant to take expansionary measures, as they believe that higher rates of inflation will result. This view seems to be based on the continued dominance in thinking about macroeconomic policy of concepts such as the so-called 'natural rate of unemployment' or 'NAIRU' (non-accelerating inflation rate of unemployment), which suggest that if unemployment falls below some specific level expansionary measures (implicitly, of whatever sort) will cause rising, or accelerating, inflation. This concept is, however, liable to be highly misleading if the rise in prices during the period that is of interest to the policy maker depends not only on the level of unemployment but also on the precise combination of measures (monetary expansion, tax rates and government outlays), and changes in those instruments, in the period.

There are a number of reasons (discussed more fully in earlier chapters) for believing that, at any given level of unemployment, the upward pressure on prices will be greater (other things being equal) if monetary policy is relatively expansionary, tax rates relatively high and government outlays also relatively high as a percentage of GDP. Those *a priori* arguments operate not only through the relative exchange rate effects of monetary expansion compared with fiscal expansion in an open economy, but also through certain direct effects on prices of those two groups of measures in a closed economy. Differentiation between the relative effects of each of the two groups of fiscal instruments is also likely to be important so far as tax increases have certain cost-increasing (or money wage-increasing) effects not shared by reductions in government outlays having the same effect on real output or employment. Indeed, so far as that is true, the dichotomy between fiscal policy and monetary policy is likely to be dangerously misleading, and needs to be replaced by a trichotomy between monetary policy, tax policy and government outlays policy.

If different macroeconomic instruments have different relative effects on the price level for a given effect on real output, a simple application of the principle of comparative advantage shows that it is possible to reduce both unemployment and the upward pressure on prices over a given period by moving the more inflationary of two instruments in a contractionary direction, and the less inflationary in an expansionary direction. So long as there are at least two macroeconomic instruments that have different relative effects on the two main objectives of macroeconomic policy, therefore, and provided that there are unused resources that can be brought into production, expansionary measures need not be forgone simply because any *individual* expansionary measure is likely to be inflationary. A combination of macroeconomic measures that will stimulate output without upward pressure on prices will thus be available unless *all* the available macroeconomic instruments that raise output have an *equal* upward effect on prices for a given upward effect on real output.

The condition that if there are at least two macroeconomic instruments that raise the price level to different extents for a given effect on real output or employment is a sufficient requirement for there to be a change of mix that will increase real output or employment without increasing inflation. But there may also be other combinations of assumptions under which appropriate changes of macroeconomic instruments would be available to deal with the two basic macroeconomic problems simultaneously or to deal with one of them without making the other problem worse.[1]

For example, there may be an instrument that will both raise real output and reduce the upward pressure on prices – and thus 'kill two birds with one stone' – certain types of tax cuts being potentially in this category as having both upward effects on real output and considerable cost-reducing effects. Or there may be an instrument that affects only one of the two main objectives, while another instrument affects them both – monetary expansion perhaps eventually affecting only prices, whereas there may be a fiscal instrument that affects real output only, or both real output and the price level. In such cases as these, combinations of measures are available that can raise employment or real output whilst reducing the upward pressure on prices – or at least making it no worse.

It is therefore crucially important for the macroeconomic health of the world economy that we should obtain as much evidence as possible on the relative effects of different macroeconomic instruments upon prices and real output; and yet such evidence has until fairly recently been remarkable by its absence. This may be because the thinking of most macroeconomists has been dominated by two sets of assumptions according to which no mix is available to deal simultaneously with both of the principal macroeconomic problems. For monetarism assumes or asserts that fiscal measures by themselves have no real effects, and that monetary measures affect only prices in the long run. 'Keynesian' approaches, on the other hand, tend to assume that, for all forms of macroeconomic stimuli, the relative 'split' between prices and output depends solely on how close the economy is to full employment – rather than on the choice of macroeconomic measures.

But recently a number of results of simulations (and some other forms of econometric testing) have been published that provide evidence as to the relative effects of alternative forms of macroeconomic stimuli upon the price level and on real output, respectively. No doubt econometricians will be able to pick holes in any one of these tests or simulations; and it is to be hoped that increasingly sophisticated methods of assessing these relative effects will be devised and applied in future. The present purpose is simply to assemble and use derivations from these simulations to draw conclusions about what are the most defensible combinations of assumptions about the direction and the relative extent of the effects on the price level and on real output of alternative forms of macroeconomic stimuli. The second section below describes the most extensive set of simulations of which the present author is aware, that undertaken at the University of Warwick in Britain, which uses all the principal available econometric models of the UK to test a wide range of different forms of macroeconomic stimuli. The third section examines the simulations undertaken by the OECD (for seven major countries, but for a more limited range of types of macroeconomic stimuli than in the models for the UK). The fourth section compares these various results among themselves and with the results of simulations for a number of alternative fiscal measures made for the (then) EEC as a whole at the European Commission, using their econometric model of the EEC in the world economy. The fifth section summarises the policy conclusions that seem to be suggested by all this evidence.

Evidence from UK models

An extensive set of simulations for an individual country – which compares the apparent effects of a number of alternative macroeconomic stimuli by the use of all the major available econometric models for that country – are those undertaken for the United Kingdom at the University of Warwick.[2]

The most recent simulations available from that source (Fisher *et al.* 1989) are for various forms of fiscal stimuli, with an accommodating monetary policy directed at holding nominal interest rates constant; and also for a cut in interest rates. (Earlier simulations, with less recent versions of the models, also included one for a rise in government expenditure with some monetary aggregate held constant.)

The models used are the four large quarterly models of the UK economy. The results of the simulations are for the annual changes, compared with the base run, in the variables (real GDP and consumer prices being the two used here) over the five-year period following the change of policy. The change of policy is in each case a once-for-all change at the beginning of the period, held at the new level for the rest of the period. In order to use this evidence to assess the comparative advantage of alternative macroeconomic instruments for increasing real output with a minimum upward effect on prices, a simple statistic has been derived from their results and is reported in Table 5.1. The average level of real output over the five years following the policy change is expressed as a percentage of the corresponding figure for the average of each of those years in the base run. Similarly, the average price level (the consumer price index, or CPI) is expressed as a percentage of its average level for those years in the base run. The first of these ratios is then expressed as a percentage of the other. This index might be called an 'output–price ratio'.[3] This means that a policy measure that increases output with only a small upward effect on prices – or one that actually reduces prices – scores more highly than one that increases output by the same amount but with a large upward effect on the price level.

76 The Reform of Macroeconomic Policy

Table 5.1 Simulated effects of alternative forms of macroeconomic stimulus in UK models on real GDP as a percentage of their effects on consumer prices

Form of stimulus	LBS[a]	NI[b]	HMT[c]	BE[d]	Average of the four models
Cut in VAT	99.7 (98.8)[e]	99.3) (97.8)	101.7 (102.4)	101.1 (101.7)	100.4 (100.2)
Cut in employers' national insurance contributions	99.0 (97.9)	99.6 (98.3)	101.2 (101.8)	100.9 (101.6)	100.2 (99.9)
Cut in income tax	98.8 (97.4)	98.4 (97.2)	100.1 (99.8)	100.6 (100.9)	99.5 (98.8)
Rise in government expenditure	99.7 (98.9)	97.8 (96.4)	99.5 (98.4)	100.1 (99.6)	99.3 (98.3)
Cut in interest rates	99.7 (99.4)	97.7 (96.7)	99.5 (97.6)	100.4 (100.2)	99.3 (98.5)

Notes:
[a] LBS = London Business School.
[b] NI = National Institute of Economic and Social Research.
[c] HMT = Her Majesty's Treasury.
[d] BE = Bank of England.
[e] All the fiscal measures are simulated on the assumption of a monetary policy that holds nominal *interest rates constant*. Figures in parentheses show the results for the fifth year after the introduction of the measure as a percentage of the corresponding figures for the base run. The measures are shown in the ranking order from the least inflationary (or, for the cut in VAT, the one having a downward effect on prices), for a given real stimulus, to the most inflationary, as indicated by the average for the four models over the whole five-year period.
The figures are calculated in the following way: (1) The average annual level of real GDP over the five years after the change in policy is first expressed as a percentage of the base figure (e.g. for a cut in VAT, the simulation with the LBS model showed the average annual level of real GDP after the policy change as 100.4 of the figure in the base run). (2) The same procedure is then applied to the level of consumer prices following the change of policy (e.g. for the cut in VAT, the simulation with the LBS model showed prices on the average of the five years as 100.7 per cent of the base run). (3) The index so calculated for real GDP is then expressed as a percentage of the index calculated as above for consumer prices. (For a cut in VAT, the simulation with the LBS model would thus show the figure of 99.7 given in the table).

Table 5.1 summarises the evidence from the most recent available simulations from this source, which are for various alternative forms of fiscal stimuli with interest rates held constant by monetary policy, and also for a reduction in interest rates. As that table shows, both the ranking for the average of the simulations with these models and that for two of the individual models (*HMT* and *BE*) provide strong evidence that cuts in the value-added tax score more highly on the present criterion than any of the other measures tested. Indeed, in two of the models (and the average of the four) cuts in VAT not only stimulate output but also have a downward effect on prices over the average of the five years, and in two models over the period to Year 5. The simulations for cuts in employers' national insurance contributions provide evidence (from two of the four models) that this form of stimulus may also operate in a helpful direction on both objectives. Income tax cuts score less well on this criterion (on the balance of the evidence) than do the other types of tax cut. But they score better than either increases in government expenditure or cuts in interest rates – two measures that have more or less the same effect on real output for a given effect on consumer prices, both on the average of the results for the models and also for three of the individual models. (These conclusions hold for the individual models apart from *LBS*; the simulations with that model – the only one that does not allow for any effect on wages – confirm only that a cut in VAT scores better than other types of tax cuts.)

This suggests the important conclusion that the dichotomy of fiscal/monetary, policy is thoroughly misleading. For the balance of the evidence from these results shows that, when each of the fiscal measures is financed in the same way (that is, with a setting of monetary policy to hold interest rates constant) the appropriate dichotomy is between tax cuts, on the one hand, and government outlays together with monetary policy, on the other, the two latter measures having broadly the same effect on prices for a given real stimulus (in three of the models and on the average of the four), whereas the various tax cuts all appear to have either a downward or an appreciably smaller upward effect on prices than government outlays or a reduction in interest rates for a given real stimulus – to judge from the bulk of this evidence.

In summary, then, this extensive evidence for the UK suggests that monetary expansion (to bring about a reduction in interest rates), or the creation of money to finance higher government outlays (or, in one model, to finance income tax cuts) is the least satisfactory form of stimulus assuming that the aim is to hold down inflation while stimulating output. Cuts in VAT are clearly the best, followed by cuts in employers' national insurance contributions. The same conclusions hold if the comparison is between the effect on output and prices in the final year (Year 5) of the simulations, rather than for the average of the whole period.

Evidence from the OECD INTERLINK model

Simulations by Richardson (1987, 1988) at the OECD relating to the seven major OECD countries show the estimated effects of certain forms of macroeconomic stimuli in those countries upon a number of variables, including real GNP/GDP and the GNP/GDP price index. The policy measures that are simulated are: (1) a rise in government outlays equal to 1 per cent of GNP/GDP; (2) a cut of two percentage points in nominal interest rates (by an easing of monetary policy); and (3) a cut in income tax equal to 1 per cent of GNP/GDP. (The last of these is not reported in the published document, but has been kindly supplied by Pete Richardson of the OECD.) The results given here for the two fiscal measures are for simulations with a fixed quantity of money and floating exchange rates; that for a cut in short-term interest rates used here is also the simulation with floating exchange rates. The outcome of the simulations is given by the OECD publication for each of the five years following the adoption of the measure in question. The figures given in Table 5.2 are for the effect of the policy change on the average annual level over the five-year period in real output or prices (as defined above) relative to the base used for the simulation. A similar comparison in parentheses is given for their values in the fifth year after the change in policy.

The first and most important conclusion is that each of the various measures simulated has different relative effects on prices for a given effect on real output. This is true for each of the seven countries, except that for France three of the four fiscal measures show the same figures for the annual average. Considerations of comparative advantage are therefore, on this evidence, relevant and applicable in determining appropriate macroeconomic policies in situations where the aim is to raise real output without worsening inflation (or, preferably, while reducing it). On this evidence, therefore, it would not be rational to resist the taking of some expansionary measures merely because of a fear the *any* form of expansion will increase inflation. For there are *combinations* of these three measures that would (on this evidence) both raise real output and reduce prices.

The second important conclusion is that the hierarchy of these three measures is, on the overwhelming balance of this evidence, consistent with that which previous chapters have suggested as being likely on *a priori* grounds. That is to say, a monetary measure of expansion (in this case a reduction of two percentage points in short-term interest rates) is generally more inflationary than bond-financed rises in government

Table 5.2 Simulated effects of alternative forms of macroeconomic stimulus on real GNP/GDP as a percentage of their effects on the GNP/GDP price index, seven major OECD countries with floating exchange rates[a]

	USA	Japan	West Germany	France	UK	Italy	Canada
Cut in income tax							
Money	99.5	100.3	100.5	100.6	100.4	100.5	99.7
	(98.3)	(99.4)	(100.4)	(100.7)	(100.1)	(100.0)	(98.6)
Constant							
Cut in income tax							
Interest rates	99.4	100.7	100.2	100.6	99.5	100.3	99.7
	(96.7)	(99.5)	(99.6)	(100.6)	(97.7)	(99.5)	(98.3)
Constant							
Rise in government outlays,							
Money	99.2	100.3	100.4	100.6	100.3	100.4	99.2
	(97.8)	(99.1)	(100.3)	(100.3)	(99.8)	(99.6)	(97.4)
Constant							
Rise in government outlays,							
Interest rates	98.5	100.6	100.1	100.5	98.9	100.2	99.1
	(95.6)	(98.9)	(99.2)	(99.9)	(96.3)	(99.0)	(96.7)
Constant							
Cut in short-term interest rates	99.0	100.2	99.7	99.8	98.8	99.2	99.9
	(97.1)	(99.9)	(99.3)	(99.6)	(97.0)	(98.3)	(99.3)

Note:
[a] Annual average over five years, with effect in Year 5 in parentheses. Figures calculated as explained in notes to Table 5.1.
Source: Derived from Richardson (1988) and data supplied by him.

outlays, or bond-financed income tax cuts – which are in most cases the least inflationary of these three measures. Each of the bond-financed forms of fiscal expansion (and also those that are accommodated, apart from the USA and Canada) is less inflationary than an expansionary change in the setting of monetary policy, for all these countries except Canada, and on both types of comparison (five-year average and final year).

A partial exception to these generalisations about the ranking of the instruments among the seven countries is Canada. For that country, these simulations suggest that government outlays are the *most* inflationary and a reduction in short-term interest rates the *least* inflationary of the three instruments, with income tax cuts being intermediate between the other two instruments simulated. But, for Canada also, income tax cuts raise prices by less for a given stimulus to real GDP than does an increase in government outlays financed in the same manner.

Furthermore, for any given fiscal stimulus, the non-accommodated form (that is, with money held constant) is in almost all cases less inflationary than the accommodated form of the stimulus (with interest rates held constant). For Japan, however, each of the fiscal measures scores less well (on one or both of the comparisons given in the table) when it is bond-financed than when it is accommodated. Both for France and for Canada the two methods of financing give the same results for tax cuts over the five-year average.

For a rise in government outlays there is also available from the OECD a (more recent) interlinked simulation, which assesses the total effects of the measures after allowing for feedback effects from other countries on to the country adopting the measure (Table 5.3). For six of the countries this simulation does not change appreciably the effect of government outlays on real output for a given effect on prices. But for the USA there is a slightly greater difference than for the other countries between the two models in the case where interest rates are held constant. Simulations for income tax cuts are not at present available for the interlinked model, and the results from a simulation of a cut in short-term interest rates with that model are not available on an exactly comparable basis to that for changes in government outlays. It is therefore not possible to say whether the relative ranking of the three instruments would be different if the results of an interlinked simulation were available for all of the three measures. The presumption would be, however, that for the USA these feedback effects are slightly more likely to be of significance than for the other countries.

Table 5.3 Simulated effects of a rise in government outlays on real output as a percentage of their effects on prices, seven major OECD countries with floating exchange rates[a]

	With fixed quantity of money		With fixed interest rate	
	Single-country model	Interlinked model	Single-country model	Interlinked model
USA	99.1	99.0	98.7	99.5
Japan	100.2	100.2	100.6	100.7
West Germany	100.4	100.4	100.4	100.4
France	100.6	100.7	100.6	100.6
UK	100.3	100.3	99.5	99.4
Italy	100.4	100.4	100.5	100.5
Canada	99.2	99.2	99.4	99.4

Note:
[a] Method of calculation as described in notes to Table 5.1.
Source: Derived from Richardson (1987, Annex Table C1).

Taken as a whole, the OECD simulations reinforce the conclusion drawn from the University of Warwick simulations for the UK, to the effect that the dichotomy of 'fiscal versus monetary' policy may be misleading and even dangerous. For, on this evidence, the two fiscal measures tested – income tax cuts and increases in government outlays – have different effects on prices for a given effect on output. At the same time, on the basis of the results of other simulations reported here, income tax cuts appear to be much closer in their relative effects on these two objectives to rises in government outlays than are other types of tax cuts. In general, however, it is true that the effects of the particular fiscal measures simulated with the OECD model are closer to one another than to those of monetary policy. For Canada, however, monetary policy appears on this evidence to be the least inflationary form of stimulus, whereas for the others it is the most inflationary.

Evidence from EEC COMPACT model

Simulations undertaken by the staff of the European Commission (Dramais, 1986) relate to the effects of alternative forms of fiscal stimulus, but do not include a simulation of monetary expansion. They are, however, interesting and helpful as being consistent with most of the evidence for the UK relating to the ranking of different types of tax cut considered on p. 76 above. The EEC simulations were made under the assumption of a constant quantity of money, whereas those with the

UK models were with interest rates held constant. The respects in which these results confirm those for the UK are that cuts in VAT, and probably also reductions in employers' social security/national insurance contributions, are likely to have a helpful effect on both objectives – tending to stimulate real output and to reduce the upward pressure on prices. Moreover, the comparison between government outlays and income tax cuts gives a result that is consistent with those of the OECD simulations, as well as with the majority of the evidence from the simulations for the UK. For the EEC results imply that, on the criterion used above (that is, the least upward effect on prices for a given real stimulus) income tax cuts score better than a general rise in government outlays (see Table 5.4).

The broad conclusion about different fiscal measures that can be derived both from the University of Warwick simulations for the UK and those from the OECD is therefore strongly confirmed by the EEC simulations. The precise type of fiscal measure employed has a considerable bearing upon the outcome, in respect of the *extent* of any effect on prices and (where there are simulations for several forms of tax cut) even in terms of the *direction* of that effect. Even the trichotomy of monetary policy, government outlays and tax rates is therefore insufficient to replace the inadequate (and often misleading) dichotomy of monetary policy and fiscal policy. For we need to consider also at least two types of tax rate cuts. Those that may reduce prices while stimulating output should be distinguished from those that may have an upward effect on prices. These, in turn, may normally be expected to be less inflationary than government outlays having the same effect on real output.

Table 5.4 Simulated effects of alternative forms of fiscal stimulus on real GDP as a percentage of their effects on prices, EEC[a]

	Cut in:			Rise in public investment
	Indirect taxes	Employers' social security contributions	Household direct taxes	
Change over 5 years	102.2	102.1	100.1	100.0
Change in Year 5	(101.9)	(102.9)	(99.7)	(98.8)

Note:
[a] Average annual change over five years, with change in Year 5 in parentheses. All the fiscal measures are simulated on the assumption of a constant quantity of money. Index numbers are calculated as outlined in notes to Table 5.1.
Source: Derived from Dramais (1986).

Policy conclusions

The principal conclusions for policy that are suggested by the evidence considered in this chapter are as follows.

If a government's macroeconomic aims (at any rate over the medium term of up to five years or so to which these tests relate) are to reduce unemployment and stimulate real output with minimum upward effect (or with some downward effect) on prices, there are mixes of measures available that seem likely to achieve those aims. One such mix is to keep monetary policy tight and to use certain forms of fiscal stimulus. The evidence from the EEC simulations suggests that cuts in indirect taxes such as VAT or in taxes on labour inputs, such as employers' social security/national insurance contributions in Europe, may be even better. Indeed, even taken on their own, tax cuts of these two last types may actually contribute to both macroeconomic objectives, by exerting downward pressure on prices while having an upward effect on real output and employment. (Note that, by the same token, this also means that if one of those two last-named instruments is moved in the wrong direction it will have adverse effects on both macroeconomic objectives.) If the fiscal stimulus is accommodated to the extent of holding down nominal interest rates in the face of the fiscal stimulus, it appears likely still to be true that a price-reducing stimulus can result from appropriate combinations of fiscal and monetary measures (to judge from the evidence from the UK models and from the OECD).

It is possible, however, that in the longer run, and for some countries and in some circumstances, other considerations relating to productivity or incentives might dictate a greater use of indirect taxation and less use of direct taxes on household income than would be justified on these medium-run macroeconomic considerations. Further (convincing) evidence would, however, be required to overthrow the presumption that can be derived from the foregoing evidence that a shift from direct to indirect taxes intensifies the medium-run macroeconomic problems facing a country. This evidence also suggests that a shift away from indirect taxes (and from taxes on labour inputs) towards direct taxes is likely to improve the medium-run macroeconomic outlook.

The evidence that different fiscal measures have different effects on prices (different in direction, in some cases, as well as different in degree) for a given effect on real output implies that changes in the cyclically adjusted (or 'structural') fiscal balance is not a good guide to whether a change in that balance towards deficit is likely to have a stimulatory effect on real output. For some combinations of measures that bring about a given change in that balance will, on this evidence, tend to raise real output and others to reduce it. By the same token, an unchanged fiscal balance within which the combinations of different taxes, or of taxes with outlays, change appreciably may either raise or reduce real output. This also means that one should not equate stimulatory fiscal measures with a move towards budget deficit. If reluctance on the part of a government to increase the fiscal deficit is inhibiting fiscal expansion, this need not continue to be an inhibiting factor. For changes in the *composition* of a given fiscal balance (or, indeed, even a movement towards surplus by an appropriate combination of fiscal changes) can have real stimulatory effects.

Nor should one assume that a movement of the fiscal balance in the direction of deficit would necessarily tend to raise prices. For this evidence suggests that there are combinations of fiscal changes in the direction of deficit that would, on the evidence considered above, tend to reduce the upward pressure on prices.

To assess the likely effect of any given change in the budget balance upon real output or prices, one therefore requires to have evidence about the relative effects on each of those macroeconomic objectives of each of the main instruments. Ideally, we need to know the effect of government outlays (preferably disaggregated into its principal components if we have evidence that different types of outlay have different effects on prices for a given effect on real output), indirect taxes, direct taxes and any taxes there may be on labour inputs.

There are other macroeconomic objectives the achievement of which will also be affected by the choice of macroeconomic instruments. If a country is concerned to change its current account balance at any given level of activity or real output it will be helpful to know the relative effects on the current account balance of alternative macroeconomic instruments, for a given effect of that instrument on real output. The available evidence (notably that from the OECD simulations drawn on above) suggests that changes in monetary policy have a negligible effect on the current account (and for some countries that effect may be favourable, but for others unfavourable), compared with either of the forms of fiscal stimuli leading to the same rise in real output. (See Chapter 6 in this volume.) For the adverse effects on the current account of the expansion in nominal aggregate demand to which monetary expansion gives rise is likely to be more or less offset by the expenditure-switching effects through the depreciation resulting from the consequent reduction in capital inflow. The OECD evidence also suggests that income tax cuts have a less adverse effect on the current account balance than does a rise in government spending, for a given real stimulus to GDP. The EEC simulations confirm that, and also suggest that a cut in VAT and cuts in employers' social security contributions will have an even less adverse effect on the current account.

If a country is also concerned with the level of private investment as a ratio of GDP it will need to take account also of the relative effects of different instruments on that objective. The available evidence (contained in Chapter 6 in this volume) confirms the *a priori* view that reductions in interest rates tend to stimulate investment. But it also suggests that (bond-financed) tax cuts encourage private investment. while (bond-financed) government outlays tend to crowd it out. These conclusions may be derived from the results of the simulations in Richardson (1987, 1988) and supplementary data provided by him for simulations of the effects of income tax cuts on the same basis.

Putting these various considerations together, therefore, a provisional conclusion would be that tight monetary policy and cuts in certain types of tax will tend to minimise the upward pressure on prices for a given real stimulus. Moreover (as we shall see in Chapter 6), tax cuts appear to have a less adverse effect than increases in government outlays on the current account at any given level of activity or for any given degree of real stimulus. They are also more likely to have a favourable effect on (private) real investment. A country that is concerned to hold down its current account deficit and to maintain or increase the ratio of private investment to GDP would consequently use restraint in government outlays rather than income tax increases – largely to minimise the upward pressure on prices, but also for the relatively helpful effects of restraint in government spending on private investment and its more favourable effect than tax increases on the current account. It would simultaneously use cuts in taxes (especially in those on employment or in the general level of indirect taxes) to stimulate real output, whilst refraining from making monetary policy too tight, so long as it wishes to stimulate real investment. If this last objective is not a pressing aim, however, it would do well to keep monetary policy tight as the most effective way of minimising inflation at any given level of activity.

There does not, therefore, appear (on this evidence) to be a conflict between choosing appropriate changes in combinations of different fiscal measures with the aim of stimulating output with minimal upward effect on prices, on the one hand, and minimising any adverse effects on the current account deficit, on the other.

It is to be hoped that econometricians will continue and extend their work with macroeconomic models to provide more evidence about the influence of a wide range of different macroeconomic instruments on the various objectives of policy for different countries.

Finally, we need to take account in our analysis of macroeconomic policy issues of the relative effects of each of the available instruments on each of a number of objectives, and to build that approach into our teaching from first year upwards.

Notes and references

1. See Chapter 4 in this volume, pp. 53–70.
2. See Wallis *et al.* (1987); Fisher *et al.* (1988, 1989).
3. A summary measure of this sort was first suggested to me by J. Kirker Stephens, though he used a 'price–output ratio', with the price change as the numerator and the output change as the denominator. I have preferred the opposite convention, as it seems more natural to give the higher index figure to a policy measure that is more successful in minimising any upward pressure on prices when a stimulus raises real output by a given amount than to one that is less successful in achieving that aim of policy.

6
Empirical Evidence about the Macroeconomic Mix in the Open Economy*

This chapter brings together empirical evidence from econometric simulations by the OECD, the EEC and the University of Warwick using the four main econometric models of the UK. It uses these results to throw light on the relative effects of different macroeconomic instruments on the current account of the balance of payments.

It relates these conclusions to the effects of the respective instruments upon output and prices that can be drawn from the same models. It then considers the policy implications that can be drawn from this evidence about the principles for determining the appropriate combinations of changes in the available instruments for dealing with current macroeconomic problems, in a framework of three macroeconomic objectives and three or more macroeconomic instruments.

There are good reasons, both on *a priori* grounds and on the basis of empirical evidence, to believe that different macroeconomic instruments have different effects on prices for a given effect on real output or employment.[1]

The greater inflationary effect of a monetary expansion (compared with either government outlays or tax cuts) for a given real stimulus is reinforced in the open economy by the tendency for monetary expansion to bring about depreciation. But that also means that a monetary expansion is likely to have a less adverse effect (and may even have a favourable effect) on the current account, and certainly a favourable effect on the level of private investment less any deterioration (or plus any improvement) in the current account balance.

---

* Originally published as University of Melbourne, Department of Economics, *Research Paper*, 234, (September 1989).

The *a priori* presumption is thus that, for a given upward effect on real output or employment, an easing of monetary policy would have the least unfavourable effect on the current account. It may even have a favourable effect on it in a world of generally floating exchange rates. For the consequent reduction in net capital inflow weakens the exchange rate. By contrast, fiscal measures of expansion, by raising interest rates, tend to attract capital inflow and to that extent strengthen the exchange rate. Comparing the two sets of fiscal measures with one another, the presumption is that government outlays, by reason of their greater upward effect on prices and money wage rates, would tend to have a more unfavourable effect on the current account than does a tax cut (for a given real stimulus).

Governments ought generally to be concerned to ensure that any measures they take to improve the current account of the balance of payments are not of a sort that would have a (fully offsetting) downward effect on useful forms of productive investment within the country. For an improvement in the country's international net debtor/creditor position (a reduction in the current account deficit or increase in the current account surplus) that is brought about only with a fully offsetting reduction in the level of its productive forms of domestic investment is unlikely to constitute an increase in the country's net wealth. Any such repercussions – positive or negative – of alternative measures on the level of private investment therefore ought also to be taken into account.

In particular, an expansionary monetary policy is likely to have a greater upward effect on private investment (for a given real stimulus, or for any adverse effect it may have on the current account balance) than are typical fiscal measures. At any rate, this is likely to be true provided that the tax cuts or government outlays in question are not specifically directed at encouraging investment. If this consideration is taken into account, therefore, the margin of advantage from using fiscal measures of restraint to improve the current account, rather than a tightening of monetary policy, would be enhanced.

On the other hand, an expansionary fiscal measure may also have some favourable effects on private investment. If this is so, that favourable effect should be deducted from any adverse effect on the current account balance that results when that fiscal instrument is moved in an expansionary direction. For that would give a measure of the effect of that change in policy upon the country's total domestic private investment plus (or minus) any change in its net overseas investment (in the shape of a change in the net current account balance) – hereafter to be termed 'thrift'. For completeness, any change in the government's own capital investment ought also to be brought into the calculation; but we shall here ignore this consideration, in effect making the assumption that the government's outlays that are being increased or reduced are not those on capital goods (or human capital).

Similarly, if a fiscal measure of expansion has an adverse effect on private investment, that effect ought to be added to the likely adverse effect of these measures upon the current account – if a government is trying to assess the likely effect on the country's thrift.

Table 6.1 shows that for all seven major OECD countries measures of monetary expansion have a negligible effect on the real current account balance, and that any small effect there may be is for some countries slightly positive and for others slightly negative, taking the average level for the five-year period as a whole. The figures for the average year-to-year change over the five-year period as a whole show that by the end of the five-year period any effect on the real current account balance has disappeared except for the USA (for which it is slightly positive) and the UK and Japan (for which it is slightly negative).

Table 6.1 also shows that for all seven major OECD countries, both a rise in government outlays and a cut in income tax rates (whether with money or interest rates held constant) would have an adverse effect on the real foreign balance; but that, for each of these countries, with an income tax cut the adverse effect would be less per unit of stimulus to real GNP/GDP than with a rise in government outlays financed in the same way. Each of these fiscal measures has a more adverse effect on the real value of the current account balance with money held constant than the same measure with an accommodating monetary policy (one that holds interest rates constant), taking the average of the five years after the change of policy. (Taking the change from the beginning to the end of the five-year period, there are some cases where, with interest rates held constant, these two fiscal measures have virtually the same effect on the real value of the current account balance for a given real stimulus.)

Table 6.2 also shows that, with money held constant, a cut in income tax again had a less unfavourable effect on thrift than a rise in government outlays (or in some cases a favourable effect when outlays had an unfavourable one).

Table 6.2 shows that these simulations suggest that, as the use of a monetary measure of expansion always had also a favourable effect on private investment, it thus had a favourable effect on thrift. On the other hand, for a given upward effect on real GNP/GDP, all the forms of fiscal expansion had either an unfavourable, or a much smaller favourable, effect on thrift than a purely monetary measure of expansion.

Table 6.1 Simulated effects of alternative measures on change in real foreign balance for 1 per cent stimulus to real GDP, with floating exchange rates, seven major OECD countries

Change in annual average level over five years as percentage of base GNP/GDP, with average annual change over the period in parentheses

	USA	Japan	West Germany	France	UK	Italy	Canada
Cut in short-term interest rates	−0.03 (+0.02)	−0.02 (−0.05)	0.00 (0.00)	+0.19 (0.00)	−0.09 (−0.03)	+0.11 (0.00)	0.00 (0.00)
Cut in income tax, interest rates constant	−0.23 (−0.05)	−0.18 (−0.06)	−0.46 (−0.11)	−0.38 (−0.07)	−0.51 (−0.10)	−0.36 (−0.07)	−0.47 (−0.09)
Rise in government outlays, interest rates constant	−0.40 (−0.09)	−0.24 (−0.06)	−0.49 (−0.15)	−0.40 (−0.07)	−0.57 (−0.11)	−0.40 (−0.10)	−0.48 (−0.10)
Cut in income tax, money constant	−0.38 (−0.13)	−0.42 (−0.04)	−0.77 (−0.23)	−0.51 (−0.13)	−0.80 (−0.25)	−0.39 (−0.09)	−0.90 (−0.50)
Rise in government outlays, money constant	−0.73 (−0.30)	−0.57 [a]	−0.83 (−0.28)	−0.64 (−0.18)	−0.96 (−0.33)	−0.49 (−0.13)	−1.04 [a]

Note:
[a] These figures are undefined, as this measure gives no stimulus to real output by Year 5 for Japan and Canada.
Source: Derived from Richardson (1987, 1988) and data supplied by him.

Table 6.2 Simulated effects of alternative measures on change in 'thrift' for 1 per cent stimulus to real GDP, floating exchange rates, seven major OECD countries

Change in annual average level over five years as percentage of base GNP/GDP, with average annual change over the period in parentheses

	USA	Japan	West Germany	France	UK	Italy	Canada
Cut in short-term interest rates	+0.84 (+0.11)	+0.83 (+0.05)	+0.52 (+0.10)	+1.02 (+0.17)	+0.93 (−0.12)	+2.01 (+0.13)	+0.54 (+0.11)
Cut in income tax, interest rates constant	+0.58 (+0.04)	+0.33 (+0.04)	+0.01 (−0.06)	+0.23 (−0.04)	−0.12 (−0.01)	+0.25 (+0.01)	+0.04 (+0.05)
Rise in government outlays, interest rates constant	−0.03 (+0.03)	+0.19 (+0.03)	0.16 (−0.08)	+0.06 (+0.04)	−0.18 (−0.01)	+0.03 (+0.01)	−0.06 (+0.05)
Cut in income tax, money constant	0.24 (−0.27)	−0.33 (−0.26)	−0.35 (−0.15)	+0.03 (−0.02)	−0.84 (−0.37)	+0.14 (−0.17)	−0.20 (−0.36)
Rise in government outlays, money constant	−0.83 (−0.41)	−1.01 [a]	−0.67 (−0.24)	−0.34 (−0.08)	−1.18 (−0.07)	−0.27 (−0.12)	−0.72 [a]

Note:
[a] These figures are undefined, as this measure gives no stimulus to real output by Year 5 for Japan and Canada.
Source: Derived from Richardson (1987, 1988) and data supplied by him.

The same broad conclusions follow when interest rates are held constant in the face of expansionary fiscal measures: the cut in income tax always scores better than the rise in government outlays in terms of its effects on the average level of thrift over the five years. As a stimulus of this sort is midway between a monetary expansion (a cut in short-term interest rates in these simulations) and a fiscal expansion with money held constant, it is not surprising that the effects of a given fiscal change on thrift (as also those on the current account) are intermediate between those of a monetary stimulus and those of the same fiscal stimulus with money held constant.

More often than not, income tax cuts with interest rates held constant have a favourable effect on thrift (on either of the statistical measurements given in Table 6.2) – the exceptions being Britain (marginally) for the five-year average level, and France, West Germany and Britain for the average annual change over the course of the period. Government outlays (with interest held constant) have a downward effect on thrift in a majority of the countries over the five-year average, though in only two of them for the change over the whole period.

As the different fiscal measures have different effects on the average level of thrift over the five years (as also on the current account taken alone) for a given real stimulus, there are clearly combinations of fiscal measures that can be used to increase real output without an adverse effect on thrift (or on the current account, or both). In particular, there are clearly combinations of tax cuts and reductions in government outlays that can be used to raise real output (with the quantity of money held constant or, alternatively, with an accommodating monetary policy) to give a stimulus to real output without bringing about a net adverse effect on the real foreign balance or thrift. In order to do this it must be given by way of the fiscal measure with the less adverse effect (or the greater favourable effect) on the current account (or on thrift), with the other fiscal measure being operated in a contractionary direction, if necessary, to an appropriate extent. Clearly no contractionary adjustment of another measure would be needed if a form of stimulus is used that has a net favourable effect on thrift (or the current account), even taken by itself.

For several of these countries a stimulus could be provided without a worsening of the current account by a combination of measures that included a monetary expansion (Table 6.3). But this evidence from the OECD simulations shows that, for all countries except Canada, monetary expansion has a much greater upward effect on prices (per unit of real stimulus) than any of these forms of fiscal expansion; so that if

Table 6.3 Combinations of income tax cuts with reductions of government outlays equal to 1 per cent of GNP/GDP to give non-inflationary stimulus, floating exchange rates and fixed quantity of money, seven major OECD countries

Annual average over five years as percentage of base GNP/GDP; range of income tax cuts that will give a non-inflationary stimulus if coupled with 1 per cent cut in government outlays with money held constant

	USA	Japan	West Germany	France	UK	Italy	Canada
Total range	0.9–1.24	1.06–1.29	1.00–1.40	1.15–1.86	1.08–2.17	1.08–1.61	1.29–1.81
Of which							
Range with constant or improving real foreign balance	0.9–1.24	1.06–1.29	1.00–1.07	1.15–1.45	1.08–1.30	1.08–1.33	None
Range with constant or increasing 'thrift'[a]	0.9–1.24	1.06–1.29	1.00–1.07	1.15–1.45	None	1.08–1.33	1.29–1.47

Note:
[a] Private investment *plus* any rise or *minus* any fall in real foreign balance.
Source: As for Table 6.1.

the country in question is concerned to hold down prices as well as to give a real stimulus with minimal adverse effect on private investment and the current account, it will not necessarily be well advised to use a monetary stimulus merely because it has the largest favourable effect on thrift – unless, of course, the consequently greater upward pressure on prices is not a matter of serious concern to the government.

This being so, it is important for a country that also wishes to hold down prices to know whether there are combinations of the fiscal instruments, or of fiscal instruments together with monetary policy, that will give a non-inflationary stimulus while improving the current account or also giving a stimulus to thrift – or at least avoiding any adverse effect on these. There are a range of combinations of income tax cuts that could, on the evidence of these OECD simulations, be combined with a reduction in government outlays in such a way as to give a non-inflationary stimulus. We need now to enquire whether or not those combinations of reductions in government outlays and income tax cuts will tend also to have a favourable effect on the real foreign balance or on thrift.

Table 6.3 shows the range of income tax cuts that can be combined with a reduction in government outlays equal to 1 per cent of GDP to give a non-inflationary stimulus in each of these countries, with a constant quantity of money; and also the range of these income tax cuts that will give a non-inflationary stimulus without worsening the real foreign balance. The table also shows that for all these countries except Britain there is a range of income tax cuts that would, on the same assumptions, give a non-inflationary stimulus without having an adverse effect on thrift.

Furthermore, Table 6.3 shows that those simulations also imply that in all these countries except Canada there is a range of income tax cuts that could be combined with a reduction in government outlays to give a non-inflationary stimulus without worsening the real foreign balance; and that for all these countries except Britain that would also be consistent with avoiding a fall in thrift.

Table 6.4 shows a more detailed working of these calculations for the USA, partly to show the method of calculation, and partly because of the importance to the world generally, and not only to the USA, of knowing whether or not there are combinations of fiscal measures that can provide a non-inflationary stimulus in the USA while still improving the US balance of payments on current account. The results cast considerable doubt on the justification for the constantly re-iterated advice to the USA to reduce its budget deficit in order to reduce its current account deficit.

Table 6.4 Simulated effects of alternative fiscal measures in the USA, floating exchange rates and fixed quantity of money

Change in five-year annual average

	Effects on			
	Real GNP	GDP price index	Fiscal balance	Real foreign balance
			(% of base GNP)	
Policy change (% of GNP)				
Rise in government outlays (1%)	0.66	1.52	−1.14	−0.48
Income tax cut (1%)	0.74	1.22	−1.08	−0.28
Rise in government outlays (l%)	+0.66	+1.52	−1.14	−0.48
Rise in income tax (1.1%)	−0.81	−1.34	+1.16	+0.31
Both the above	+0.15	+0.18	+0.02	−0.17
Cut in government outlays (1%)	−0.66	−1.52	+1.14	+0.48
Income tax cut (1.6%)	+1.18	+1.96	−1.78	−0.46
Both the above	+0.52	+0.44	−0.64	+0.02

Source: As for Table 6.1.

Table 6.4 shows that (according to the OECD simulations for the USA) alternative combinations of changes in government outlays and income tax in the USA would be possible that would either: (1) lead to an *improvement* in the fiscal balance with a deterioration of the real foreign balance; or (2) lead to a deterioration of the fiscal balance with an improvement in the real foreign balance.

This emphasises that the 'twin deficits' approach – which argues that a reduction in the fiscal deficit is necessary in order to achieve a reduction in the current account deficit – is highly misleading; for the above figures illustrate that a reduction in the fiscal deficit is neither a sufficient nor a necessary condition for an improvement in the current account balance.

Indeed, if an attempt is made to reduce the fiscal balance by a combination of measures that includes a rise in government outlays together with a rise in income taxes sufficient to bring about a reduction in the fiscal deficit, these figures suggest that only if the tax increase were sufficient to reduce the fiscal deficit by nearly 0.9 per cent of GNP would this result in a fall in the real foreign deficit. It also suggests that in the process it would lead to a net fall of 0.7 per cent in GNP. (A balanced budget increase of government outlays and income taxes would, on these figures lead to a fall in real GNP.)

If the movement towards reducing the external deficit was by way of reductions in both income tax and government outlays, however, by reversing the signs in the preceding example it may be seen that a cut in government outlays equal to 1 per cent of GNP combined with a cut in income tax equal to under 1.7 per cent of GNP could bring about an *improvement* in the current account balance, though with a substantial increase in the fiscal deficit – and a substantial net stimulus to real GNP. This emphasises how attempts to reduce the external deficit by reducing the fiscal deficit may rule out combinations of these two fiscal measures that could improve the external deficit without reducing (and, indeed, even while actually increasing) real output.

If simulations were available for the USA of other types of tax cut, notably cuts in indirect taxes, one might reasonably suppose that – on the basis of the results for the EEC reported in a later section – it would be even more likely that an improvement in the current account could be brought about by combinations of measures (including cuts in indirect taxes) that would not reduce the fiscal deficit; and that reductions in the fiscal deficit that were brought about by way of increases in indirect taxes would not necessarily reduce the external deficit, and might be expected to reduce real output and exert upward pressure on prices.

Evidence from simulations with UK models

Table 6.5 shows that simulations at the University of Warwick with the four main quarterly models of the UK economy indicate that, on the average of the following five years, of the measures of macroeconomic stimulus that were simulated in these tests, a cut in short-term interest rates has the smallest adverse effect on the current account for a given stimulus to real output in two of the four models and, in one model,

Table 6.5 Simulated effects of alternative macroeconomic measures on UK current account balance for 1 per cent rise in real GDP

(change in average annual level of current account over five year as per cent base GDP)

	LBS	NI	HMT	BE	Average
Cut in short-term interest rates	−0.72	−0.08	−0.18	+0.30	−0.17
Cut in income tax[a]	−0.67	−0.29	−0.66	−0.17	−0.45
Cut in VAT[a]	−0.79	−0.43	−0.51	−0.17	−0.48
Cut in employers' national insurance contributions[a]	−0.52	−0.40	−1.74	−0.53	−0.80
Rise in government outlays[a]	−0.43	−0.35	−0.53	−0.72	−0.46
Rise in government outlays with money constant	−0.96	−0.44	−1.98	−0.26	−0.91

Notes:
[a] Signifies 'with interest rates held constant'.
LBS = London Business School.
NI = National Institute of Economic and Social Research.
HMT = Her Majesty's Treasury.
BE = Bank of England.
Source: Derived from Fisher et al. (1988).

even a positive effect on the current account. In the remaining model, two of the tax cuts simulated (with interest rates held constant), as well as an accommodated rise in government outlays, have a less adverse effect on the current account (per unit of stimulus to real GNP) than does a monetary expansion.

But in all four models a rise in government outlays with money held constant had the largest adverse effect on the current account (for a given real stimulus) among the measures tested (all the other fiscal measures being tested with interest rates held constant), except that in one model a cut in employers' national insurance contributions had an even bigger adverse effect on the current account. If, therefore, a reduction in government outlays, with money held constant, were accompanied by an appropriate cut in income tax (all models) or by a cut in VAT or in employers' national insurance contributions (each in three of the models), with interest rates held constant, these figures suggest that it would be possible to provide a real stimulus with a simultaneous improvement in the current account.

Over the average for the five-year period, in three of the four models a tightening of monetary policy would be the worst way (in terms of the amount of real output that would have to be forgone) among those tested to achieve a given improvement in the current account of the balance of payments (and in one model it would actually worsen the current account). In every model it would be clearly less efficient for this purpose than a cut in government outlays with money held constant, and also inferior to a rise in VAT or to a cut in government outlays with interest rates held constant. In three of the four models it would also be inferior to a rise in employers' national insurance contributions. Reductions in government outlays (with money held constant) could thus (on this evidence) be combined with one or more of these alternative forms of fiscal stimulus in such a way as to increase real output without worsening the current account.

Trying to improve the current account by tight monetary policy would also be inferior to an accommodated rise in VAT in all four models and to an accommodated rise in employers' national insurance contributions in three of them; so that some combination of an easing of monetary policy with a rise in VAT, and perhaps a rise in employers' national insurance contributions, would be another way of bringing about a net improvement in the current account.

It was shown in Table 6.1 that the results of the OECD simulations indicated (consistently with the balance of the results for the UK given in Table 6.5) that, of the measures simulated by them, tight monetary policy was the worst way of trying to improve the current account, in view of the fall in real output needed if it were to succeed. Moreover, for the UK it would not (on those simulations, as also for the Warwick test using the Bank of England model) improve the current account at all on the average of the five years. On the OECD simulations also, it was seen that of the measures tested in their model a cut in government outlays with money held constant had the greatest effect in improving the UK's current account for a given decline in real output (that is, a smaller fall in real output was needed to effect a given improvement in the current account) than with any of the other measures tested. This was also true of three of the four UK models.

The conclusions about the UK that can be derived from the OECD simulations can thus be used to complement the Warwick tests – which assume that interest rates are held constant when fiscal measures are employed (except for one set of simulations of a rise in government outlays).

The OECD conclusions are generally consistent with the balance of the evidence from the tests using the UK models, so far as the two sets of results can be compared with one another – that is, so far as they relate to cuts in interest rates, to bond-financed government outlays, and to accommodated cuts in income tax or accommodated rises in government outlays. But the OECD simulation results imply also that if a rise in income tax rates or a cut in government outlays was employed to try to improve the current account, it would be better to hold money constant than to keep interest rates fixed; and that a cut in government outlays would be preferable to a rise in income tax financed in the same way if either of those instruments were to be used to try to improve the current account with a minimum loss of real output.

Evidence from EEC simulations

Table 6.6 shows that simulations done with the EEC COMPACT model (Dramais 1986) of alternative forms of bond-financed stimulus had varying effects on the current account balance of the EEC as a whole, for any given effect on real GDP.

Cuts in income tax had an only slightly less adverse effect on the current account than did rises in government outlays for a given effect on real GDP, but the other two types of tax cut simulated had a much less adverse effect over the average of the five years after the introduction of the measure than did a rise in government outlays (indeed, only about half as great). The main difference in the relative effects on the current account is thus between government outlays or cuts in income tax, on the one hand, and cuts in employers' social security contributions or in value-added tax, on the other.

As Table 6.6 shows, the evidence from the EEC simulations (which relate only to fiscal measures of stimulus, and with money held constant – in effect, each fiscal stimulus being bond-financed) suggests that the ranking of these four instruments is the same in terms of their respective effects on the average level of the current account as for their effects on private investment (for a given stimulus to real GDP). A cut in employers' social security contributions is the only one of these measures that has such a large upward effect on private investment as to exceed its unfavourable effect on the current account balance (its adverse effect on which is the least of the four); a cut in indirect taxes has more or less the same upward effect on private investment (per

Table 6.6 Simulated effects of alternative fiscal measures on the current account balance and on private investment, for 1 per cent rise in real GDP, EEC

Change in average annual level over five years a per cent of base GDP, with average annual change over five years in parentheses

	Change in current account	Change in private investment	Change in private investment[a] less change in current account
Cut in employers' social security contributions	–0.22 (–0.03)	+0.45 (+0.03)	+0.23 (0.00)
Cut in household indirect taxes	–0.32 (–0.02)	+0.23 (+0.03)	–0.09 (+0.01)
Cut in household direct taxes	–0.47 (–0.11)	+0.21 (–0.04)	–0.26 (–0.07)
Rise in public investment	–0.50 (–0.16)	+0.15 (–0.03)	–0.35 (–0.19)

Note:
[a] Figures for private investment, which are expressed as a percentage of baseline investment in the original, have here been converted to a percentage of GDP using the ratio of Gross Private Fixed Capital Formation to GDP in 1986 from OECD, *Historical Statistics* (1984).
Source: Derived from Dramais (1986).

unit of stimulus to real GDP) as does a cut in household direct taxes; but the cut in indirect taxes, as well as having a slightly more favourable effect on private investment than cuts in household direct taxes, has a much less adverse effect on the current account. Government outlays (in this simulation described as 'public investment' – though the source makes it clear that the model does not permit the effects of this form of public spending on goods and services to be differentiated from those of other forms) – clearly has the greatest adverse effect on the current account and the least favourable effect on private investment of the four forms of fiscal stimulus that were simulated by the EEC.

Taking together the effects upon private investment and on the current account balance (together termed 'thrift') of each of these fiscal measures, and comparing their effects with that on the current account taken by itself, it may be seen that government outlays – which were only marginally the form of stimulus that had the most adverse effect on the current account – are the measure that had clearly the most adverse effect on thrift. A cut in household direct tax, which had nearly as great an adverse effect on the current account as did a rise in government outlays having the same effect on real output, had an appreciably smaller adverse effect on thrift than did government outlays.

A cut in indirect taxes, which had only a slightly more adverse effect on the current account than did a cut in employers' social security contributions, had a small adverse effect on thrift; and a cut in employers' social security contributions had a very marked positive effect on this combined total, in contrast to its clearly adverse effect on the current account.

If one looks at the average year-to-year change from the beginning to the end of the five-year period (rather than that in the average level over the five years), the ranking of these measures is not substantially different. But on this criterion the cut in indirect taxes now scores best in terms of its effect on thrift (which is now slightly positive) or on the current account taken alone. The rise in government outlays still has the greatest adverse effect on the current account alone or on thrift, with a cut in household direct taxes being superior to a rise in government outlays, but inferior to the two other measures tested.

A non-inflationary stimulus and the current account

The EEC simulations imply that there are various combinations of tax cuts with reductions in government outlays that can be used to give a non-inflationary stimulus; and that, even taken alone, a cut in employers' social security contributions not only gives a non-inflationary stimulus to output, but (to judge from these results) does not have an unfavourable effect on the total of private investment *less* any rise in the current account deficit (though it tends to worsen the current account balance taken by itself).

Let us take first the combination of a cut in government outlays equal to 1 per cent of GDP and a simultaneous reduction in income tax sufficient to give a non-inflationary stimulus. As Table 6.7 shows, the extent to which (according to the results of this simulation) household

Table 6.7 Simulated effects on private investment and the current account of alternative forms of fiscal stimulus, EEC

Change in average annual level over five years as percentage of base GDP, with average annual change over the five years in parentheses

	Effect on:				
	Current account (1)	Private investment (% of base GDP) (2)	'Thrift' (3) = (1) + (2)	Real GDP (%) (4)	GDP price index (%) (5)
Change (as % of base GDP)					
Cut in government outlays (1%)	+0.44 (+0.08)	−0.13 (+0.02)	+0.31 (+0.10)	−0.88 (−0.34)	−0.88 (−0.34)
Cut in household direct tax (1.5%)	−0.42 (−0.12)	+0.19 (+0.05)	−0.23 (−0.07)	+0.90 (+0.21)	+0.72 (+0.30)
Cut in household indirect tax (0.9% of GDP)	−0.24 (−0.04)	+0.21 (+0.05)	−0.03 (+0.01)	+0.92 (+0.20)	−0.92 (−0.14)
Reduction in employers' social security contributions (1% of GDP)	−0.20 (−0.04)	+0.40 (+0.16)	+0.20 (+0.12)	+0.90 (+0.30)	−1.02 (−0.28)

Source: As for Table 6.6.

direct tax would need to be cut in order to give a non-inflationary stimulus by this combinations of measures would leave a substantial net favourable effect on the current account or on thrift. This can be seen from the figure in the line for cuts in household direct taxes relating to the average effect over the five years on the current account, or on the total for private investment less any rise in the current account deficit – figures that are substantially less adverse than the corresponding (positive) ones for a cut in government outlays.

Moreover, if the cut in government outlays equal to 1 per cent of GDP were combined with either of the other two types of tax cut there is a also a range of combinations with these tax cuts that would provide a non-inflationary stimulus without a deterioration of the current account and without a reduction in thrift. For in each case the table shows that the adverse effect on the current account of the tax cuts in question is much less than the favourable effect of the cut in government outlays (for the same effect on real output); and that the upward effect on private investment of the tax cuts exceeds the downward effect on investment of the cut in government outlays.

The last two columns of the table show that in each case the tax cuts of the order shown increase real GDP by more than it is reduced by a cut in government outlays equal to 1 per cent of GDP; and that the net effect on prices of the cut in government outlays coupled with tax cuts of the order shown is in each case downwards.

The household direct tax cuts illustrated in Table 6.7 are in each case about the minimum that would have a favourable effect on all the objectives (assuming the aim is to reduce the current account deficit and raise real output without raising prices). Clearly, much bigger cuts in employers' social security contributions or in household indirect taxes would have a helpful effect on all these objectives; only if the cuts in either of those taxes were equal to at least 2 per cent of GDP would the provision of a further non-inflationary stimulus in this way bring about a net deterioration in the current account. Any cut in household direct taxes appreciably larger than that shown in the table would, however, bring about a net deterioration in the current account.

If a comparison is made of the effects over the course of the whole five-year period (in effect, comparing the situation at the end of that period with what it would have been in the absence of the policy change), cuts in these taxes of the order shown in the table, together with a cut in government outlays equal to 1 per cent of GDP, could still be expected to give a non-inflationary stimulus. But the table also shows that by the end of the period cuts in household direct taxes of the order shown would lead to a rise in the current account deficit, though not to a net adverse effect on thrift. A smaller cut in household direct taxes (equal to only 1 per cent of GDP) with a cut in government outlays of the same order would, however, still leave a non-inflationary stimulus, without a worsening of the current account. Cuts in the other taxes of the order shown, with the same reduction in government outlays, would continue to have favourable net effects on all the objectives at the end of the five-year period.

Table 6.8 shows the minimum cuts in each of these three different types of taxes that would, in combination with a reduction in government outlays equal to 1 per cent of GDP, leave a net rise in real output without upward pressure on the price level.

It may be seen that the increase in the current account deficit resulting from the minimum tax cut needed to provide a net real stimulus in the face of this reduction in government outlays is in each case less than the improvement in the current account balance resulting from the reduction in government outlays; so that the minimum tax cut required to provide a real non-inflationary stimulus (coupled with that reduction in government spending) also has a net favourable effect on the current account balance as well as on thrift.

Table 6.8 Simulated effects on the EEC current account of alternative combinations of tax cuts with reductions in government outlays equal to 1 per cent of GDP[a]

Change in annual average of five years after the change as percentage of base GDP; range of tax cuts (as percentage of GDP) that will give a non-inflationary stimulus with stated effect on current account balance

	To keep current account constant	To reduce current account deficit	To reduce current account surplus
Cut in household direct tax	1.6	1.5–1.6	1.6–1.8
Cut in employers' social security contributions	2.2	1.0–2.2	More than 2.2
Cut in household indirect taxes	1.7	0.9–1.6	More than 1.6

Note: All the measures tested assume that the quantity of money is held constant.
Source: As for Table 6.6.

There is a range of tax cuts of which this is true. But it may also be seen that for cuts in employers' social security contributions or in household indirect taxes, there is a range of tax cuts that can be coupled with a cut in government outlays to give a non-inflationary stimulus but with a net *upward* effect on any current account deficit (or downward effect on any current account surplus). This is obviously an important conclusion when a country has an excessive structural current account surplus; for it means that there are combinations of fiscal measures available that will help to solve this problem *without the need for such countries to introduce inflationary forms of fiscal stimulus*. In that case, such a country would be able to reduce its current account surplus by appropriate forms of fiscal policy, even though at the same time holding domestic real output constant or even reducing it.

Conclusions

The results of these simulations (coming as they do from a variety of sources and models) afford strong evidence that there are combinations of macroeconomic instruments that can give a non-inflationary stimulus. Indeed, there are ones that can stimulate real output or employment while also exerting *downward* pressure on prices (at least over a five-year period). But that also means that such combinations are often also ones that will tend to improve the balance on current account. If a country feels inhibited from taking expansionary action (when it has unemployed resources) merely by fears that a stimulatory policy must inevitably exert upward pressure on prices or have adverse effects on the current account, therefore, a choice of appropriate combinations of two or more macroeconomic instruments will (on this evidence) generally be available to enable it to set those qualms at rest. On the other hand, there are also combinations of measures that will, on this evidence, provide a non-inflationary stimulus but which would at the same time tend to reduce a current account surplus.

It may be argued that if a tightening of monetary policy is one of the measures used to restrain prices, most of its effect operates through the exchange rate, and will to that extent be operating in a manner that exports to other countries the inflationary pressures that the country tightening its monetary policy is seeking to reduce. If, however, that is felt to be a sufficient objection to a mix of tighter monetary policy coupled with fiscal expansion, there are other combinations, of reductions in government outlays combined with certain types of tax cuts on the appropriate scale (and probably with *any* types of tax cut), that will achieve the same aim of providing a non-inflationary stimulus without relying on the exchange rate as their channel of operation, and often with net favourable effects (or at least no adverse effect) on the current account.

The alternative of changing the mix *within* fiscal policy (rather than as between fiscal and monetary measures) has the additional advantage that the use of a tightening of monetary policy to reduce inflation would have been likely also to have adverse effects on the level of private investment at any given level of activity. If this consideration is felt to be important, and if it is therefore added to the presumption that a tightening of monetary policy will have only a small effect – even the direction of which is uncertain – on the current account, this means that changes within the fiscal mix are appropriate for a country that is concerned to maintain the ratio of private investment to GDP (or to avoid reducing the total of private investment *less* any rise in the current account deficit), rather than a change in mix that includes a tightening of monetary policy.

At any given time one might hope that there will be as many countries concerned to try to reduce an excessive current account surplus as to reduce an external deficit. For if there is on balance more concern on the part of governments to reduce external deficits than surpluses, the net effect will be downward pressure on demand in the world economy; for the totality of efforts to improve the current account of the balance of payments would in that case bring about a net deflationary effect. On the other hand, if the majority of governments were trying to increase their current account deficits, that would be tending to cause excess demand in the world economy.

If, however, at any given time, the state of the current account of some countries is thought to be excessively strong, on a scale that approximately balances the extent to which other countries believe theirs to be excessively weak, it should thus not be thought to be a general disadvantage if the combinations of measures most likely to provide a non-inflationary stimulus happened to be also ones that tended to worsen the current account. One would expect that there would be some forms of non-inflationary stimulus that could be used by countries wishing also to reduce their external deficits on current account, and other forms of non-inflationary stimulus that could be used by countries with excessive external surpluses while reducing those surpluses. It is thus of special interest and importance that the evidence discussed above implies that, for some countries at any rate, there appear to be some combinations of different fiscal instruments that will tend to provide a non-inflationary stimulus and also have a favourable effect on the current account; and that for many countries there is also a different range of these or other combinations of fiscal instruments that would give a non-inflationary stimulus while tending to reduce an excessive current account surplus.

Moreover, the combinations of measures that will provide a non-inflationary stimulus will not necessarily involve an increase in a country's fiscal deficit; so that if fears that this may occur are inhibiting a government from taking expansionary action, this need not necessarily be a barrier. At the very least, the equating in so many people's minds of the provision of a fiscal stimulus with a movement of the fiscal balance towards greater (structural) deficit is not defensible. It also appears to be true that combinations of fiscal measures that will tend to improve the current account balance may not necessarily be ones that will tend also to reduce the fiscal deficit, especially if they are also to be combinations that will help to stimulate the level of employment and real output while holding down the price level. By the same token, some combinations of measures that would tend to reduce the fiscal deficit would not tend to improve the current account balance. This being so, the so-called 'twin-deficits' approach is not merely unhelpful, but it may very often lead to the adoption of measures that will make the external problem worse, even if they reduce the fiscal deficit; and it may also lead to combinations of measures that will tend to reduce real output or employment (for any given degree of upward pressure on prices), or to bring about a greater degree of upward pressure on prices for any given level or rate of increase in real output or employment.

The most general conclusion ought therefore to be that we must stop trying to assess the extent of the effects of different macroeconomic policies – whether on output, prices or the state of the current account – by looking at their effects on fiscal balances. The only analysis that is likely to be helpful is one that relates changes in particular fiscal instruments to their respective effects on all the macroeconomic objectives that are of interest – real output or employment; 'inflation' (as indicated by the upward pressure on prices over the period that is of interest to the policy maker); and the state of a country's current account ± any change in the level of useful productive investment. A framework of analysis that involves these three broad macroeconomic objectives and at least three instruments (more if different types of taxes are also included) must always be employed in appraising policy and prescribing appropriate measures to meet any given situation if rational policies are to be devised and implemented.

Notes and references
1. For reasons why different instruments may be expected to have different effects on each of the various macroeconomic objectives, see Chapter 2 in this volume.

7
Public Finance and Macroeconomic Policy (1991)*

Introduction

In a celebrated article in 1945 Colin Clark argued that when taxation reached 25 per cent or more of net national income it tended to cause inflation – not immediately, but over succeeding years.[1] In 1964, and again in a revised form of the same essay in 1970, he returned to the theme and elaborated that argument.[2] There he illustrated it with figures that he interpreted as implying that the countries with the highest tax ratios tended to have the highest rates of inflation. He pointed to the undoubted fact that inflation had been endemic in the period since the end of the Second World War – a period when the ratios of tax revenue to national income had in virtually all developed countries been well above the 25 per cent figure. More recently, in conversation with the present writer, he confirmed his view on this matter, saying that the positive relationship between high taxes and high inflation, though weak, was a clear one.[3] It is probably to be regretted that he originally put such emphasis on the 25 per cent figure – which could easily be contested on both *a priori* and empirical grounds (though his use of it probably served to draw considerably more attention than it would otherwise have attracted).[4] But it probably tended to divert attention from the importance of his basic insight that taxes have certain inflationary effects that need to be set against whatever effect they may have in holding down inflation by restraining aggregate demand.[5] Even now, it does not appear

---

* Inaugural Colin Clark Memorial Lecture, given at the University of Queensland, 7 June 1991, and published in *Economic Analysis and Policy*, 22(1), (March 1992). Helpful comments by Ian McDonald on an earlier draft are gratefully acknowledged; but he is not responsible for remaining deficiencies.

that this basic insight of Clark's has been incorporated into the conventional wisdom of macroeconomists.

But there has (to the best of my knowledge) been no convincing argument raised in the literature that would lead one to reject the basic idea that taxes (at least above a certain level) have cost-push effects. Governments have, in recent years, come to act to some extent as though they accept the basic Clark proposition. For they have begun to hold down the ratio of taxes (and government outlays) to GDP during the 1980s, after its almost uninterrupted rise in most countries between the late 1960s and the early 1980s. They have on this issue thereby shown a good deal more perspicacity than virtually all the contributors to the mainstream literature of macroeconomics.[6]

Clark's thesis was not merely a statistical observation. He adduced *a priori* arguments for his views, more fully and convincingly in his Hobart paper of 1964:

> taxation (some forms of which may have less effect than others) raises costs partly through discouraging productive effort; more significantly, perhaps in causing industrialists to become careless about costs (if half of any increase is 'on the Treasury', they will make much less effort to avoid it, whether it be a wage increase, interest charges, or an expense account) and, finally, and in rather a subtle manner, the existence of a high level of taxation alters the whole climate of politics: politicians tend to lose their capacity to resist pressures, whether governmental or private, leading to cost increases, in the more or less unconscious knowledge that a rise in prices will lower the real value of all fixed charges on the budget and in that way lighten their burden.[7]

He might also have added – though perhaps he meant it to be implicit in what he said – that the taxes on business inputs are presumably passed on in the prices that businessmen quote. Moreover, so far as wage and salary earners are interested in post-tax income, increases in taxes cause them (*ceteris paribus* – in particular, at a given level of unemployment) to demand higher wages and salaries ('shift their supply curves to the left') in pre-tax terms. This would then exert upward pressure upon costs and prices at any given level of unemployment.

The clear policy implication to be drawn from this is that governments ought to have refrained from using increases in taxation (rather than other instruments) to try to hold down inflation. Governments have, however, often raised taxes in the post-war period when demand appeared excessive – in preference to reducing government outlays and also (at least up to the early 1980s) in preference to tightening monetary policy. This meant that the (supposedly) 'anti-inflationary' macroeconomic instrument that they have often preferred was one that tended (on this view) to some extent to make inflation worse. At the very least, it certainly tended to make it worse at any given level of real output or employment, by comparison with the alternative macroeconomic measures of restraint. In other words, the rate of inflation – or the rise in prices in any given period – does not depend (on this view) solely on the level of (nominal) aggregate demand relative to capacity (or perhaps on changes in that relationship). It also depends on the level of taxation, and perhaps especially (as Clark's 1964 essay suggested) on the level of particular types of taxation.[8]

An indirect corollary of that conclusion is that there is no point in tolerating a higher level of unemployment than would otherwise have been chosen merely in the hope of thereby reducing inflation. For so long as there are taxes that can be reduced (at any rate down to the lower limit of 25 per cent of national income, or whatever that limit may be), they could reduce taxation and simultaneously move a more inflationary instrument in the contractionary direction. This should be done to whatever extent is needed to hold employment constant on balance (or even to give a real stimulus). It would thus be possible to exert downward pressure on prices without incurring the social and economic costs of high unemployment and lost output.

It is worth emphasising that one can draw that conclusion about policy even if tax increases do not actually increase inflation, provided that they do not reduce inflation as much as a reduction in government outlays having the same effect on employment.

If one accepts also the view that expansionary monetary measures are more inflationary than either fiscal instrument for a given real stimulus (whether because of their relative effects on the exchange rate or for reasons internal to the economy), one has more than one appropriate combination of macroeconomic measures.[9] For in that case one can tighten monetary policy while reducing taxes or increasing government outlays. This will be so provided that a contractionary monetary policy has a greater downward effect on prices than the rise in prices brought about by an increase in government outlays having a fully offsetting effect on employment.

Clark's 1945 article also argued that a ratio of government spending to net national income above 25 per cent tended to increase inflation when government spending exceeded tax revenue. Clark did not pursue this point in his 1964 essay. But perhaps his arguments relating to taxation (even taken alone) are sufficient to justify this second point. For they imply that, at any given level of aggregate demand – or of total fiscal stimulus – rises in government outlays are more likely to raise prices than are tax cuts (which may, indeed, on Clark's thesis, even be expected to hold inflation down).

Note that this hypothesis rules out the use of figures for changes in the budget deficit as any indication of whether a given change in fiscal policy is tending to make inflation worse; or of the extent, or even of the direction, in which the change will affect employment. For the net effect on the budget balance of the chosen combination of higher government outlays and lower taxes (either or both of which tend to increase the deficit) does not tell us whether it will tend to worsen inflation, or even whether it will raise real aggregate demand. If both a rise in government spending and a rise in taxation tend to increase prices at any given level of activity, the relative extent of changes in both sides of the budget determine the increase in nominal aggregate demand. The effect on inflation will also be partly determined by how far the changes occur on the outlay side, and how far on the revenue side. Moreover, that will also determine the effect on real output or employment for any given stimulus to nominal aggregate demand, or for any given rise in the budget deficit. Even a balanced budget 'expansion' (better termed an 'increase') can actually be contractionary in real terms, provided that the price-increasing effects of the tax increases or government outlays (or both) are large enough.[10]

What Clark said about inflation underlines the misleading nature of the widespread use of the dichotomy of 'fiscal' versus monetary policy (as if fiscal policy were a single instrument). For an implication of what he said was that tax increases have an upward effect on inflation (presumably, other things being equal), whereas cuts of the same order in government outlays do not tend to increase prices at any given level of activity – and may, indeed, reduce inflation. Tax cuts thus tend to reduce inflation and government outlays to increase it (at any given level of employment), so that fiscal policy cannot helpfully be regarded as a single instrument.

Furthermore, if we take up Clark's hint (in 1964) that some taxes are more inflationary than others, we can, with still greater advantage, subdivide the different forms of taxation into those that are most likely to worsen inflation from the cost side, and those that are less likely to do so. This diversity of the effects of various taxes upon inflation renders the simple dichotomy of fiscal versus monetary policy even more misleading.

For it means that the revenue instrument ought itself to be subdivided into the (most) price-increasing forms of taxes and the other types of taxes (some of which may reduce inflation, at least if their effects through the level of activity are included).[11]

But even with only two macroeconomic instruments we can in principle tackle both inflation and unemployment simultaneously. The perception that this is 'too good to be true' arises only because economists and policy makers have for so long had in the back of their minds the idea that a crude type of Phillips curve relating inflation to unemployment is a unique relationship. For if that were so it would justify tolerating at least temporarily high unemployment as the only way to reduce inflation. It would, however, be a very odd state of affairs if that were true. For it would be the only law in economics that was not subject to the *ceteris paribus* condition. It is even odder when one observes that the crude type of Phillips curve (while it still lurks in the minds of policy makers) appears to have been replaced in the literature by the equally dangerous reversal of causation that is called the expectations-augmented Phillips curve. For that suggests that the only way to reduce unemployment (and then only temporarily) is to accept a temporary and unexpected rise in inflation.

But neither version of the Phillips curve constitutes a useful guide to policy if the particular combination of policy measures – including the level of taxation – with which a given level of employment is established is itself one influence on the rate of inflation. For, in that case, it is possible to reduce inflation by appropriate changes of the macroeconomic instruments that hold employment constant (lower government outlays coupled with lower taxation, or lower taxation coupled with tighter monetary policy). It is in that case also possible to stimulate employment without accepting a higher rate of inflation – provided that an appropriate combination of macroeconomic measures is chosen to reduce inflation (to a fully offsetting extent) at any given level of activity.

Clark did not introduce the question of monetary policy into the discussion. But if we accept the basic Clark hypothesis about cost-push taxes, we need to dichotomise fiscal policy into an outlay side and a revenue side, and thus view macroeconomic policy as at least a trichotomy of government outlays, revenue, and the setting of monetary policy.

If we take up Clark's 1964 hint that some taxes are more inflationary than others, we may expect to find that both indirect taxes, which tend to raise the consumer price index or other price indexes, and payroll taxes, which increase the cost of labour, may be more likely to raise inflation (or to increase it by more) than are income taxes. At the same time, high marginal rates of income tax may also raise inflation, at any given level of employment, by making wage-earners bid for higher pre-tax wages. It is thus an empirical matter which of these effects – that operating through the level of aggregate demand and tending to hold down inflation, and that operating through the cost side, and tending to increase it – predominates for any given type of tax increase or reduction. We shall now look at the evidence on this point from a number of simulations conducted with large macroeconomic models that appear to throw some light on this matter.

Simulations with UK models

The various simulations done at the University of Warwick using five quarterly models of the UK economy in 1990 provide strong evidence that decreases in indirect taxes and in employers' national insurance contributions (as well as decreasing unemployment) reduce inflation. They suggest that this reduction in inflation exceeds any upward effect on it

Table 7.1 Simulated change in rate of consumer price inflation for 100 000 rise in employment, UK, [a]per cent per annum

Average change in inflation in Years 1,3 and 5 after the change in policy

Model:	LBS[b]	NIESR[c]	HMT[d]	BE[e]	OEF[f]	Average
Effect of:						
Income tax cut	0.76	1.30	0.11	0.34	0.43	0.60
Cut in VAT	1.20	0.67	0.41	–1.20	–0.40	–0.03
Cut in employers' national insurance contributions	0.64	0.76	–0.33	–0.50	–0.17	0.08
Rise in government expenditure	0.37	4.34	0.27	0.28	0.19	1.09

Notes:
[a] These simulations assume that interest rates are held constant by means of monetary policy.
[b] LBS = London Business School.
[c] NIESR = National Institute of Economic and Social Research.
[d] HMT = Her Majesty's Treasury.
[e] BE = Bank of England.
[f] OEF = Oxford Economic Forecasting.
Source: Derived from simulations in Fisher *et al.* (1990).

through aggregate demand that may result when those taxes are decreased. This means that cuts in those taxes not only reduce unemployment but also reduce inflation (at least over the five-year period covered by those simulations). By contrast, those simulations indicate that cuts in income taxes, as well as increases in government outlays, appear to raise inflation in the process of reducing unemployment (see Table 7.1).[12] Much the same results can be derived from simulations (undertaken at the European Commission) for the European Community (see Table 7.3)

Evidence from OECD simulations (shown in Table 7.2) for the seven major countries suggests that cuts in income tax (the only form of tax cut simulated with their model) are for all of the seven countries less inflationary than a rise in government outlays for a given stimulus to real output and employment. This result is clearly consistent with income tax cuts having certain cost-reducing effects that are not (or not fully) shared by increases in government outlays having the same effect on real output or employment. This is true whether the fiscal

Table 7.2 Simulated change in average annual rate of inflation (GNP/GDP price index) over five years, resulting from alternative fiscal measures for 1 per cent stimulus to employment, seven major OECD countries, per cent per annum

Stimulus	USA	Japan	West Germany	France	UK	Italy	Canada
Income tax cut (money constant)	2.30	1.60	0.13	0.20	0.20	0.70	1.20
Rise in government outlays (money constant)	[a]	1.80	0.20	0.24	0.21	1.00	[a]
Rise in government outlays (interest rate constant) (interest rate constant)	1.74	1.16	0.25	0.57	1.25	1.80	2.25
Income tax cut (interest rate constant)	1.13	0.93	0.23	0.40	0.97	1.30	1.30

Note:
[a] Signifies that there is no rise in employment over the period as a whole for those countries, so that the figure is undefined, making it the most inflationary of the measures tested.
Source: Derived from Richardson (1987, 1988). For income tax cuts, the data have been supplied by the same author.

Table 7.3 Simulated change in consumer price inflation for 1 per cent average rise in employment in five years after the change in policy, EEC,[a] percent per annum

Cut in households' direct taxes	2.72
Cut in employers' social security contributions	−1.08
Cut in household indirect taxes	1.85

Note:
[a] These simulations assume that each form of fiscal stimulus is financed by bond sales.
Source: Derived from Dramais (1986).

measure in question is bond-financed (money being held constant) or if interest rates are held constant by monetary policy. For six of the seven countries an easing of monetary policy (the simulation for which is not shown in Table 7.3) is more inflationary than either of the two fiscal forms of stimulus tested. This evidence is consistent with the view that even income taxes have certain cost-push effects that are not shared (or not fully shared) by cuts in government spending or by tighter monetary policy having the same effect on real output or employment.[13]

On the basis of the balance of the evidence from these various simulations with a number of different models, policies intended to stimulate employment may be ranked according to the extent of their inflationary effects over the five-year period after the stimulus is given. The least inflationary – or the ones most likely to reduce inflation – are cuts in indirect taxes and payroll taxes (such as employers' national insurance contributions), followed by income taxes, with government outlays being typically the most inflationary of the fiscal measures, and monetary policy more inflationary still.

The policy conclusion from this evidence from major econometric models is thus that Clark's insight that high tax rates have marked inflationary effects appears to be justified for indirect taxes and for taxes on labour inputs, in particular. The evidence relating to income taxes is, however, that whatever cost-increasing and price-increasing effects they may have fall short of the downward effects exerted through the reductions in activity that follow income tax increases. On balance, however, the evidence suggests that even income tax increases are less likely to reduce inflation than are reductions in government outlays having the same effect in increasing unemployment. This conclusion is consistent with Clark's original insight, if we interpret that as a hypothesis about the effects on inflation of high taxation and high government outlays at a given level of employment.

Some other evidence

The policy implications of the evidence of the University of Warwick simulations and those for the EEC and the OECD is also consistent with the very different approach of Tran Van Hoa and the present writer. This analysis (reported in Chapter 4 in this volume) tested the apparent effects of changes in the general level of taxation and of government outlays, as well as of changes in monetary growth, upon inflation and unemployment in the two years following the changes, using the evidence from 15 OECD countries over the period 1967–84. The conclusions were that monetary expansion and rises in government outlays in an individual country had a statistically significant (positive) relationship with inflation over the two immediately succeeding years, but not with unemployment. This study found also that increases in total tax revenue tended to be followed by increased unemployment, but not to have a significant apparent effect (in either direction) on inflation. This last result is clearly consistent with some types of taxation making inflation worse and others reducing it (which is also suggested by the evidence from the simulations by the University of Warwick group, as well as those from the EEC). It is also consistent with the cost-push effects of tax increases approximately balancing whatever downward effects on inflation they may have by holding down employment. Moreover, it throws considerable doubt on the wisdom of trying to restrain inflation by increasing the general level of taxation – which appears (on this evidence) to increase unemployment without necessarily reducing inflation.

In another study, we also found (Tran Van Hoa and Perkins, 1987) that if one uses aggregate data for the whole of the OECD from 1971 to 1985, there was no evidence that tax reductions tended to increase inflation over the two subsequent years. (In this study the effects of monetary growth rates were also taken into account.) Indeed, in any such period that included the years since 1981 there was a statistically significant tendency for decreases in the general level of taxation to be followed by lower inflation.

A third objective?

In many countries, governments have often been concerned with a third macroeconomic objective – the state of the current account of the balance of payments. Two points relating to this debate about whether this is defensible objective of macroeconomic policy should be made in the present context. In the first place, the choice between present and future consumption certainly constitutes an important objective of macroeconomic policy. It may be identified with the level of useful productive investment *less* any current account deficit. That is to say, governments should be concerned with the level of internal *plus* external saving or investment (the current account balance). This aggregate, which we may call 'thrift' (following McDonald, 1985), or 'a wealth variable' (following Weale *et al.*, 1989) is inevitably affected by governments through their choice of macroeconomic measures. Through this aggregate, government policy influences the level of current consumption relative to future levels of consumption. Because of this influence, this objective ('thrift' or 'wealth') should be one of the objectives of macroeconomic policy.

Perhaps this concept of 'thrift' as a macro policy objective requires further explanation. We may be trying to reduce the current account deficit on the grounds that the increased indebtedness to foreigners to which it leads will inflict an unduly high cost on posterity (in the shape of the reduction in the level of consumption in future years needed to service the additional external debt). If so, we should be concerned also about the effects on the level of useful productive investment that may result from the policy measures we adopt to improve the current account, especially if they involve reducing the level of economic activity. For posterity will certainly not thank us if we bequeath to it a lower level of the stock of useful productive capital, if that leads to a bigger reduction in its consumption than any benefit posterity may derive from our having reduced the deficit on current account. It is thus the combined aggregate of changes in the country's stock of useful productive capital *less* any net increases in liabilities to foreigners (that is, the level of productive investment *less* the current account deficit) that should be the appropriate policy objective, and not the state of the current account taken alone.

Secondly, the biggest objection that can be raised to governments adopting measures to reduce the current account deficit is that it may lead them to tolerate a lower level of employment and consequently higher social costs (and a lower level of useful productive investment) than they would otherwise have chosen. There do, however (as we shall see), appear to be alternative combinations of macroeconomic measures that can reduce the current account deficit without involving the economic waste and social cost of holding the economy at a lower level of activity than would otherwise have been chosen, and without reducing useful productive investment. If so, there is correspondingly less objection to governments pursuing the state of the current account as an additional objective.

In any event, it appears that (rightly or wrongly) governments do take some account of this objective in framing their policies – whether of the state of the current account alone, or of this broader objective of the level of productive investment *less* the current account deficit. We therefore need to ask whether the same principle of choosing the right combination of two or more macro instruments can also be used to move the economy towards the government's desired external balance (or towards the level of internal *plus* external investment – the balance of present versus future consumption – that it desires), as well as towards full employment without inflation.

The use of even two instruments to hold down inflation at a given level of activity may also be expected in most cases to improve the current account balance at that level of activity. For a country with less inflation (at any given level of employment) is more competitive internationally than one with a higher level of inflation (at any given nominal exchange rate). Certainly, on this evidence, a shift from indirect taxation and payroll taxes towards income tax, or reductions in government outlays coupled with lower tax rates (at least of certain types of taxes) may be expected to increase international competitiveness (at a given nominal exchange rate) for any given level of employment or real output (and also for a given total revenue).

Moreover, so long as there are some types of taxes, cuts in which reduce both inflation and unemployment, the provision of a stimulus by way of those tax cuts is likely – on the balance of the evidence of

Table 7.4 Simulated effect of alternative fiscal measures on UK current account balance for 100 000 rise in employment, billion pounds sterling

Model:	LBS	NI	HMT	BE	OEF	Average
Effect of:						
Cut in income tax	−1.46	−1.47	−1.15	−1.19	−1.81	−1.41
Cut in VAT	−1.33	−1.14	−1.18	−0.75	−1.39	−1.16
Cut in employers' national insurance contributions	−1.78	1.46	−1.48	−0.88	−1.34	−1.39
Rise in government expenditure	−0.82	−0.69	−0.72	−0.61	−0.51	−0.67

Source: As for Table 7.1.

the Warwick simulations for the UK (evidence from which is shown in Tables 7.1 and 7.4) – to improve the current account as well as reduce both unemployment and inflation, provided that there is a sufficient increase in income taxes at the same time. For increases in income tax had (on this evidence from all but one of the five UK models used) a greater effect in holding down the current account deficit than the upward effect on the external deficit that results from a cut in indirect taxes or employers' national insurance contributions having the same effect on real output or employment. This conclusion is confirmed by the simulations for the EEC taken as a whole (see Table 7.5).

This implies that a country that thinks of shifting some of its tax burden towards indirect taxes and away from income taxes will have to tolerate a higher current account deficit, as well as a higher rate of inflation, at any given level of activity; or, by the same token, to tolerate a higher level of unemployment if it tries to achieve a given reduction in the current account deficit or hold inflation down to a certain figure by that means. The EEC simulations also indicate that income

Table 7.5 Simulated effects of alternative fiscal measures on the current account balance and private investment for a 1 per cent rise in employment,[a] EEC

Change in average annual level over five years as percentage of GDP

	Change in current account (1)	Change in private investment (2)	(1) + (2)
Cut in employers' social security contributions	−0.21	+0.41	+0.20
Cut in households indirect taxes	−0.32	+0.29	−0.03
Cut in households direct taxes	−1.27	+0.56	−0.71
Rise in government spending	−2.00	+0.59	−1.41

Note:
[a] These simulations assume that the fiscal changes are bond-financed. The figures for private investment, which are expressed as a percentage of baseline investment in the original, have here been converted to a percentage of GDP using the ratio of gross private fixed capital formation to GDP in the EEC in 1985, from OECD, *Economic Outlook*, p. 40, December 1986.

Source: Derived from Dramais (1986).

tax cuts coupled with a rise in value-added tax on a scale that holds employment (or real output) constant would reduce the level of private investment less the current account deficit.

Cuts in indirect taxes coupled with cuts in (at least some forms of) government outlays could also, on the above evidence, be expected to reduce both inflation and unemployment and to improve the current account balance (as well as the level of private investment). Furthermore, evidence from the OECD simulations for the seven major countries indicates that, for all except one of those countries, cuts in income tax and simultaneous reductions in government outlays on a scale to hold employment constant would have an upward effect on 'thrift'. Moreover, this would be true whether or not the fiscal changes were accompanied by monetary policy action to hold interest rates constant (see Table 7.6).

Combinations of tight monetary policy with tax cuts (on a scale that would reduce both inflation and unemployment), could not, however,

Table 7.6 Simulated effects of alternative fiscal measures of stimulus on 'thrift' (private investment ± change in real foreign balance) for 1 per cent rise in employment,[a] seven major OECD countries

Change in average annual level over five years as per cent of base GNP/GDP

	USA	Japan	West Germany	France	UK	Italy	Canada
Stimulus:							
Cut in income tax (interest rates constant)	+1.06	+1.67	+0.01	+0.83	−0.19	1.50	+0.07
Rise in government outlays (interest)	−0.06	+0.89	−0.19	+0.19	−0.26	+0.16	−0.10
Cut in income tax, (money constant)	−0.52	−1.56	−0.82	+0.11	−1.24	+0.66	−0.32
Rise in government outlays (money constant)	−2.11	−4.42	−1.38	−0.90	−1.39	−1.23	−1.02

Note:
[a] Original data for private investment were expressed as a percentage of base private investment. Here those results are converted to a percentage of base GNP/GDP by using the ratio of gross private fixed capital investment to GNP/GDP in 1985, from OECD, *Historical Statistics 1960–1985*.
Source: As for Table 7.2.

necessarily be expected to improve the current account. For even the direction of the net effect of a tightening of monetary policy on the current account balance is uncertain. It may be positive or negative, according to whether its effects on the current account balance through the level of activity exceed or fall short of those through the exchange rate. Tax cuts, on the other hand, will certainly worsen the current account. Certainly, monetary policy should not be varied with an eye to trying to deal with the current account, as its comparative advantage on that objective (even if helpful at all) is small relative to its effects on inflation or employment.

The evidence (as well as *a priori* reasoning) suggests, however, that monetary policy has a substantial effect upon the level of productive investment. If, therefore, our third objective is the trade-off between current and future consumption, that is, the level of internal plus net external investment) – 'thrift' (as in McDonald, 1985, pp. 6–19) or 'a target value for national wealth' (as in Weale *et al.*, 1989) – monetary policy can usefully be directed largely towards that objective.[14] Appropriate combinations of fiscal measures (rather than primarily a tight monetary policy) could then be used to reduce inflation and maintain full employment. There may, however, be a still better way of influencing 'thrift': namely, variations in some form of tax concession for productive investment, such as investment allowances; and if this further separate tax instrument is introduced into the discussion, it then becomes possible to focus monetary policy primarily on reducing inflation.

In principle, provided that we know enough about the ranking and direction of the relative effects of all the available instruments on the three objectives – inflation, employment and the current account (or 'net wealth') – we ought to be able to use the three instruments to work towards all three of these objectives (especially if there is an instrument – cuts in certain taxes – that in itself reduces both inflation and unemployment). Certainly, if that amount of information is available there is no need to accept higher unemployment than we would otherwise have chosen simply in order to improve the current account, or the level of thrift, any more than to reduce the rate of inflation. This is true provided that one or more of these instruments has a greater effect on the current account (or thrift, as the case may be) than do the others for a given effect on the other objectives.

Even without using monetary policy, we may be able to change the mix of two types of tax (perhaps together with the level of government spending) in such a way as to improve the current account, or thrift, as well as to reduce both inflation and unemployment.[15]

The available evidence suggests that the appropriate directions in which to move these various instruments so as to improve the current account (or thrift), and also simultaneously to reduce both inflation and unemployment, is to reduce indirect taxation (and any taxes on business inputs such as payroll taxes). It may also be possible to do this by reducing government outlays and keeping monetary policy tight. If, however, we want at the same time to stimulate investment (or raise national wealth) we should move monetary policy in an expansionary direction. But we would then need also to change the combination of fiscal measures (mainly by cutting indirect taxes and taxes on employment) in a direction tending to offset the inflationary effects of the more expansionary monetary policy; or, alternatively, to give a tax incentive to raise productive investment.

Conclusions

If there is any justification for Clark's basic insight that taxes may have inflationary effects (even if those effects offset only part of any downward effect on inflation that tax increases may have through the level of activity), there are important implications for policy.

In the first place, a government that wants to reduce inflation should be very unwilling to try to reduce it by increasing taxes – even when it is sure that the inflation is the result of excess demand. If the taxes that it increases are ones that have such large cost-push effects as to exceed any downward effect they have through the level of activity, increases in them will make both unemployment and inflation worse.

Secondly, the particular combination of tax rates with other macroeconomic instruments that a government chooses may be expected to have an effect on the rate of inflation over the period that the government has in mind. There is consequently no justification for holding unemployment higher (and real activity lower) than would otherwise have been chosen merely in order to hold down inflation (even assuming that a higher level of unemployment, taken alone, would tend to reduce inflation).

Indeed, there may well be some types of taxes (indirect taxes and payroll taxes) that are so inflationary that reductions in them actually reduce both inflation and unemployment without the need to move some other (more inflationary) instrument in a contractionary direction. This would be consistent with Clark's 1964 insight that some taxes are more inflationary than others. In particular, it appears likely from the available evidence (as well as from *a priori* reasoning) that cuts in indirect taxes (and also in payroll taxes such as employers' national insurance contributions in Britain) reduce both unemployment and inflation; so that a shift from income tax towards indirect tax (or payroll taxes) would make inflation worse at any given level of activity.

Holding down government outlays – or some forms of those outlays – may also help to hold down inflation (at any given level of employment). But governments have shown a lack of wisdom in concentrating restraint in government outlays upon capital works – many of which would have helped to hold up the stock of productive capital. One may understand the reasons why they have done this in terms of voter preferences. But there is a risk that all forms of government outlays may be thought of as tending to make inflation worse (at any given level of real output or employment). In fact, however, it is far more likely to be mainly those forms of government outlay that have immediate appeal to voters, and which are thus least likely to be cut, that do most to hold up inflation.[16] There is evidence that government outlays are more inflationary than income tax cuts. But there is stronger evidence that government outlays (on the average), and also income tax cuts, are more likely to increase inflation than are cuts in indirect taxes and cuts in taxes on business inputs, such as the indirect taxes paid by businesses, and cuts in the payroll taxes such as employers' social security contributions.

Thirdly, one needs to add a third objective – the state of the current account, or the level of productive investment *less* any increase in the deficit in the current account. One can, in principle, work towards all three macro objectives simultaneously by varying government outlays, indirect taxes (or payroll taxes) and income taxes in appropriate ways. This is true provided that the different instruments have different relative effects on these various objectives (and both the available evidence and *a priori* reasoning suggest that they do). Furthermore, the use of an expansionary monetary policy probably has a greater upward effect on inflation (and perhaps a still greater upward effect on national wealth) for a given effect on the other objectives. A further instrument is thus at hand that may be varied (together with two or more of the others) in such ways as to bring about an improvement in the macroeconomic state of the economy in all three respects.

We need considerable research on the relative effects of different instruments on different objectives, and about whether these relative advantages differ as between one country and another. But we have sufficient evidence to confirm Clark's basic insight that some taxes (at least) have cost-push effects; and also that some have much greater inflationary effects than others at any given level of activity.

The application of that knowledge to policy decisions would make it possible to work towards the achievement of two or three macroeconomic objectives without the need to sacrifice full employment in the pursuit of other objectives. The social and economic benefit from the application of that principle in the past would have been considerable. Its application in future could be immensely beneficial to the world economy.

Notes and references

1. Clark (1945).
2. Clark (1964, 2nd edn 1970).
3. It is unlikely that any of the evidence on this point that was adduced by Clark would convince a modern econometrician; and that is probably true also of the limited literature on the subject that has appeared since. (See, for example, Carmichael and Stebbing, 1983, who believed that the available evidence relating to Australia on the effects of taxation on inflation up to 1981, when their paper was written, was scanty and, at best, unconvincing.) But we might have to wait a long time before econometricians are convinced about the evidence on this point – and meanwhile macro policy decisions have to be taken. It seems that over the short and medium-run (towards which macro policy decisions are normally directed), at any rate, some or all forms of tax increases are likely to have a smaller downward effect, or a greater upward effect, on inflation over that period than alternative fiscal or monetary measures having the same effect in reducing real output or employment.

   This is not to deny that all macroeconomic measures that hold down aggregate demand will to that extent probably have some effect in the direction of holding down inflation. But whatever money wage-increasing, price-increasing effect taxes may have must be set on the other side. There is no general presumption about which of these two effects on inflation will be the dominant one.
4. I have discovered with interest that Heinz Arndt (1985, p. 34) had exactly the same reactions to Clark's 1945 article as I did (see Perkins, 1949) – immediate scepticism about the limit of 25 per cent, but, subsequently, appreciation of the importance of the insights in the article. There Clark also commented on what he saw as a tendency – during the inter-war period to which his statistics related – for inflation to be brought back to 25 per cent once that figure was exceeded. He commented, however, that as people's living standards rose they were apparently willing to tolerate a higher proportion of their income being taken in taxation (and quoted from a work of Confucius relating to ancient China by way of substantiation). He did not return to this question in his 1964 contribution.
5 I recall that in the 1940s many businessmen said that tax increases were inflationary, and derided economists for saying that taxes should be increased to hold down inflation. It now seems to me that there was a good

126 *The Reform of Macroeconomic Policy*

deal of validity on both sides of this argument. For holding down aggregate demand is likely to have some effect in the direction of restraining inflation; but if the means chosen to do this is a tax increase, this 'supply-side' effect (as it would now be called) exerts some upward effect on costs and prices. This effect may, over some period, equal, or even exceed, the downward pressure on prices resulting from the fall in aggregate demand.

6. Among some policy makers, however, from time to time, the extraordinary view appears to have been taken that it is not desirable or feasible to vary the setting of particular fiscal instruments anti-cyclically, simply because they are being used for the long-term purpose of reducing the share of government outlays and taxation in GNP/GDP. It would, however, be perfectly possible to vary one or more fiscal instruments anticyclically around whatever long-term trend is thought appropriate.
7. Clark (1964), pp. 23–4.
8. One important contribution to the literature that does build into its policy analysis the cost-push effects of high taxation upon wage rates is Weale *et al.* (1989) (for example, pp. 18–19, where it is also pointed out that certain taxes, such as VAT, may have more cost-push effect than others, such as income taxes). Their analysis appears to be addressed only to the effects of taxes upon wage settlements, however, whereas both Colin Clark's original contributions and also the approach of the present writer would include also other possible cost-push effects.
9. For reasons why this might be so, see Chapters 2 and 3 of this volume.
10. A. Knoester (1987) found that, for all four countries for which he tested, a cut in income tax balanced by an equal cut in government outlays, namely, West Germany, the Netherlands, the UK and the USA, over the five-year period for which he ran his tests (and even in the first year for all except the UK), this balanced budget reduction was expansionary in its effect on output and employment. It also reduced the rate of inflation in all four countries, both in Year 1 and Year 5 after the changes.
11. That is to say, those taxes may increase inflation *at a given level of activity*: but increases in them may nevertheless tend to hold down inflation through their effects on activity to a greater extent than they increase it through the effects on costs and the decisions of governments and businesses to which Clark referred. At any given level of activity, therefore (if that is what we may interpret Clark as meaning), increases in any and all taxes could be 'inflationary' in the sense that Clark presumably had in mind. And those taxes that, in the 1964 essay, he thought to be more inflationary than others may well, on the evidence discussed in the text, be more inflationary in the sense that Clark presumably had in mind. Moreover, those taxes that he thought in the 1964 essay to be more inflationary than others, may well be indirect taxes and taxes on business inputs such as labour.
12. Perkins (1990a), Chapter 3. The figures given in Tables 7.1 and 7.2 are derived from simulations by the same group published in 1990. (See Fisher *et al.*, 1990).
13. This evidence is brought together in Perkins (1990a), Chapter 3. It is derived from results most of which are given in Richardson (1987, 1988).
14. Weale *et al.* (1989), argue that if the macroeconomic objectives are nominal GDP and a wealth variable (which includes the state of the current account)

monetary policy should be geared partly to influencing the wealth variable and partly towards inflation, its relative advantage compared with taxation (of which they consider only one type) depending largely on the system of wage-setting.

15. The reluctance of Weale *et al.* (1989) to include government outlays as one of the instrument variables in their approach to macroeconomic policy (a matter on which the authors appear to be ambivalent) is based on their view that such outlays are (and presumably, in their view, should be) directed towards other ends than macroeconomic policy. But this view is unconvincing. If a closer approach to macroeconomic goals may be achieved by more restraint in some form of government spending, then the welfare gains from making use of that instrument to approximate more closely to macroeconomic goals must be set against any welfare loss that results from a lower level of government spending on a particular object. The optimal decision is not to refrain from using changes in government outlays for macroeconomic purposes, but to ensure that, at the margin, there can be no net gain by changing the level of government outlays, taking due account of all the ways in which changes in those outlays may affect welfare.

16. Weale *et al.* (1989) show a marked reluctance to use changes in government outlays as a macroeconomic instrument – though they do countenance the idea of having a shelf of public works available to be introduced in a recession. Variations in government outlays do not, however, constitute one of the instruments in their analysis, nor do variations in the composition of taxation between those taxes that are more inflationary and those that are less inflationary. The fact that they can, nevertheless, come up with a convincing policy prescription using only two instruments and two objectives suggests that a government that is willing also to make some use of variations in the tax structure, and perhaps some variations in government outlays (as recommended in the text of the present chapter), should have more than one combination of changes in instruments available to work towards all of its macroeconomic objectives without having to sacrifice full employment.

8
Of Budget Deficits and Macroeconomic Policy (1996)[*]

The amount of attention given to reducing, or at least holding down, the government's budget deficit (on some definition or other) in recent years has been at the expense of a rational approach to macroeconomic policy. This chapter outlines the reasons why that approach may have damaging macroeconomic effects. It draws attention to ways in which the costs and benefits of a reduction or increase in government borrowing ('the budget deficit') should be considered only in the context of the macroeconomic (and other) effects of the particular combinations of government outlays and revenue with which any change in the budget deficit is brought about.

Simulations for a number of countries and areas are drawn upon to illustrate that different combinations of outlays and revenue items can have widely varying effects on the various macroeconomic objectives for the same effect on the budget deficit. These illustrate the basic point that it is not helpful to try to couch macroeconomic policy in terms of the effects that it has on the budget deficit, on whatever definition a government may be choosing to apply. Moreover, defensible definitions are so many that the deficit can be made to show almost any figure by an appropriate choice of definition. (See Perkins, 1995; Robinson, 1996.)

The possible benefits and costs of a reduction in government borrowing are first considered – as distinct from those resulting from the changes in outlays and revenues with which the change in borrowing

---

[*] An earlier version of this chapter appeared in D.T. Nguyen (ed.), *Queensland, Australia, and the Asia-Pacific Economy*, Economic Society (Queensland) (Brisbane, 1996). The ideas in this chapter are considered in greater detail in Perkins (1997).

is brought about. Some *a priori* reasons are then suggested for expecting different items of revenue and outlay having the same effect on the budget balance to have different effects on any or all of the main macroeconomic objectives. That being so, the effect on the budget balance can never be a useful guide to policy.

A range of simulations for different countries or areas are then brought together, to throw light on the ranking of some of the main fiscal instruments in terms of their effects on different macroeconomic objectives. A final section draws some conclusions for policy.

Fundamental considerations

Advocates of cuts in a government's budget deficit often have in mind the reduction in its interest outgoings that will result, and the cut in future taxation that can be expected to be associated with the cut in its borrowing. But they also seem to imply that a reduction in government debt is (always) desirable in itself, so that terms such as 'deterioration' and 'improvement' are used to describe, respectively, increases or reductions in the budget deficit – as if any reduction were always desirable. The only sense that can be made of such judgements is that, *other things being equal*, an individual, a company, a country or a government would always prefer to be saddled with a lower, rather than a higher, level of debt.

But no-one in their senses borrows in order to leave other things equal. They borrow to make possible additional consumption or investment in the near future that they believe will benefit them sufficiently to leave them better off over the whole period of the loan and its servicing and repayment. It therefore makes no analytical sense to assert that a borrower will benefit by having a lower level of debt, except in the context of the costs or benefits of the changes in that borrower's consumption or investment made possible by the borrowing (or made impossible by reducing its borrowing).

People will usually say that it is a bad thing for a government to be in debt. But then, when they are asked whether they or their family has a mortgage, and whether they believe this to be beneficial, they agree that they consider this form of borrowing to be worth while. Similarly, there are social benefits as well as costs associated with borrowing by a government. Indeed, one task of a government is to ensure both that the costs inflicted on posterity by its borrowing are not excessive, and also that the current generation does not make undesirably large sacrifices of welfare merely in order to benefit posterity.

Discussions about the budget balance are usually implicitly discussions about whether the country is saving too much or too little (in this sense); for the budget balance is one factor that has a bearing on these policy decisions relating to inter-generational transfers. The principal question that will concern us here, however, is the various social costs and benefits associated with the different combinations of government outlays and revenues to achieve a given reduction in the budget deficit. These costs and benefits must be considered (together with the costs and benefits of any consequent inter-generational transfers) before one can reasonably assert that there are net social benefits to be derived from reducing or increasing that borrowing.

Different multipliers

There is one very familiar set of reasons why different fiscal measures may have different effects on the level of demand for the same effect on the budget balance. These arise from the different multiplier effects associated with different fiscal measures. In the first place, government spending on goods and services fully and immediately affects the level of aggregate demand. By contrast, tax cuts and transfer payments influence spending only when (and so far as) the recipients change the level of their spending as a result of the consequent changes in their disposable income.

Secondly, different income groups are likely to have different marginal propensities to consume and save; and this will affect the multiplier to be applied to taxes or transfers (as well as payments for goods and services) that affect their disposable incomes.

Thirdly, different individuals will have different marginal propensities to import, and different government outlays will be spent to varying extents on imported goods.

Supply-side considerations

But there is a further relevant set of considerations, which relate to the supply side. In addition to influencing aggregate (nominal) demand many (perhaps all) taxes, and sometimes also certain government outlays, affect costs and prices (the aggregate supply curve). Tax increases are likely to be passed on in varying degrees to consumers of those products whose input costs have been raised by taxes. Furthermore, indirect taxes may lead directly to increases in the prices of goods on which the taxes are levied, and those price increases may have further effects through wage bargains. Wage demands may also be affected by changes in the tax rates applicable to the incomes earned by wage-earners; and the prices charged by producers may also be affected by increases or reductions in the tax rates payable on their profits. Some government subsidies may reduce costs, and indirectly prices.

So far as any of these (or other) effects on the supply side may arise, for any given effect in reducing (nominal) aggregate demand, some or all taxes will have certain upward effects on costs and prices, and thus reduce the level of real output that will be associated with any given level of nominal aggregate demand. Government outlays may also increase or reduce costs of production. So far as different fiscal measures may have different effects on real output and prices, there can then be no presumption that a rise in the budget deficit will be expansionary or that it will be inflationary. For this will depend on the particular combination of revenue and outlay items that is used to bring that change about.

This may be readily seen by taking any assumption about two fiscal measures having different effects on real output for a given effect on the budget balance, and combining them in various quantities so as to either reduce or increase real output in the face of a given rise in the budget deficit.

Empirical evidence

Evidence for the OECD

We turn now to some empirical evidence that different fiscal measures having the same effect on the budget balance may have different effects on real GDP and on the price level or the rate of inflation. A set of simulations for two fiscal measures covering the seven major OECD countries was conducted with the OECD's INTERLINK model in 1987. These simulated the effects of two fiscal measures (government non-wage expenditures and income tax cuts) on a number of different macroeconomic objectives; these included the rate of growth of real GDP, the price level and the current account balance. They also included private investment – which is here aggregated with changes in the current account balance to give an indication of the relative effects of these two instruments on private net wealth. For this appears to be the concept that people have in mind when they speak of the need to increase 'national saving'. To illustrate how measures having the same effect on the government's deficit may have varying effects on any given macroeconomic objective, the figures in Table 8.1 have been standardised for a rise in the government deficit of 1 per cent of GDP.

Table 8.1 Simulated effects of government non-wage expenditure and personal income tax cuts for a rise in financial deficit equal to 1 per cent of GDP/GNP, seven major OECD countries, percentage of points, five-year totals[a]

	Effect on:								
	Price level (1)		Level of real GDP (2)		(3) = (1)/(2)		Net wealth[b] (4)		(5) = (4)/(2)	
	A	B	A	B	A	B	A	B	A	B
USA	1.33	1.13	0.58	0.69	2.29	1.64	−0.48	−0.27	−0.83	−0.39
Japan	0.37	0.30	0.58	0.58	6.33	0.52	−0.42	−0.22	−0.72	−0.38
West Germany	0.25	0.20	0.69	0.70	0.36	0.29	−0.46	−0.22	−0.72	−0.38
France	0.14	0.10	0.48	0.53	0.29	0.19	−0.17	+0.03	−0.35	+0.06
UK	0.18	0.09	0.38	0.39	0.47	0.23	−0.43	−0.32	−1.13	−0.82
Italy	0.20	0.16	0.39	0.47	0.51	0.34	−0.11	+0.01	−0.28	+0.02
Canada	0.75	0.49	0.31	0.29	2.42	1.69	−0.24	−0.17	−0.77	−0.59

Notes:
[a] 'A' = Government non-wage outlays; B = Personal income tax cuts
[b] Change in real current account balance *plus* change in private investment, as percentage of GDP.
Source: Derived from Richardson (1987).

It may be seen from Table 8.1 that for six of the seven major OECD countries over the five years as a whole income tax cuts had a greater upward effect on real GDP/GNP than a rise in government non-wage expenditure for a given rise in government borrowing. (The exception was Japan, for which country the two effects were the same.) The detailed tables in the simulation show, however, that government expenditure had the greater upward effect on output for the first two years (the first three years for France).

It may also be seen that for six of these countries, government outlays were the more inflationary of these two instruments for a given effect on government borrowing, the exception being Germany, for which the two effects were the same. Column (3) in this table puts these two considerations together. It shows that for each of these countries the upward effect on the price level for a 1 per cent stimulus to GDP is greater for a rise in non-wage government expenditure than it is for a cut in personal income tax, the difference being especially marked for the USA.

Table 8.1 also shows that a rise in government non-wage expenditures has, for all these countries, a greater negative effect on private net wealth than does a cut in personal income tax (or in two cases a negative effect when income tax cuts have a positive effect). Assuming, therefore, that a government wishes to reduce the budget deficit without a downward effect on private net wealth, it should (on this evidence) reduce government non-wage expenditure rather than increase personal income tax. If it was concerned only with reducing the budget deficit with no reduction in real GDP, it would (on these figures) do better to reduce government non-wage outlays, while reducing personal income tax by somewhat less. For the USA, for example, a cut in government non-wage expenditures equal to 1 per cent of GDP, offset by a cut in personal income tax of anything more than about

Table 8.2 Simulated effects on rate of inflation and real GDP growth rate of changes in government non-wage expenditures and cuts in a package of direct taxation having the same effect on budget balance, OECD, Percentage of points, five-year average

	Rate of inflation (1)	Real (2)	GDP Growth rate (3) = (1)/(2)
Government non-wage expenditure	1.1	0.8	1.4
Cut in direct taxation	0.3	1.9	0.2

Source: Derived from Richardson et al. (1994).

Table 8.3 Simulated effects of various fiscal measures over five years, EEC

Percentage points

	Effect on:				
	Real GDP (1)	Unemployment (2)	Inflation (3)	'Net wealth'[a] (4)	Inflation/GDP (5) = (4)/(3)
Cut in employers' security contributions	1.8	−1.72	−0.60	+0.41 (−0.40)[b]	−0.33
Cut in indirect taxation	1.6	−1.12	−0.25	−0.04 (−0.41)	0.16
Rise in public consumption	1.3	−0.31	0.49	−1.54 (−1.77)	+0.38
Rise in public investment	1.3	−0.31	0.49	−0.54 (−1.77)	+0.38
Cut in household direct taxation	0.8	−0.30	0.27	−0.21 (−0.38)	+0.34

Notes:

[a] 'Net wealth' = Effect on investment ± effect on current account balance.

[b] Effect on current account balance alone is shown in parentheses.

Source: Derived from Dramais (1986).

0.8 per cent of GDP (but less than 1 per cent of GDP) would raise the rate of growth of real GDP. It would also increase net wealth. A later OECD simulation (also with the Interlink model) for the OECD as a whole, shown in Table 8.2 (Richardson *et al.*, 1994) provides evidence that a rise in non-wage government expenditure is more inflationary, though having less upward effect on real GDP, than cuts in a package of various forms of direct taxation.

Taken along with the conclusions from Table 8.1 about personal income tax cuts, this implies that other direct taxes, especially employers' social security contributions, and perhaps also taxation on corporations, are the direct taxes that affect real output more than does government non-wage expenditure.

Evidence for the EEC in the mid-1980s

The simulation from which the results in Table 8.3 are derived is for the area of the EEC in the mid-1980s. If the aim of a government is to raise real GDP and reduce unemployment without increasing inflation, clearly the most appropriate measure is to reduce employers' national insurance/social security contributions; and the next most appropriate measure of those simulated would be a cut in household indirect taxation. On this criterion, a cut in household direct taxation would be the least appropriate form of stimulus. But if account has to be taken of the effects on the country's net wealth (or on the current account taken alone), increases in government consumption would be the least appropriate measure of those in this table.

By the same token, if a government is aiming to reduce its budget deficit with as small as possible a reduction in real GDP, and as large as possible a reduction in inflation, an example of an appropriate fiscal mix would be a cut in employers' national insurance contributions equal to 1 per cent of GDP and a reduction in public consumption equal to anything more than 1 per cent of GDP but less than about 1.4 per cent of GDP. But the choice of measures depends partly on the relative weight the government attaches to holding up the level of national net wealth, compared with minimising the fall in output or the increase in inflation.

Evidence for the USA

The simulations used as a basis for Table 8.4 were part of a paper (using the MSG2 computable general equilibrium model (see McKibbin and Bagnoli, 1993) appraising the US government's fiscal proposals in 1993. These results (which relate to effects on the level of real GDP,

Table 8.4 Simulated effects of various fiscal measures for an increase in the budget deficit equal to 1 per cent of GDP (percentage deviation from trend relative to deviation of budget deficit from trend as percentage of GDP over first five years after the change), USA

	Employment (1)	GDP (level) (2)	Inflation (3)	'Net wealth'[a] (4)	[a]Inflation GDP (5)
Permanent investment tax credit	1.86	3.32	−0.21	+3.10	−0.06
Temporary investment tax credit	1.16	2.38	0.89	+2.17	0.37
Permanent labour tax credit	2.19	1.88	−0.28	+0.04	0.15
Indirect tax cut	2.75	1.69	−1.52	−0.14	−0.90
Temporary labour tax credit	1.36	1.07	0.75	−0.07	0.70
Corporation tax cut	0.65	0.94	0.03	+0.36	0.03
Government infrastructure investment (gradual)	0.66	0.75	0.18	+0.09	0.24
Lump-sum transfers to households	0.48	0.36	−0.24	−0.07	−0.67
Government non-investment spending	0.52	0.56	0.09	−0.11	0.16
Income tax cut	0.53	0.20	0.14	−0.26	0.70
Memorandum items[a]					
Rise in public spending[b]	n.a.	1.56	1.30	(0.42)	0.83
Cut in direct taxation[b]	n.a.	0.81	0.72	(0.29)	0.89
Non-wage government spending	n.a.	0.89	0.52	n.a.	0.58
Income tax cut	0.31	0.69	0.46	−0.27	0.67

Notes:
[a] 'Net wealth' = effect on private investment ± effect on trade balance.
[b] Average of Years 1 and 5 only.
Source: Derived from graphical data in McKibbin and Bagnoli (1993) and data supplied by them.

rather than growth rates) strongly suggest that tax concessions for private investment and a permanent labour tax credit (which may be thought of as analogous to a cut in employers' social security contributions in Europe), or a cut in corporation tax, would have the greatest effect on output for a given effect on the budget deficit. A temporary labour tax credit would have somewhat less. Government infrastructure investment has more effect on real GDP than government non-investment spending (which is termed 'military spending' in the model, but is not differentiated in its effects from other types of government spending apart from infrastructure investment).

Clearly, on this evidence, over the five years as a whole both forms of government spending have less effect on real GDP than the various types of tax concessions or reductions simulated, apart from the cut in income taxation in the form simulated here. But this is a cut that mainly affects higher income groups. It should therefore not be taken as indicative of the effects of a cut in income taxation generally, especially of one concentrated in lower income groups – which would presumably have much greater stimulatory effects. A cut in personal income tax in the USA of the type simulated in Table 8.1 (presumably a much wider range of income being affected than those in the McKibbin and Bagnoli simulations) had a greater effect on real GDP than a rise in government non-wage expenditures for a given effect on the budget balance over the whole five-year period. On the evidence of Table 8.1, together with Table 8.2, therefore, a general cut in personal income tax should in the USA probably be ranked higher than some or all types of government expenditures, in terms of its effects on real GDP for a given effect on the budget balance.

The ranking of these measures is not radically different over the period of three years from that over five years, except that a corporation tax cut has a much smaller effect than government spending over this shorter period, and government investment spending has a relatively greater effect over the shorter period than the longer one. These various results suggest that it is government expenditure on wage items (rather than non-wage expenditure) that has a clearly greater effect on real GDP than do cuts in personal income tax of the same size as, and perhaps also greater than, cuts in direct taxation generally.

It may be seen from Tables 8.3 and 8.4 that indirect taxation had a greater effect on real GDP than does either of the forms of direct taxation simulated, and also greater than any of the forms of government outlay (though not greater than certain types of tax credit) for a given effect on the budget balance. The upward pressure on inflation for a given stimulus to real GDP when income tax is cut appears on the figures in Table 8.4 to be less than that which results from non-wage government expenditure. But a cut in direct taxation in general appears to be more inflationary for a given stimulus to real GDP than cuts in personal income tax alone, and more so than an increase in government expenditure generally.

If the effect of indirect taxation is added, clearly the cutting of taxation in general becomes less inflationary (and more likely to reduce inflation) over the five years than if direct taxation alone is cut. If, therefore, the proportionate extent to which indirect taxation is cut is reasonably large, a general cut in total taxation may be expected to have a downward effect on inflation over the five-year period, or at any rate less upward effect than government expenditure. In the only result among those included in Table 8.4 where a cut in direct taxation has a greater upward effect on inflation than does a rise in public spending, a small cut in indirect taxation occurring at the same time would reduce the upward pressure of the total tax cut on inflation below that of government spending for a given stimulus to real GDP. Table 8.4 also shows that a permanent investment tax credit reduces inflation over the period, and also has a larger upward effect on both real GDP and net national wealth (on this measure) than any of the other measures simulated there. These results are consistent with those for the EEC (in the mid-1980s) – the other large area for which indicators of effects of a range of fiscal measures on all these macroeconomic objectives are available – which were discussed above. (See Table 8.3.) In both cases, government outlays are almost always more inflationary than some or all of the tax cuts simulated for a given rise in the budget deficit and for a given stimulus to real GDP. The exception is that it is uncertain from these simulations for the USA whether income tax cuts are more or less inflationary than government outlays, in view of their concentration on higher income groups in the McKibbin and Bagnoli simulation and conflicting conclusions on this point from other simulations.

But as indirect tax cuts tend to reduce inflation, combinations of cuts in indirect and direct taxation together could readily be found that would reduce inflation, whereas government expenditure would increase it.

Evidence for Nordic countries

It may be seen from Table 8.5 that in the five Nordic country models used for these simulations government employment expenditure has a consistently upward effect on inflation. Again, in all the models, cuts

Table 8.5 Simulated deviation of GDP price index from baseline for change in general government financial balance of 1 per cent of GDP, four Scandinavian countries

Percentage of points

Model:	ADAM (Denmark)	MODAG (Norway)	KOSMOS (Sweden)	KESSU (Finland)	BOF4 (Finland)
Rise in government employment expenditure	2.40	0.83	4.71	0.00	0.51
Cut in local income tax	1.75	0.41	0.70	0.00	1.29
Cut in VAT	−5.73	−2.29	−3.54	−2.29	−0.13

Source: Derived from Wallis and Whitley (1991).

in VAT reduce inflation over the five years. Cuts in local income tax generally increase it, but to a smaller extent than government employment expenditures.

Conclusions for policy

The pressure for governments to reduce their budget deficits appears to spring largely from a view that the present generation is inflicting excessive costs on future generations – and on itself in future years – by not saving enough, and thus devoting correspondingly less of its resources to increasing the stock of human and material capital. The servicing of the extra debt thus created also means higher taxation in future. The pressure from business, journalists and some politicians and academics to reduce the budget deficit and increase net saving may well be a useful correction to what would otherwise be an excessive preference for present satisfactions. For, in the absence of this pressure, governments might be unduly inclined to keep taxes too low and outlays too high (borrowing the difference), thereby achieving popularity at the expense of future generations. Yet one task of a government ought to be to see that the present generation does not sacrifice *too much* in the interests of posterity. Future generations are likely to be richer than the present one – at least in rich countries – and, in any case, it is always worth asking: 'What has posterity done for me that I should do so much for posterity?' It is, however, probably true that on a global scale it is by no means certain that future generations will be better off than we are. Excessive wastage of world resources, as well as need to make adequate resources available to finance development in the poorer countries, may well be problems calling for public and private increases in net saving to be made, coupled with efforts to make available a greater flow of public and private aid to them, and a greater use of resources in ways that will reduce damage to the environment.

But that is likely to require higher government outlays – in the form of foreign aid and in conserving the environment; and merely reducing budget deficits will not in itself contribute to those aims. If the focus of policy is the budget balance (or the level of government borrowing or government debt), attention is likely to be diverted from the significant matters of the combinations of government outlays and taxation with which any given balance is achieved.

In the same way, by focusing on the current account of the balance of payments attention is diverted from the more important question of the use to which the extra resources obtained by means of a current account deficit are being put; and thus from consideration of the additions to the country's stock of capital – or flow of overseas aid – that would become impossible if certain types of measures were used to reduce the current account deficit.

When the government is urged to borrow less, it is usually because this is expected to add to the country's total saving, and thus to the resources available for real investment (or reducing overseas debt). But such an analysis neglects all the different repercussions of the various ways in which a budget deficit may be reduced. Obviously, reductions in disposable incomes that will result from higher taxation or lower government spending will have repercussions on the saving undertaken by the private sector, so that the proportion of a given level of income that will be saved will not necessarily rise, and will certainly not rise to the full extent of any reduction in the budget deficit.

Perhaps more important, attempts by the public and private sector to save more, if they are not complemented by adequate measures to ensure that these additional savings are employed to make possible a higher level of real investment (or overseas aid) will not necessarily lead to a higher total level of saving. For the 'paradox of thrift' is that attempts by individuals or governments to save a higher proportion of a given income will, in themselves, reduce the flow of incomes, and to that extent also total saving.

The crucial matter is, therefore, whether any additional saving is being employed to make possible a higher level of other (presumably more useful) forms of outlay than those that would have occurred in the absence of the additional saving. Furthermore, a decision by a government to run a smaller budget deficit does not necessarily lead to an increase in the country's net wealth – a better description of this aim of policy than 'saving', because (unlike the word 'saving') it incorporates the idea of the saving being devoted to the production of useful capital, or to the reduction of external debt. It also directs attention to total saving, rather than merely the propensity to save.

We have seen that different fiscal measures having the same effect on the budget balance may have widely varying effects on the country's private net wealth, and – if the government's own investment is included on the outlay side of the budget balance – also on the stock of national net wealth. This means that some combinations of measures that reduce the budget deficit will also reduce net wealth, and others that increase the budget deficit will increase net wealth. But this is not the only objection to using the budget balance as a focus of policy. In particular, different fiscal measures having the same effect on the budget balance will have widely varying effects on the rate of growth of real GDP, on employment and on inflation. This means that some combinations of outlays and taxation that will increase the budget deficit will make inflation and unemployment higher, and the rate of growth lower, whereas other combinations of measures will have the opposite effect on some or all of these for the same effect on the budget balance. As different budgetary measures having the same effect on the budget balance can have widely varying effects on real output, employment and inflation, there is no necessary link between a movement of the budget balance in the direction of a lower deficit and a reduction in real output and employment. The net effect on either of these (as well as on inflation) depends on the particular combination of measures with which a given reduction in the budget balance is achieved. This also means that some types of expansionary fiscal measures are available than do not increase the budget deficit, and may even reduce it.

It is true that pressure to reduce the budget deficit may sometimes lead governments to adopt measures that are desirable. But it is equally likely that it will lead them to adopt combinations of measures that will reduce real output and employment, to reduce net wealth and even increase inflation (especially if they try to reduce the budget deficit by increasing indirect taxation – which appears to increase inflation over at least four to five years, to judge from the evidence of the simulations that have been drawn upon above). It is not surprising that many studies have found conflicting or uncertain relationships between changes in the budget balance and the level of activity. For this is what one would expect if different forms of government outlay and of taxation have different effects on activity. But that conclusion should not be distorted to say that fiscal measures are ineffective in influencing activity. That would be true only if changes in the budget balance were indicative of the expansionary or contractionary effects of a budget – which they certainly are not. For, as we have seen above, different outlays and forms of revenue have different effects on output or employment for a given effect on the budget balance.

It may be mentioned in passing that the argument that business confidence may be increased by cutting the budget deficit does not have any bearing on the foregoing discussion, as it will (if it is valid) operate equally for all the fiscal instruments having a given effect on the budget balance, and so not affect their ranking in relation to their effects on output or employment.

To sum up: the budgetary balance is important only because it is the resultant of the various forms of outlays and taxation that make it what it is; and it is those various forms of government outlay and taxation that require to be considered each on its own merits. The social costs and benefits of reducing government borrowing as such should certainly come into the calculation of what policy is appropriate, but only in the context of the costs and benefits of measures that are adopted on the outlay and revenue sides to bring about a given change in that balance. Failure to adopt that approach will mean that the measures adopted are as likely to bring net social costs as net social benefits, and are certain to be less beneficial than an approach that gives due weight to all the costs and benefits of the various alternative changes that may be made on either side of the budget to effect a given change in the budget balance.

9
The Dangers of Targeting the Budget Deficit (1995)*

The intermediate target most widely used in discussions of macroeconomic policy in many countries in recent years been the budget deficit, or in Britain the Public Sector Borrowing Requirement (the PSBR): what its level should be, and whether it should be increased, and if so by how much. This chapter considers a number of the dangers involved in this approach, looking first at some widely known objections (which are, nevertheless, almost completely ignored in most of the public discussion). It then discusses in more detail a particular set of problems that arises out of the fact that different ways of bringing about a given level, or a given change, in the budget deficit (on some definition) can have varying effects on any of the various possible fundamental objectives of macroeconomic policy.

One should first call to mind the unhappy experiences of many countries with a number of intermediate policy targets – especially those relating to monetary aggregates and exchange rates and the current account deficit – over recent decades. The attempt to base policies on hitting any of these targets – *a fortiori* several of them at once – not surprisingly prejudices efforts to hit the fundamental macro targets of (1) a high rate of growth of real output or employment, (2) low and steady inflation and (3) an adequate, though not excessive, emphasis on investment rather than consumption. For none of the intermediate targets has proved to have a reliable and reasonably constant relationship to particular fundamental objectives – still less to the complex combination of fundamental objectives that is the real aim of policy.

---

* Originally published in *The Economic and Labour Relations Review*, 6 (1) (June 1995).

The most likely explanation one can suggest for the popularity of intermediate objectives in public discussion is their superficial simplicity – which makes them easy to write or talk about, while avoiding the complexities of discussing the relative merits of alternative combinations of policy measures as means of achieving the real objectives of macroeconomic policy. Moreover, for any endogenous target it will be true that other factors besides government (or central bank) action affect the actual outcome, so that changes in the intermediate target magnitude are not good indicators of changes in the settings of policy.

The extensive experience we have had of the follies of focusing attention on intermediate, endogenous, targets ought to have warned us against trying to base policy on yet another such target – 'the' budget deficit. Indeed, this concept is open to particular objections arising in part out of the fact that there are many alternative defensible definitions of 'the' budget deficit. One eminent British financial journalist has said (Brittan, 1993): 'There is an almost unlimited number of respectable ways of defining the budget deficit.' This means, of course, that 'the' budget deficit can rise on one definition in a period in which it may fall on another (perhaps equally or more defensible) definition.

One can, for example, define it: to include, or to exclude payments for capital outlays (on some definition – before or after allowing for depreciation on government owned assets); to include, or to exclude, investment by government business undertakings; to consider only the central government or the general government sector (which includes local government); or to include, or to exclude, unfunded liabilities for pensions and for similar official transfer payments. Or one can concentrate on the 'primary' surplus or deficit – that is, netting out from outlays interest on the national debt (on the ground that there needs to be a net surplus on other items if the level of national debt is to be reduced; and as a very approximate way of discounting for the effect on spending of changes in real interest rates and inflation) (Blanchard, 1990).

There is also the matter of adjustment of the budget balance (and so the national debt), for the effects of inflation. When the price level rises, the real level of government liabilities, and so the wealth of the owners of the government securities, is reduced as surely as if a tax had been levied upon them. Obviously, this consideration is less important now that inflation is at much lower levels; but, on the other hand, the total nominal level of the national debt is almost everywhere now higher, and thus also the base on which this adjustment has to be calculated. This adjustment ought to be calculated each year and subtracted from the budget deficit (or added to the budget surplus) if we are interested in seeing how the real level of the government's liabilities has changed during the year. (Definitions of the budget balance that include the proceeds of the sale of public assets as revenue are so clearly indefensible that it does not seem justifiable to include them in this list of reasonable definitions: for they are clearly a means of financing deficits analogous to the sale of bonds by the government.)

Perhaps most important of all, there are various ways of adjusting the budget balance for cyclical factors, so as to obtain what is often known as the 'structural' deficit or surplus (an unfortunate term in view of the fact that at least one other meaning is already attached to the term 'structural' in economics). Certainly, changes in the budget balance are no sort of indication of discretionary changes in government fiscal policy unless some appropriate form of cyclical adjustment is made to the figures to allow for the effect of cyclical changes in the economy upon the budget balance. It is true that there is a large element of discretion in deciding how to make such an adjustment; but it will always be true that any reasonably justifiable adjustment must be preferable to using the unadjusted figures as a guide to the discretionary changes that have been made to fiscal policy. On the other hand, one may take the view that governments may refrain from making a discretionary change because they know, and are allowing for, the effects of the so-called 'built-in stabilisers'; and one may wish to assess the effects of all changes in government outlays and revenue items, whether discretionary or automatic (so that some more general measure than the cyclically adjusted ones would be appropriate for that purpose).

Reasons why alternative ways of changing the deficit by a given amount may have different effects on macroeconomic objectives

It might make some sense to discuss changing the budget deficit (on some agreed definition) by a given amount if all the possible ways of bringing about that change had the same effect on the macroeconomic objective, or objectives, that one wanted to achieve. But if that is not so it is not merely unhelpful but dangerously misleading, to talk in terms of what should be done to the budget deficit. For alternative ways of having a given effect on the budget deficit may have different effects on any given objective. In other words, this means that to bring about a given effect on the objective in question some combinations of fiscal measures that might be used would raise, whereas others would reduce, the budget deficit, and others leave it unchanged. This means that anyone who advocates a change in the budget deficit of a given order, or in a given direction, with the aim of working towards some macroeconomic objective, is implicitly asserting that every possible way of changing the budget deficit in the way they are suggesting will affect the macro objective they have in mind in the same way – or, at the very least, in the same direction – over the period they have in mind.[1]

Yet this is, at the very least, such an extraordinarily extreme assumption that anyone who discusses policy in terms of changes in the budget deficit (on some expressly stated definition) should feel it incumbent on them to state the evidence they have that any change of outlays or revenue that affects the net balance in the way they are advocating will have the same effect on the policy objective(s) that they have in mind as any other combination of measures that changes the budget deficit by that amount.

Let us recall the principal reasons why different sorts of budgetary measures having the same effect on the budget balance might be expected to have different effects on the basic macro objectives of real output and employment. In the first place, outlays on goods and services by a government directly and immediately create employment and output (at least in nominal terms, and normally also in real terms). By contrast, transfer payments (or their obverse, tax increases) affect at the first instance only the disposable incomes of those affected by them; so that they affect actual employment and output only when those who are directly affected change their expenditures as a result of the change in taxes or transfers.

Clearly, the extent to which this occurs will depend on many factors, especially the income level of those directly affected and their expectations about the future (including whether the taxes or transfers in question are thought of as being likely to be once for all or continuing), as well as the level of activity relative to full employment. If different outlays or items of expenditure have different effects on real output or employment for a given change in the budget balance, a move in the direction of deficit will not necessarily be 'expansionary'; nor is it necessary to move the budget towards deficit in order to have an expansionary effect. This can be readily illustrated by taking any assumption to the effect that one fiscal measure raises the level of output or employment by more than some other measure (for a given change in the budget deficit); and then using the two measures in various combinations. It will be seen that a move towards deficit can be either expansionary or contractionary, and an expansionary policy may or may not involve a move towards deficit.

Secondly, for a given change in the disposable income of the first-round recipients, the effect on the country's output and employment will be affected by the proportion of the rise in income that is spent on imported goods and services. This is also true of any increase in government outlays, some forms of which may be expected to have a higher import content than others. Indeed, some of the outlays may themselves take place overseas (on diplomatic missions, foreign aid and so on). The effects of alternative budgetary measures on inflation (for any given rise in real output) may also be expected to vary considerably, as some types of tax (especially on business inputs) will be more likely to raise wages and other costs than are others. Tax increases may even have such unfavourable effects on output from the supply side as to reduce output by more than it is stimulated by an equivalent rise in government outlays. (See Knoester and Kolodziejak, 1988.)

Some forms of government outlays (subsidies on labour costs, for example) are more likely to reduce the upward pressure on costs or prices (at a given level of activity) than are others – many of which may, indeed, increase the upward pressure on prices. The more inflationary ways of increasing the budget deficit by a given amount may indirectly be expected to reduce the upward effect on real output or employment (for any given setting of monetary policy and of budget measures in nominal terms). Thirdly, the varying distributional effects of different government outlays and revenue will mean that the marginal propensity to consume of the country will vary for different combinations of fiscal instruments having the same effect on the budget balance. Attempts to reduce the budget deficit by imposing more taxes on high income groups may have little effect on demand.

The points made in the preceding paragraphs ought to be self-evident and familiar. The reason for mentioning them is to point out that they are implicitly being ignored whenever anyone advocates an increase or reduction of 'the budget deficit' (or the Public Sector Borrowing Requirement) in general terms or by a specific amount and to a particular level.

Discussions of fiscal policy should therefore always be in terms of what changes should be made in particular forms of outlay or revenue, and with explicit attention to the real policy objective that they are intended to affect (rather than the effect on the budget balance).

It is true that one particular objective – which is not, strictly speaking, a macroeconomic one – is probably in the minds of those who talk in terms of budget deficits as an intermediate policy objective. This is the level of public debt and thus the level of interest on it. Implicitly or explicitly, the aim of those who say that the budget deficit should be cut is to reduce the national debt (or its rate of increase) or the interest payments to which it gives rise. But it is indefensible to advocate measures to achieve that objective without paying due attention to the possible macroeconomic costs and benefits that will follow from the particular combination of measures that is adopted with the aim of reducing the level of public debt by the amount in question. For alternative ways of having a given effect on the public debt will clearly have different macroeconomic effects.

It is obviously true that any individual, or household, or business, or government, will always prefer to incur less debt, rather than more – *other things being equal*. But this is a trivial statement of no use for economic analysis. For the purpose of borrowing is, or should be, to make it possible to invest in forms that will increase the output of the firm, country or government, or at least its economic welfare in some sense, sufficiently to leave the borrower with a net gain after servicing the additional debt. The only qualification to this is that a household (and also a government) may borrow with an eye to bringing forward its level of consumption (or that of the country as a whole in the case of a government) at the cost of a reduction in its consumption at some future time. For a family (in particular) this may be a rational decision – as the claims on its income may be high in the present and near future, and its ability to meet them low by comparison with what it is likely to be in some future period. But for a government, it may be the imminence of an election that leads it to adopt policies that in effect borrow from the more distant future – by maintaining consumption in the immediate future at an unsustainably high level, or at the cost of a fall in the available level of consumption after the election, and with a net social cost to the country over time.

But the 'burden' of any rise in the debt of an individual, family, business, government, or country ought to be set against any increase in its potential future output that the borrowing makes possible. (Irrespective of the prevailing level of the national debt, it is only if potential output – or economic welfare more generally – can be increased by the borrowing sufficiently to service the debt that the extra debt should be incurred.) This will clearly vary greatly according to the direction of any outlays involved in the process of changing the budget deficit, or any effects on output or employment that result from the tax changes that reduce the deficit. The 'burden' of servicing any additional public debt should be considered only in relation to any change it makes possible in the output of the country – or its economic welfare in general. It makes no sense to discuss the effects of changes in the public debt apart from the effects on the country's output (and so its ability to service that debt) that result from the measures of revenue and outlay directed towards reducing the public debt.

The same principles apply to policies directed towards reducing the level or rate of increase in a country's external debt. Whatever the prevailing level of external debt, the only criterion of whether it should be increased or reduced should be whether, at the margin, the use made of an increase in external liabilities (or fall in external assets) of a given size will add more to the country's welfare (in the shape of additional output or in other ways) than the costs of raising that additional overseas capital (or the loss of benefits of reducing external assets) over (appropriately discounted) future years.

If the aim is to increase the country's net wealth (that is, its stock of useful productive capital *less* any rise in external liabilities, or fall in net external assets), the direction and size of any change in the budget balance that will work towards that end clearly depend on the particular combination of fiscal measures that is chosen to effect that change.

In the first place, different combinations of fiscal measures will have different effects on the level of private saving (at a given level of employment or real output). The net addition to saving by the government – represented by any given fall in the budget deficit – will therefore not be a good indication of its effects on net saving by the country as a whole. Some ways of reducing the budget deficit by a given amount will tend to reduce the level of net saving by the non-government sector by more than will others (and some may even reduce private net saving by more than the addition to government net saving). If the addition to public sector saving is not offset by other measures to ensure that output is not consequently reduced, there will of course be important welfare losses to set against whatever benefits may result from the increase in the proportion of the national income (at a given level of income) that is saved. (Discussion of these issues should, in any case, be in cyclically adjusted terms.)

Secondly, the level and form of the government's own capital outlays are an important constituent of total additions to net wealth. If, therefore, one is discussing a definition of the budget balance that includes government capital outlays among the debits, a reduction in the budget deficit that is brought about by a fall in useful government capital outlays will tend to reduce the level of additions to net wealth in the year in question, and will often reduce the productivity of private capital. (See Otto and Voss, 1994.)

This is an important practical matter in view of the extent to which governments have, in pursuit of lower budget deficits, reduced their capital outlays, and those of the rest of the public sector (at least as a proportion of GDP) in recent years. Especially in view of this fact, it would be best always to differentiate between capital budgets and current budgets when talking about fiscal policy. At the same time, not all potential forms of government capital outlay will be likely to lead to additions to net wealth – but nor will all forms of private capital outlay.

The matter is complicated by the fact that some items of government outlay classified as 'current' are in fact investments in human capital – most obviously, a good deal of government spending on health and education, the social return on some of which may equal or exceed that available on many public and private capital outlays. A study by economists at the Australian Treasury (Depta *et al.*, 1994) has attempted to make a rough adjustment to the figures to include part of government spending on health and education as 'capital' outlays.

A further complication is that some forms of government capital outlays are more likely than others to 'crowd out' useful forms of private outlay, and some forms of government outlay may tend to complement, and to that extent to encourage ('crowd in') private capital outlays. (For a survey of studies on this matter, see Dowrick, 1994.) For this reason also, the net addition to government capital outlays is not a good indicator of the size of the net change in national wealth to which those outlays may give rise.

Those who advocate a reduction in the budget deficit often argue that this will bring about a fall in interest rates, or that it will make possible a discretionary reduction in interest rates, and that this will tend to increase net national wealth – by stimulating investment and reducing the level of net capital inflow, and so the current account deficit. Assuming that the overall setting of macroeconomic policy is such as to ensure that total real output or employment is unchanged, a shift of fiscal policy in the direction of a lower deficit or greater surplus, and monetary policy in the expansionary direction, will often have these effects. But it is by no means certain to do so. In particular, if the tightening of fiscal policy took the form of a reduction in worthwhile government capital outlays (including those in human capital), or a rise in taxation in forms that predominantly reduced investment or the private propensity to save, it is quite possible that the net effect of the shift would be to reduce net national wealth. In any event, the size, or even the direction, of the net effect cannot be simply assumed to follow from a 'tightening' of fiscal policy (however defined) and an easing of monetary policy. For the existence and possible extent of any such effect depends on the particular combination of fiscal (and monetary) measures used to move the budget in the direction of smaller deficit or greater surplus.

The budget deficit as a 'constraint' on governments

The strongest argument that may be raised by those advocating the use of the level of the budget deficit as an intermediate target of policy is that it may impose a desirable constraint on governments that are inclined to make irresponsible fiscal decisions. Governments have often imposed such targets on themselves, in the hope of convincing the electorate or the financial markets of their fiscal rectitude. The IMF frequently includes such targets in the programmes that it agrees with the governments of countries that are making large drawings on the Fund: and the OECD often asserts that most member countries should reduce their budget deficits.

Such targets *may* have the desired effect, and this may often tend to increase economic welfare. But they may also lead governments to take unwise decisions. Certainly, the fiscal balance is a simpler intermediate target than ones incorporating suggestions about what combination of changes in outlays and revenue would be in the country's best interests, and as such it may be thought more likely to be understood and implemented by politicians. There may be cases where any form of reduction in the fiscal deficit – almost irrespective of the measures whereby this is achieved – may be advantageous. But the cases where that is true are most likely to be where the country in question starts from a very high rate of inflation, and where increases in the fiscal deficit are likely to be financed by the creation of central bank credit. Even in those cases, however, there will always be better and worse ways of effecting a given reduction in the budget deficit (and some ways that will carry a net social cost), But in the typical OECD country, where inflation is low and where resort to central bank credit to finance a deficit is much less likely to occur, it is always appropriate to consider what combinations of measures to reduce the deficit (or, indeed, to increase it) will tend on balance to increase economic welfare, and which will not. For some combinations of measures to cut the deficit will have worse effects on welfare (by reducing employment and output, or by bringing about an inferior allocation of resources or distribution of income) than whatever favourable effects are expected to follow from the reduction of the national debt and the interest upon it. This means that the imposition of such a budget deficit constraint in such countries must be assumed to be potentially welfare-reducing if implemented in some ways, even if it can be expected to be welfare-increasing if it is carried out in others. The 'constraint' on governments imposed by this intermediate target may therefore turn out to be a constraint against the implementation of good policies, and not necessarily a constraint against the adoption of bad ones.

It is said that the imposition of more detailed targets for spending or taxation may be unacceptable politically to governments that are making drawings on the IMF – though sometimes targets for some types of spending are now often included in the conditions imposed by the IMF. On the other hand, some governments welcome such more detailed targets, as making it politically easier for them to implement policies that they know to be necessary. If the IMF specifies a target purely in terms of the budget balance, this may also lead the government concerned to push certain outlays 'off budget'; though, provided that they remain within the public sector, the imposition of a public sector borrowing requirement, rather than a budget deficit target, should make this less likely.[2]

Table 9.1 and 9.2 draw upon some simulations by the OECD for the whole OECD area, to illustrate how the effects of different fiscal measures (of direct taxation and government non-wage expenditure) having the same effect on the budget balance can have different effects upon real GDP and inflation in the whole OECD area.

The conclusion drawn from these and related simulations by OECD economists (Richardson *et al.*, 1994, p. 12) is as follows:

> Comparing the two cases without monetary easing, adjustment through higher taxes was found to be more costly in terms of real GDP and unemployment ... In effect, the scale of real adjustment and their longer-term real-side effects appear to be greater for the case of tax adjustment .... The same broad conclusions apply with respect to the cases of fiscal changes with a simultaneous monetary easing.

That is to say, for a given change in the budget balance, rises in taxation have a greater downward effect on real output and employment,

Table 9.1 Simulated percentage-point differences from baseline reference scenario for effects of alternative fiscal policies (with given real interest rates), OECD, 1994–2000[a]

	1994	1995	1996	1997	1998	1999	2000	7-year total
Effects on:								
Real GDP growth (%) of								
Cut in government spending	0	0	−0.2	−0.2	−0.4	−0.7	−1.0	−2.5
Increase in taxes	0	0	−0.2	−0.5	−0.7	−1.2	−1.8	−4.4
Level of real GDP (%) of								
Cut in government spending	0	0	−0.2	−0.4	−0.8	−1.5	−2.5	−5.4
Increase in taxes	0	0	−0.2	−0.7	−1.4	−2.6	−4.4	−9.3
Inflation (% per annum) of								
Cut in government spending	0	0	0	−0.3	−0.6	−1.1	−2.0	−4.0
Increase in taxes	0	0	0.1	0.1	−0.1	−0.5	−1.2	−1.7
Unemployment rate (%) of								
Cut in government spending	0	0	0.1	0.3	0.6	1.1	1.9	2.5
Increase in taxes	0	0	0.1	0.3	0.7	1.3	2.1	3.9
Government net lending (as % of GDP) of								
Cut in government spending	0	0	0.1	0.3	0.7	1.3	2.1	4.5
Increase in taxes	0	0	0.1	0.3	0.7	1.3	2.1	4.5

Note:
[a] The table gives the simulations for the OECD as a whole for each of the two forms of fiscal tightening simulated (for the same effect on government net lending – in effect, the budget balance). The assumption is that real interest rates are kept *unchanged* (meaning that monetary policy is used to prevent the tightening of fiscal policy from causing a fall in real interest rates). The cut in taxation is in an (unspecified) range of direct taxes. The results may be sensitive to these assumptions.

Source: Leibfritz *et al.* (1994).

Table 9.2 Simulated percentage-point differences from baseline reference scenario for effects of alternative fiscal policies (with lower real interest rates), OECD, 1994–2000[a]

	1994	1995	1996	1997	1998	1999	2000	7-year total
Effects on:								
Real GDP growth (%) of								
Cut in government spending	0	0	0.2	0.4	0	-0.5	-0.9	0.1
Increase in taxes	0	0	0.3	0.3	-0.2	-1.0	-1.4	-2.0
Level of real GDP (%) of								
Cut in government spending	0	0	0.2	0.6	0.6	0.2	-0.6	1.0
Increase in taxes	0	0	0.3	0.6	0.4	-0.6	-2.0	-1.3
Inflation (% per annum) of								
Cut in government spending	0	0	0	0.2	0.4	0.2	-0.4	0.2
Increase in taxes	0	0	0.1	0.4	0.7	0.7	0.3	2.2
Unemployment rate (%) of								
Cut in government spending	0	0	0	-0.1	-0.2	-0.1	0.3	-0.1
Increase in taxes	0	0	-0.1	-0.2	-0.2	0.2	0.8	0.5
Government net lending (as % of GDP) of								
Cut in government spending	0	0	0.1	0.3	0.7	1.3	2.1	4.5
Increase in taxes	0	0	0.1	0.3	0.7	1.3	2.1	4.5

Note:
[a] See note to Table 9.1.
Source: Leibfritz *et al.* (1994).

and a smaller effect in reducing inflation, than do cuts in government outlays, taking the OECD as a whole (thought not necessarily, of course, for every individual country taken alone). The OECD gives simulations also for the major seven OECD countries and for OECD Europe, and this comparison of the relative effects of the two forms of fiscal tightening holds good for those aggregates also.

The obverse of these propositions is that if a government tries to use fiscal expansion as a *stimulus*, a *rise* in government spending will raise inflation by more, and have a smaller upward effect on real growth over the seven years than will a *cut* in taxation having the same effect on the budget balance (as may be seen by reversing the signs of the figures in the tables).

Notes and references

1. As different lags characterise different items of outlays and revenue, the net effect will depend also on the period under consideration.
2. In drafting this section I have benefited greatly from discussions with Max Corden, Graeme Dorrance and Jocelyn Horne.

10
Of Wage–Tax Trade-offs and Macroeconomic Mixes (1981)[*]

This chapter discusses the relationships between the choice of an appropriate combination of macroeconomic instruments, on the one hand, and the rate of increase in money incomes, especially money wage rates, on the other. It makes no assumptions or assertions about the possibility of achieving any particular form of prices and incomes policies, nor about the costs and benefits of achieving such policies either by direct controls or by agreement. It merely takes the view that, whatever the desirability or feasibility of prices and incomes policies may be, the likelihood of their being successful will be enhanced by an appropriate choice of macroeconomic instruments. It is also argued that any sort of prices and incomes policy is virtually certain to be ineffective if resorted to in the hope of thereby escaping the consequences of using inflationary combinations of macroeconomic instruments.

The basic proposition (argued in detail in Chapter 2) is that it is pointless, unnecessary and inexcusable to tolerate a temporarily higher level of unemployment than would otherwise have been chosen, merely with the aim of checking inflation, provided that even one form of macroeconomic stimulus has less upward effect on the price level than some other. For if that is true there is always the possibility of altering the setting of the more inflationary instrument in a contractionary direction, whilst moving some other (less inflationary) instrument in an expansionary direction. This should be done to an extent that holds employment constant (but with a consequent downward impact on prices over the period in which the change is being made).

---

[*] This paper (also written in 1981) is complementary to that reprinted as Chapter 2 of this book.

By combining a sufficient switch of this sort with a net real stimulus, it is therefore possible, if the economy starts at less than full employment, to increase employment without upward pressure on the price level. The least inflationary form of stimulus is a cut in tax rates accompanied by a sufficiently tight monetary policy. In this chapter, a number of aspects of this policy prescription that relate to wage bargaining are outlined in more detail.

Wage bargains and real post-tax interest rates

The choice of macroeconomic mix is likely to affect both wage demands and the readiness of employers to accede to them.

Wage demands are likely to be increased if wage-earners find that a large proportion of their pre-tax wages, and of any increment of them, is being swallowed up either by higher marginal income tax rates or by increases in indirect taxation on the items they purchase.

There have been a number of investigations of this effect in different countries, and there seems to be ample empirical evidence for its existence. It is true that at very low rates of tax wage-earners may well take little or no account of taxes in their wage-bargaining. But with the ratio of taxes to incomes rising in recent years, this tax effect on wage demands has presumably been of steadily increasing importance.

A tightening of monetary policy, leading to a rise in nominal interest rates, *might* have *some* upward effect on wage demands. For some wage-earners, at least, may take account in their wage demands of any rise in the nominal interest rates they have to pay on their mortgages and any other borrowing.

But against this must be set the consideration that any such upward effect on wage demands is unlikely to be as significant as that of a tax increase (on wage-earners' incomes and on the items they buy) having the same effect in restraining demand. For *all* wage-earners are directly affected by higher taxes.

In any case, the net effect of a tax cut coupled with a rise in real post-tax interest rates will not necessarily be a rise in nominal interest rates, even in the short run. For the tax cut will increase the demand for financial assets (at any given level of employment), and the various cost-reducing and price-reducing effects of the tax cut and of the tightening of monetary policy will tend to reduce the actual and expected rates of inflation. It will therefore also to that extent reduce nominal interest rates. Indeed, in anything but the very short run a tightening of monetary policy coupled with a tax cut is likely to result in holding *down* nominal interest rates. A shift to a mix with tighter monetary policy is likely for this reason to work in the direction of *restraining* wage demands (at any given level of employment).

The other alternative to a tax increase as a measure for restraining demand is a cut in government outlays.

If wage-earners take account in their wage demands of the level of government outlays on items of importance to them, this might also have some effect on their wage demands. For example, a reduction in government spending on health may well be analogous (in its effects upon their real disposable income) to a tax levied upon them as a health charge. But they may not consider it as such when formulating their wage demands. Moreover, any given government outlay is usually less clearly identifiable by wage-earners as affecting their real living standards than is a direct or indirect tax levied upon them or on their purchases. It may sometimes be possible to persuade unions generally, when there is some form of centralised bargaining, to take account in their wage demands of the so-called 'social wage' represented by certain forms of government outlay. But it will usually be difficult to persuade any individual wage-earner or negotiator that it is *their* wage demand that ought to be restrained (rather than someone else's) in consideration of the government outlay in question being kept at a relatively high level.

In short, a tightening of monetary policy or a cut in some forms of government spending may sometimes have some upward impact on wage demands. But any such effects are unlikely to be comparable in their effect on wage demands to those of a tax increase having the same effect in restraining the real level of aggregate demand. Mixes with high tax rates (and correspondingly lower real post-tax interest rates or higher government spending) are thus more likely to give rise to rapidly increasing wage demands than are the opposite mixes.

But we have now to consider whether a mix of high taxes and relatively low real post-tax interest rates will have effects upon the willingness of employers to accede to wage demands (at any given level of unemployment). For if such a mix stiffened the resistance of employers to wage demands there might be no presumption that wages would rise more rapidly under such a mix than under its opposite (even though it is, as we have seen, likely to stimulate wage *demands*). In fact, however, it is likely that the mix of high tax rates and low real post-tax interest rates will make employers *readier* to accede to wage demands.

The presumption must be that a relatively high level of company/corporation tax will make employers readier to agree to pay higher wage rates. For if there is a company tax of, say 46 per cent, this means that employers will generally think of 46 per cent of any given wage rise as being, in effect, 'paid by the treasury'. If, at the other extreme, there were no company tax the firm's readiness to pay a wage rise would therefore be markedly less, as its profits would fall by the whole of the wage rise, rather than by only 54 per cent of it.[1]

Furthermore if, in addition, shareholders have to pay a marginal income tax rate of 42 per cent, another 58 per cent of the remaining 54 per cent (i.e. 31 per cent of the wage rise) goes to reduce their post-tax earnings. In all, then, the treasury effectively pays 69 per cent (the 46 per cent of the company tax rate – plus the 42 per cent income tax rate levied on shareholders of the remaining 54 per cent – which equals another 23 per cent, making 69 per cent in all of any wage rise).[2] In that situation companies are likely to be relatively ready to accede to wage demands when both these forms of direct taxation are relatively high.[3]

Moreover, if the firm in question has to borrow more (or sell income-earning assets) in order to pay a given wage increase, it will presumably be readier to do so if real interest rates are relatively low. If company tax is high a relatively large proportion of any extra interest payments will be a deductible expense against profits.

It is thus not surprising that the past decade of progressively rising effective tax rates and low or negative real post-tax interest rates has been a period of rapidly rising money wage rates, despite the high levels of unemployment. If we want to reduce the upward pressure on prices and wages at any given level of employment, the first priority should be to reduce real tax rates and to raise real post-tax interest rates – towards the levels that prevailed in the macroeconomically happier days of the mid-1960s. It is not, of course, necessarily to be expected that the rate of increase in money wage rates and inflation would then at once return to the lower levels of the 1960s; for it will take time to adjust habits acquired during the past decade. It may even be necessary to raise real post-tax interest rates to levels higher than those of the 1960s, and to reduce tax rates below those levels for a while, in order to restore something like the combinations of inflation and unemployment that prevailed during those years.

Trade-offs and 'social contracts'

We have hitherto considered only the automatic effects on wage demands and wage settlements that operate through the choice of mix (without any special agreement being reached to this effect between employers and employees). If, however, some form of understanding can be reached between the government, unions and employers (and, where they exist, arbitration authorities) the process might be rendered more effective.

For example, if the arbitration authority, or trade union negotiators, moderate their wage rises in the light of a commitment by the government to reduce tax rates (income tax rates on the average worker, or indirect tax rates generally) it may be easier to achieve a slowing down in wage increases, with a given level or rate of reduction in tax rates.

The essence of any such arrangement would be that the average worker would obtain a given real post-tax income primarily by way of a lower level of tax rates than would otherwise have prevailed, rather than by way of higher pre-tax wage rates. Clearly, if this can be accomplished everyone will be better off, as the rate of inflation will be less, and the government thus less inclined to tolerate high levels of unemployment (in the hope of thereby checking inflation). Indeed, as the economy can be operated nearer to full employment if this means of checking inflation is successful, real living standards generally can be higher.

Even if a government is unable or unwilling to reach any formal agreement on these lines with trade unions, it might be possible to announce two or more alternative income tax schedules. The lower of these would operate if money wage increases are kept below a stated rate of increase in the coming year. Ideally, the tax rates would be chosen so that wage-earners in general would have nothing to gain in terms of real post-tax incomes by achieving a faster rate of increase in money wage rates. There might even be built in a slight incentive for them to prefer lower rates of pre-tax wage increases rather than achieving the same real post-tax income with more rapid wage increases and correspondingly higher tax increases.

In any case, if there is any sort of commitment to wage indexation, it should be in terms of incomes *after tax*. For wage indexation of the type some countries (Italy and Australia, for example) have had in the past perpetuates and intensifies inflation. If inflation has been rapid and has led to demands for large wage increases, it is absurd to permit this to lead to additional rapid wage increases through wage indexation, and so to more rapid inflation, as the consequent rise in wage costs leads to further price increases. The way in which wage-earners should be protected – so far as it is feasible to protect their living standards at all – should be by way of bond-financed tax cuts, so as to maintain the real value of their *post-tax* incomes. Businesses will not then have to suffer a further rise in wage costs. Indeed, if inflation has already been excessive, it would be best to reduce money wage costs: reverse indexation of *pre-tax* wage rates (so as to bring inflation down to the desirable level) would thus be the ideal, coupled with positive indexation of the *post-tax* pay packets, in order to protect the real living standards of the wage-earners.

Incidentally, to trade off the promise of an interest rate reduction for wage restraint would be a very misguided approach. For the consequently higher tax rates (for a given level of activity) and lower post-tax interest rates (for a given degree of overall restraint on the economy) would worsen the trade-off between inflation and unemployment, and tend to nullify the effect on inflation of whatever wage restraint might have been achieved under the agreement.

Tax-based incomes policies ('TIP')

In a paper in the early 1980s (Scarth, 1981), Scarth argued persuasively that of the various possible forms of incentives to employers and employees to restrain price and income increases, the only form that will not increase the instability of the economic system is a tax levied on employers on the basis of the extent to which the rise in the wages they pay exceeds some guideline rate of increase. It would presumably be difficult or impossible to apply such a system in a country where there was an arbitration system imposing award wage rates that were not consistent with the guideline for wage increases upon which the tax system was based. But if this problem could be overcome, there would still be the problem of enforcing the system, and especially of preventing the avoidance of it by changes in the classification of labour.

Consideration might be given to enforcing such a system by way of a rebate of payroll or company tax to companies that held down their wage and salary increases below a stated level. The tax incentive would then be the same. But it would operate in a way that would reduce the general level of costs (including tax) to companies, rather than in a way that would increase their costs (as would occur if excessive wage increases led to a net rise in company tax bills). If there were no reason to favour general tax cuts (coupled with tighter monetary policy), rather than the opposite mix, this might not matter. But if a tax incentive to check wage increases were given in a way that reduced the overall tax bill, the general upward pressure on costs would be less, whereas the opposite type of incentive (that proposed by Scarth) would tend to increase inflation by way of higher taxation.

But, whatever the extent to which any such schemes were applied, it would still be true that the general level of tax rates would themselves affect the general level of price and wage increases. It is also true that the structure of taxes (at any given general level of taxation) presumably also influences the rate of wage and price inflation at any given level of employment. But an appropriate setting of macroeconomic instruments generally would probably make it unnecessary to experiment with tax-based income policies. Moreover, a proper choice of macroeconomic instruments generally will always reduce the burden placed on any sort of tax-based income policy, and provide a setting in which it will have the best chance of success. In any event, tax-based income policies are so contentious that the chances of their being adopted are so slim that there are grounds for placing all the weight on adopting appropriate combinations of taxation and monetary policy.

If the main aim is to discourage wage increases above a certain level being granted by employers, it seems unnecessary to go so far as to introduce a tax-incentive for them not to pay excessive wage rises. For the obvious first step would surely be to reduce the rates of tax on companies and their shareholders, and so reduce the extent of the effective subsidy being given to the granting of wage increases.

'MAP'

Another form of incentive to restrain inflation is the proposal of Lerner and Colander (1980) for a 'Market Anti-inflation Plan' ('MAP' – their rival to 'TIP').

These writers argue that a deficiency of 'TIP' schemes is that they tax only wage increases in excess of some norm, whereas all wage increases are inflationary and should therefore be discouraged in the public interest in inflationary periods. (Even particular changes in wage rates that are negative may need to be made still more negative when the general wage level is rising too rapidly.) The same incentive should therefore be provided for all wage increases to be less than they would otherwise have been (and for wage reductions to be greater than they would otherwise have been).

The MAP proposal has the merit of avoiding the risk of apparent bias against wage-earners and unions that is involved in a tax that aims merely to discourage increases in wages. For the intended effect of MAP is to hold down *the total of both wages and profits*. It operates in a context where the government is assumed to be keeping the overall level of effective demand rising at an appropriate rate for maintaining full employment. In effect, the right to increase prices (defined as value added) is traded among firms, and the total of such rights available is held down to a figure that keeps price increases below the rate desired by the government (which may be zero). But the scheme leaves employers and employees free to fix individual prices and wage rates. The idea is basically simple, but the administration of it might present serious problems, involving as it does assessing each firm's value added on an appropriate definition – though the authors of the plan argue that this need not be more difficult than assessing taxable profits. It would also involve ensuring that businesses do not increase their value added in a particular year without purchasing sufficient MAP units to authorise them to do so.

Even if some form of MAP were introduced, it would still be important to have an appropriate macro policy in order to make a given price level (or rate of inflation) consistent with full employment. It is also likely that the choice of the combination of instruments with which the required rate of increase in aggregate demand was achieved would still be relevant to determining the rate of change in real output, employment and prices. If anything like MAP is unlikely ever to be introduced, it becomes correspondingly more urgent and important to use the orthodox instruments appropriately for minimising inflation and for maximising employment. But MAP shares with the proper use of the macroeconomic mix the advantage of not being apparently directed at restraining money wage rates in particular, but as being concerned with the rate of increase in money incomes and prices generally (the total of profits plus wages – that is, value-added). By contrast, wage–tax trade-offs – whether they are in the form of agreements between unions and governments, or are imposed by arbitration – usually have the disadvantage of being directed primarily at restraining money wage increases (at least in appearance). They are thus less likely to be viewed as equitable by employees, and so less likely to be feasible.

The Corden approach

One approach to the problems of wage restraint and macroeconomic policy is that of Corden (1981) and Corden and Dixon (1980). The aim of this proposal is to reduce wages as a cost, without reducing wages as an income, by a wage–tax trade-off. But a criterion Corden suggests for this trade-off to be successful is that it should not reduce investment or government spending in relation to total output. The possible objections to the use of this macro mix seem to me to be threefold:

(1) First, the Corden analysis may give the impression that the case for adopting a more appropriate mix rests solely on the effect upon wages as a cost relative to wages as an income. This is not so. For there are more important channels through which the mix can operate. One of these is through its effects on prices by way of consequent rises in productivity. They could also be expected to affect the price level directly, even if productivity were not increased. These channels of operation are quite independent of any effect through changes in the relationship between real wage costs and real wage incomes that may result from changes in tax rates. (Corden states at the outset that he is discussing only the 'real' aspects.)
(2) In the second place, the main way in which a better mix can affect the chances of stopping stagflation is through discouraging governments from tolerating high unemployment in the hope of thereby checking inflation, when they might be able to use the mix for this purpose.
(3) The main objection to the Corden analysis is that it defines a 'free lunch' as being a situation where less unemployment and less inflation is possible *only if* government spending and the ratio of investment to output are not reduced by the wage–tax trade-off. But 'investment' is implicitly defined – in this as in virtually all macro models – as meaning 'those types of outlay that are influenced by the rate of interest'. There is, however, no presumption that these types of outlay are predominantly productive forms of investment such as one would wish to encourage with an eye to maintaining real incomes in future. Indeed, the forms of outlay most susceptible to changes in the rate of interest are probably dwelling construction and consumer spending on durables, especially motor vehicles. To rule out policies of the types suggested by Corden on the grounds that they may lead to higher interest rates at a given level of activity and a lower level of 'investment' simply because that is thought likely to damage the interests of future generations, therefore, seems curious. For the best thing to do to further their interests is to restore and maintain a high level of output – preferably in the least inflationary way possible. Moreover, the level and form of government spending should not be regarded as sacrosanct; and, as we saw above, it too may affect wage rates and productivity.

One should therefore add to the Corden analysis of real wage costs and incomes the various other effects of tax cuts and tighter monetary policies (higher real post-tax interest rates) on the price level. The scope for slowing down price and wage inflation by means of a given tax cut (with correspondingly higher real post-tax interest rates) then becomes correspondingly greater. None of these effects is allowed for in the Corden analysis or in the estimates outlined in the Corden–Dixon article applying the analysis to the Australian economy.

These points are not, of course, criticisms of the Corden analysis within its own assumptions: they are merely considerations that must be borne in mind before any conclusions are drawn from that analysis about the use of tax cuts coupled with tighter monetary policy in the real world. The Corden analysis is concerned with the real shares in output that go to wage-earners, profit-earners and the treasury, respectively. Certainly this approach is an important advance on the sort of analysis that speaks only of 'real wage rates' – without differentiating wages as a cost from wages as an income. In a world where there are taxes, the dichotomy of wages and profits ought always to be replaced by a threefold division into wages, profits and taxes. But these relative real shares, important though they are, are not the only elements in determining the macroeconomic effects of changes in monetary policy, taxation and government spending. For even if the ratio of wages to total output remains unchanged, each of these instruments is likely to have different effects (relative to the others) on prices and real output.

Conclusion

It may be concluded that, whatever may be done by way of TIP, MAP, or some form of social compact or wage–tax trade-off, the adoption of a less inflationary mix is essential. Moreover, if such a mix were adopted it is far from certain that any of the other devices would be required.

Notes and references

1. Some may argue that this reaction on the part of employers would not really be rational. For a high rate of company tax also reduces the post-tax benefit to them of paying lower wages; and this may tend to offset the greater post-tax benefit to them of the tax-deductibility of the wage rates paid by them. Nevertheless, many (if not all) employers are likely to think of part of the cost to them of any wage rise as being 'paid for by the treasury'.

166 *The Reform of Macroeconomic Policy*

2. Tax rates assumed here are those applicable in Australia at the time; but since this passage was written dividend imputation has been introduced in Australia. This means, in effect, that company tax paid by the employers is deducted from the income tax that the shareholders would otherwise have to pay.
3. I am grateful to Alan Gunther for saving me from an arithmetical error in this analysis.

11
Deregulation and Macroeconomic Policy (1989)*

This chapter considers the implications for the choice of macroeconomic policy instruments of various forms of financial deregulation, and some of the concomitant forms of financial innovation, that have occurred in recent years.

The various effects of different forms of deregulation and financial innovation do not all operate in the same direction: in particular, some of them seem likely to enhance the influence of monetary policy upon aggregate demand, and others to reduce it. But the general conclusion would be that, for a given change in interest rates resulting from monetary measures, the effects are probably, on balance, to weaken the overall influence of monetary policy on aggregate demand.

There are also important implications for the effectiveness of monetary policy in influencing the exchange rate and, through that channel, the state of the current account. Here the conclusion is that the use of a tightening of monetary policy to try to improve the current account is much more questionable than it was prior to deregulation; but that the use of fiscal measures for this purpose has probably been enhanced.

This chapter brings together a number of arguments that may be raised about the impact of various forms of financial deregulation on the efficacy of monetary policy for achieving the principal macroeconomic objectives, including its relative effectiveness as compared with fiscal policy.

---

* I am indebted to Jerry Stein for very helpful discussions about a number of the matters raised in this chapter. I am of course alone responsible for remaining deficiencies. I have discussed several of these issues in an Australian context in Perkins (1989a).

Deregulation of bank deposit rates

The process of deregulation has been accompanied and followed by a process of financial innovation leading to the payment of something closer to market rates of interest on many liquid assets that are either forms of money or near-money. To the extent that this is true, a rise (or fall) in nominal interest rates does not change the opportunity cost of holding money. There will still be a change in the demand for money (at a given level of aggregate demand) in response to a change in the general level of interest rates. But this change will not be as great as when most forms of money were much less likely to bear something close to market rates of interest. This change to the payment of near-market rates of interest on many forms of near-money has much the same effect as a reduction in the interest-elasticity of demand for money. But it is not appropriate to describe it as such, for the response of the demand for money to a give change in the opportunity cost of holding money may be the same as it was before the deregulation of interest rates. Nevertheless, it constitutes a change in the slope of the LM schedule to a more nearly vertical position. It therefore has much the same consequences for monetary policy (that is, it tends to make it more effective) as a reduction in the elasticity of demand for money in response to a given change in interest rates.

This has certain implications for macroeconomic policy. Take first a closed economy, and compare the effects of a given tightening of monetary policy with those that would have ensued prior to deregulation of bank interest rates.

When monetary policy is tightened, the consequent rise in interest leads to some economising in the holding of cash balances (at any given level of nominal aggregate demand); that is, to a rise in the velocity of circulation. This weakens the effect of a tightening of monetary policy. But the payment of something closer to market rates of interest on a number of types of money or near-money means that when monetary policy is tightened the opportunity cost of holding money does not rise as much as it did prior to the deregulation of bank deposit rates. This means that a given tightening of monetary policy (measured as a given rise in the general level of interest rates resulting from monetary tightening) exerts a greater downward effect on aggregate demand than it did before deregulation (as the velocity of circulation does not rise as much as it did when monetary policy was tightened in the past).

Now let us apply a similar analysis to the effects of a tightening of fiscal policy (and assume that it does not make any difference from this point of view whether this occurs by way of a rise in taxes or a fall in government outlays).

The effect of a tightening of fiscal policy, with a given quantity of money, is to reduce the demand for money (so far as it depends on aggregate demand), and so to reduce the general level of interest rates. When, before deregulation, that reduced the opportunity cost of holding money, the effect was to lead people to hold more money at a given level of activity than they would have done when interest rates were higher. The velocity of circulation therefore fell. This exerted a further downward pressure on aggregate demand – thus *reinforcing* the downward effect on activity of the tightening of fiscal policy, whereas the corresponding effect when monetary policy was tightened was (as we saw above) to *diminish* the effect of a change in that policy instrument.

Post-deregulation, however, with something closer to market rates of interest now payable on many forms of 'money', when market interest rates fall there will not be as great an increase in the demand for cash balances at a given level of aggregate demand as would have occurred in the past. That means that the payment of market rates of interest on many forms of money reduces the incentive for people to hold more money when interest rates fall as a result of a fiscal tightening. This consideration tends to make fiscal policy less effective in influencing aggregate demand (other things being equal) than it was prior to the deregulation of interest rates – especially relative to monetary policy.

On the other hand, in the years during and following financial deregulation, monetary authorities have probably become readier to allow interest rates to rise or fall. The greater readiness of governments to let interest rates vary would thus work in the opposite direction to the effects discussed in the preceding paragraphs – which related to responses to a *given* change in the general level of interest rates.

Open economy aspects

Let us now consider some aspects of these considerations that relate to the open economy.

A tightening of monetary policy now leads to the rates of interest paid on near-money rising by more than they did before deregulation, there is now less incentive than there used to be for rising interest rates to lead to greater economising in the holding of cash balances (a rise in the velocity of circulation); and that intensifies the excess demand for money, and so the demand for additional capital from overseas. This leads to greater upward pressure on the foreign exchange value of the currency in the face of a tightening of monetary policy than would have occurred before deregulation. In addition, deregulation of capital flows and other factors relating to the international integration of capital markets now make capital flows more responsive to interest rate differentials than they were in earlier years. The consequence is that a given tightening of monetary policy (in terms of its effects on domestic demand) now makes capital inflow more responsive to any give rise in interest rates; and this further increases the extent to which the value of the currency in foreign exchange markets will rise in response to a given tightening of monetary policy. Indeed, it may be argued that capital flows are now so mobile internationally that the main impact of monetary policy is on the exchange rate (through the consequent effects on capital flows), rather than on interest rates.

This means that a given tightening of monetary policy is less likely to have a favourable effect – and, indeed, more likely to have an unfavourable effect – on the current account. For the greater appreciation of the currency that now occurs when monetary policy is tightened makes it likely that the consequent appreciation of the currency will offset (or even reverse) the favourable effect on the current account that would otherwise result from the fall in aggregate demand as monetary policy is tightened. Indeed, as a tightening of monetary policy tends to increase net capital inflow, it must (with a floating exchange rate) to that extent tend to increase any current account deficit. The general presumption ought therefore to be that a tightening of monetary policy will now tend to *increase* any current account deficit, even in the short run. In the medium run – when net interest remittances to other countries rise (or net interest receipts fall) as a result of the additional capital inflow – it becomes even more likely that the current account deficit will increase.

Are there any channels through which a tightening of monetary policy might nevertheless reduce a current account deficit?

One way in which that might occur would be if the tightening of monetary policy brought about a large fall in aggregate demand. This could happen provided that the inflow of capital was appreciably more sensitive to the level of aggregate demand than to relative interest rates. It seems very unlikely, however, that a tightening of monetary policy would, on balance, reduce net capital inflow (that is – given floating exchange rates – to improve the current account).

But even if a tightening of monetary policy could succeed in improving the current account balance through this route, it would do so only with a substantially greater reduction in output and employment than would a tightening of fiscal policy (because of their respective effects on the exchange rate are in opposite directions). This was true even before deregulation, and is likely to be true *a fortiori* since deregulation and with the increasing international integration of capital markets.

There may be other channels through which a tightening of monetary policy could improve the current account. A rise in interest rates could perhaps increase the propensity to save (at any given level of income or output) by more than a fiscal tightening (which tends to reduce interest rates). But the direction and extent of the effect of changes in interest rates upon the propensity to save seems uncertain, and a dangerous reed to lean upon for this conclusion. In any case, with highly mobile capital flows, the main effect of tighter monetary policy is now on the exchange rate, rather than on the level of domestic interest rates.

For countries where investment goods have a high import content it is possible that there might be a large change in the structure of demand resulting from a tightening of monetary policy, and that this would reduce the demand for imports considerably at any given level of activity, and to that extent bring about an improvement in the current account. This could happen if a rise in interest rates led to a curtailment of investment demand and with it a very sharp fall in imports. But if the government is concerned (as it should be) to maintain the total of the level of real investment *less* the current account deficit – the combined total of which is a more defensible objective for policy than the state of the current account taken by itself – this would surely not be an acceptable route for achieving an improvement in the current account. Indeed, no government should seek to improve the country's net external financial position at the cost of a fully offsetting reduction in its domestic wealth in the form of useful productive investment.

Deregulation and fiscal policy in the open economy

In an open economy, the downward effect on aggregate demand of a tightening of fiscal policy tends to reduce interest rates, and so lead to a fall in net capital inflow. Before deregulation of bank deposit rates, that effect was, however, to some extent alleviated by the increased holdings of cash balances (at any given level of activity) that resulted from the consequent appreciable fall in the opportunity cost of holding money.

But the widespread payment of near-market rates on many forms of money or near-money has reduced that alleviating effect. The downward effects on capital inflow of a given fiscal tightening (in terms of its effects on aggregate demand) will consequently be greater.

A given tightening of fiscal policy will therefore now lead to less appreciation (or more depreciation) than it would have done before the deregulation of bank deposit rates, and therefore to a greater improvement in the current account at any given level of activity. This means that, if a government wants to effect as big an improvement as possible in the state of the current account with a minimum downward effect on real output or employment, fiscal measures will be more useful for this purpose than they were before deregulation. This is because the opportunity cost of holding money is less than it was before deregulation of interest rates on money or near-money. A tightening of fiscal policy is therefore even more likely than before deregulation to achieve that aim than is a tightening of monetary policy.

Other considerations in the closed economy

There are some other considerations that need to be set against the effects on the demand for cash balances that result from the payment of something closer to market rates of interest on many forms of money or near-money.

In the first place, private expenditure may have become less sensitive to a given rise in market rates of interest. If so, this would tend to reduce the impact of monetary policy on aggregate demand (whereas the payment of interest on money tends, as we have seen, to *enhance* its effect on aggregate demand).

One general reason for this is that people now believe (with some justification) that they will always be able to obtain the funds they require – at some interest rate or other – now that rationing of credit is no longer an important channel for the operation of monetary policy,

It is therefore important for a central bank to make its intentions clear if a rise in interest rates is to have an appreciable effect in restraining demand. In particular, it should not give the impression that it expects that interest rates will soon come down again. This is not to say that there is any special connection between announcement effects as such and the fact that monetary tightness now operates to a greater extent through the price mechanism (and less by way of credit rationing). The argument is simply that if the process of deregulation has weakened the immediate impact of monetary tightening on aggregate demand it becomes doubly important to ensure that the intentions of the authorities are made clear to the markets.

These considerations are reinforced by the fact that many loan contracts are nowadays on a floating interest rate basis. This means that when a potential borrower is considering whether to borrow in order to finance an outlay (on a house, or a factory, for example), the borrower will be less likely to be discouraged from making the expenditure in question. For the borrower knows that if market rates fall during the life of the loan, the rates on loans will be reduced accordingly. By contrast, when rates were fixed, borrowers were locked into the high rates prevailing in a period of monetary stringency. In that situation, borrowers were more likely to postpone their expenditures at a time of high interest rates. The introduction of floating rates on loans may thus for this reason have reduced the sensitivity of investment expenditures to rises in interest rates. By the same token, in periods when interest rates are temporarily low, expenditure will not be stimulated by interest rate reductions under floating rates as much as they were when interest rates were fixed.

It may be argued, on the other hand (an argument that has been attributed to the Bank of England – though I have not been able to trace the source), that the current prevalence of floating rate loans may enhance the effectiveness of monetary policy. The argument is that a rise in interest rates now affects immediately not only those borrowers who are in the market this week, but also those who have borrowed in the past on a floating rate basis. This means that the impact of a given tightening of monetary policy is now much more widely spread over borrowers (whether they are in the market this week or not). That consideration has therefore to be set against those raised in the previous paragraph.

It is obviously an empirical question which of these two conflicting effects dominates the other (or whether they neutralise one another). But probably a temporary rise in the interest rates paid this week by people who have borrowed in the past is not likely to have a great impact on their expenditures – at least on capital investment in the immediate future.

Another consideration is that mortgage contracts are nowadays much more likely to be such that when market rates rise the lender will merely extend the period of the loan, rather than increase the monthly payments. There are also a number of other arrangements available whereby the immediate effect on the borrower of a rise in interest rates may be alleviated. In the short run, therefore, the borrower's expenditure is less likely to be reduced by a given rise in market rates of interest (though in the longer run expenditure will presumably be reduced to more or less the same extent as it would have been under the old system).

It is also likely that increases in interest rates nowadays have a greater *upward* effect on the disposable incomes of some households through the greater flexibility of the rates of interest paid on their bank (and other) deposits than was true before deregulation. So far as that is so, there may be a greater tendency for increases in interest rates to raise (some) disposable incomes and consumption expenditures than was true in the past. This effect should therefore be set against the downward effect on investment spending that may result from the rise in interest rates. Lower income groups, being on or below the lowest marginal tax rates, are most likely to be among those benefiting by the payment of interest on savings accounts (in particular) rather closer to market rates than they were before deregulation, the effect on their post-tax income (as well as the proportion of any such rise in their disposable incomes that is spent on additional consumption) is likely to be relatively high. Again, this consideration works in the direction of weakening the impact of monetary policy on aggregate demand.

It has even been suggested that in the USA the immediate upward impact of higher interest rates on disposable incomes through the widespread payment of market rates of interest on near-money is likely to be more significant in its (upward) effects on household income and expenditure than the downward effects on the spending of borrowers, which take some time to flow through, depending partly on the lag before the terms of mortgage contracts are re-negotiated. In Australia, the continued existence of a number of mortgage borrowers whose rates are subject to a fixed ceiling would have something of the same – indeed, a more marked – effect, though over only a minority of existing mortgage borrowers. The presumption should therefore be that the effects of a rise in interest rates on the disposable incomes of those households whose mortgages are still subject to the interest rate ceiling would be upwards – compared with those on floating rates.

Conclusions

Let us now draw together the threads of these various considerations.

On the one hand, the payment of market rates of interest on many forms of money or near-money tends to enhance the effectiveness of monetary policy (by operating, in effect, rather like a reduction in the elasticity of the LM schedule). Nevertheless, it remains true that the total of non-interest-bearing accounts is still large, even though they have not been rising nearly as fast as interest-bearing accounts. Many countries are therefore very far from the extreme position (to which that in the USA approximates) where market rates of interest are paid on almost all forms of money (except currency) – at any rate in those forms for which the demand is likely to be sensitive to interest rate changes.

On the other hand, a number of simultaneous changes (associated, or at least coincident, with deregulation) in the terms of many loan contracts have presumably worked in the direction of weakening the impact on household incomes and the level of expenditure of a given change in monetary policy. This is also true of the upward effect of a tightening of monetary policy on the disposable incomes, especially those of lower income groups holding near-money assets. This effect (by offsetting to some extent the effect on spending by borrowers) must presumably have worked in the direction of weakening the impact on household incomes and expenditure of a given change in monetary policy.

If policy makers have been placing undue reliance on the first of these two effects (the one tending to enhance the effectiveness of monetary policy), they would therefore be unduly inclined to have confidence in the ability of a given tightening of monetary policy to restrain aggregate demand. The progressive tightening of monetary policy that occurred over the course of 1988 and the first half of 1989 in both Britain and Australia seems to have had less effect in restraining demand than policy makers in those countries expected. But the analysis given above implies that one should not be surprised that it was difficult to achieve the desired degree of restraint in aggregate demand by means of the progressive tightening of monetary policy.

At the same time, the consequent tendency for a tightening of monetary policy to place upward pressure on interest rates, leading to a sharp rise in capital inflow and a consequent appreciation (or less depreciation) of the currency, would, on this analysis, have been tending to bring about a weakening of the current account at any given level of activity.

A tightening of monetary policy has therefore presumably become less likely to improve (and more likely to worsen) the current account at any given level of activity. By analogous reasoning, the comparative advantage of fiscal measures for dealing with the current account will therefore have been enhanced. It is even possible that monetary policy may now tend to weaken, rather than strengthen, the current account in the process of achieving a given reduction in the upward pressure on prices. This is because of the upward effect on the exchange rate of a tightening of monetary policy (and the consequent worsening of the current account at any given level of activity) which may well exceed the effect of lower activity in strengthening the current account. For the downward pressure on demand that results may well be insufficient to lead to a net improvement in the current account. In any case, a greater sacrifice of output and employment will be required (for any improvement in the current account that would result) than would the use of a fiscal measure of restraint. Fiscal measures are therefore likely to have an even greater advantage over a tightening of monetary policy for improving the current account than was true in the past.

The comparative advantage of using fiscal, rather than monetary, measures of restraint is likely to be still greater if one takes account not only of the effects of monetary policy on the current account but also of its effects on the proportion of total output that is devoted to private investment. A tightening of monetary policy is still likely to reduce appreciably the ratio of investment to total output (whereas most fiscal measures of restraint are likely to have a smaller downward effect on investment for a given reduction in output). One must therefore take account also of this greater downward effect that a tightening of monetary policy is likely to have on investment – together with the fact that it would have only a slight effect (if any) in improving the current account balance. A tightening of monetary policy will now therefore be less likely to have a favourable effect, and more likely to have an adverse effect, on this combined objective (of private investment *plus* any improvement, or *less* any worsening, in the current account balance). This is because it must now be expected to have a greater upward effect on the value of the currency in foreign exchange markets than it did before deregulation and the accompanying forms of financial innovation. This will reduce any favourable effect (and increase any unfavourable effect) that it may have on the current account.

This means that more reliance needs to be placed on fiscal measures if one aim of policy is to improve the state of the current account, especially if the aim is to do this without adversely affecting private investment.

This leaves open the question of whether the state of the current account is in fact a defensible macroeconomic objective in itself. The above analysis merely assumes that governments do in fact concern themselves with the state of the current account in deciding their macroeconomic policy. They ought therefore to take full account of the opportunity costs of measures to improve the current account in terms of the effects on the other macroeconomic objectives of using one macroeconomic instrument for this purpose rather than another.

12
Macroeconomic Policy in Conditions of Low, Zero or Negative Inflation (1998)*

Most economic analysis of macroeconomic policy during and since the Second World War has been carried out in a context of both actual and expected inflation. Indeed, for most of that period it could be said that restraining inflation was the dominant objective of macroeconomic policy. It is true that more recently the restoration of low unemployment has become in many countries (especially in continental Europe and Japan) at least as important an objective as holding down inflation. Moreover, there may be also a third objective. This may be defined as 'maintaining an adequate but not excessive level of saving or investment at a given level of activity'. This has come to be important in one form or another (often expressed – rather inadequately – in terms of keeping down the current account deficit in the balance of payments, or of holding down the budget deficit, on some definition or other).

But recently the rate of inflation of consumer prices, not only in most OECD countries but also in many others (such as Latin America and South-East Asia) has fallen to very low levels, especially by comparison with the rates of inflation that have been experienced in the past at similar levels of unemployment. Producer price inflation – which would presumably be relevant for many production decisions – had in many countries even become negative by 1998.

By the later 1990s, a low rate of inflation (even as measured by consumer prices) coupled with low unemployment has been a feature of the US economy, and to a lesser extent that of Britain, where the rate of unemployment has also been very low by comparison with recent

---

* Written for this volume.

post-war experience. But in continental Western Europe, where inflation has also been low, at the same time (in most of those countries) unemployment has been at a high level. Japan in the later 1990s had virtually no inflation, coupled with rather higher levels of unemployment than the very low levels reached there in most previous post-war years.

The widely assumed inverse relationship between unemployment and inflation appears to have broken down to a considerable extent in at least some countries. This suggests that the tendency to tolerate (at any rate temporarily) higher unemployment than would otherwise have been necessary with a view to keeping down inflation is no longer a useful guide to policy – if, indeed, it ever was. We should not, of course, assume that inflation is conquered permanently. The low rate of inflation experienced lately even in many Latin American countries (where it had until the last few years been very high) may be the result of temporary factors. One of these could be a once-for-all increase in the rate of productivity growth. Another could be a rapid increase in international competition (or 'globalisation') – which may or may not continue in future at such rapid rates. So far as that is true, no macroeconomic policy maker would be wise to ignore the risk of a return to high rates of inflation, and should certainly be prepared (when appropriate) to change the combination of policy measures in directions that will reduce the risk of the rate of inflation increasing appreciably. The present risk, however, is that central banks may be 'fighting the last war' – in the sense of risking less than full employment to hold down inflation when it is already effectively zero.

For the moment, at any rate, it is thus important to concentrate, to a greater extent than in the past, on macroeconomic objectives other than holding down inflation. In particular, it will be relatively more important to concentrate on the objective of reducing the level of unemployment, especially in those countries where it remains high. So far as that involves increasing the rate of economic growth in more developed countries, it will also tend to alleviate the poverty of the less developed countries, and the serious problems that some of them, especially in South-East Asia, have been experiencing of late. In this situation, the need to choose combinations of instruments that will minimise inflation at a given level of unemployment (as discussed in earlier chapters) becomes correspondingly less important – at least in the immediate future.

The macroeconomic literature of the 1930s (and some of that of the 1940s) was concerned primarily with dealing with unemployment.

In that situation, there was no real need to be concerned about inflation (though that did not prevent some writers worrying about inflation during the 1930s, even in the midst of falling prices and mass unemployment). This situation gave way in the immediate post-war years to one where dealing with inflation was the primary problem, and then to conditions of 'stagflation' where both inflation and unemployment were often too high. More recently, in the later 1990s (as we have seen above) in some countries, especially in the USA and in Britain, a situation has arisen where there has been something close to full employment without excessive inflation. It is the situation of *low* unemployment coupled with *low* inflation that does not so far appear to have given rise to a literature about macroeconomic policy. In this respect, the situation in some countries during the later 1990s contrasts with that of the 1930s, where high unemployment (coupled with low or negative inflation) was typical of most countries.

Another respect in which the situation in the later 1990s contrasts with that of the 1930s is that there has in the recent past been over several decades a widespread experience of varying degrees of appreciable inflation. This means that inflationary expectations have not been completely conquered, at least in most countries. It also makes central banks (especially) concerned to ensure that high inflation is not allowed to recur.

Nevertheless, the main feature of the later 1990s is that inflation is no longer a major problem; but that low inflation is coupled with low unemployment in some countries, though with high unemployment in others. One implication of this in a world of 'globalisation' is that events and policies of one country quickly spread their effects to others, especially through capital movements, often in situations where the repercussions of one country's policies upon others (with a different set of problems) may well be unwelcome.

'Deflation'

The term 'deflation' has of late been widely used (mainly by journalists) to mean 'a falling price level', especially since the chairman of the Board of Governors of the US Federal Reserve System used it in this sense. But the term 'deflation' has usually been employed in the past by economists to mean a fall in output or employment. It is true that in the 1930s falling prices often accompanied a contraction of output and employment. But there is no presumption that this will be the normal course of events. Indeed, unless these two uses of the term 'deflation' are kept separate there is a risk that a misconception will arise that they are inevitably associated with one another: that falling prices are always accompanied by falling output or employment, and that falling employment or output cannot occur without falling prices. It is especially important to distinguish between these two possible uses of the term 'deflation' as very different policy measures will be required to deal with falling output or employment accompanied by inflation from those that will be required for a situation of falling (or low) inflation combined with constant or rising employment or output. (There have been a few cases of the term 'disinflation' being used to mean 'a situation of falling prices'. But that term was coined to mean simply 'the reduction or elimination of inflation'; and it does not, therefore, seem desirable to extend its meaning in that way.)

In what follows, therefore, the term 'negative inflation' will be used to mean 'a falling price level'. The term 'deflation' will be reserved to mean 'a contraction of output or employment' – at least relative to potential.

Measured inflation and actual inflation

In a situation of low inflation, and with many central banks being committed to achieving the objective of 'price stability', there may well be periods where the general price level is actually falling. For if the central banks are successful in achieving something close to price stability over a period, it would imply that the general level of prices will be falling about as much and as often as it will be rising. This is especially likely to be true when one bears in mind that the objective of 2–3 per cent inflation as indicated by the available price indexes (usually representing consumer prices) is the target range that many central banks appear to have in mind. This may represent something close to actual price stability when due allowance is made for the extent to which the available price indexes probably over-state inflation.

It is therefore important to distinguish between the rate of inflation as measured by those indexes ('measured inflation') and the rate of inflation that is actually being experienced ('actual inflation'). Many of the problems with price indexes are well known. In the first place, there are the inevitable inaccuracies to which all published statistics are subject. There is, however, no general presumption that this will lead to an under-statement of the rate of inflation rather than to an over-statement of it.

One particular difficulty, however, is that the output of government services is generally measured by their inputs. Clearly, if the standard of services provided is being improved or the inputs needed to produce them are falling, this leads to an under-statement of the level of services available to the public, and so to an over-statement of rises in the level of prices.

Two other deficiencies are also both likely to lead the indexes to over-state inflation. In the first place, there is the problem of changing weights, as higher prices lead people to shift their consumption pattern towards products whose prices have fallen, or risen by less than those of others. They may also change their consumption pattern with fashion or changing tastes, even if all prices have been rising at the same rate. Statisticians try to take account of this problem to varying degrees by re-weighting at intervals; but this process can be undertaken only with a changing lag behind the actual changes in prices (as is true also, of course, for all indexes).

Another important set of deficiencies relates to the difficulty of adjusting the indexes to take full account of quality improvements. This is especially important when (as in recent years with information technology) those quality improvements are occurring at a rapid rate and on a large scale, and with effects on virtually all industries and consumers. As with the problem of up-to-date re-weighting, the adjustments have inevitably to be made with some considerable lag, and are often extremely difficult to measure. The quality improvements in information technology in recent years and in the prospective future probably mean that this deficiency of the relative indexes of productivity and the price level are far greater than in any other period.

Furthermore, there may be political obstacles to making the appropriate adjustments to consumer price indexes for quality, as well as for re-weighting, as there has been in recent years in the USA, where those whose incomes by way of transfers from the government would be reduced by the use of a more accurate price index have made it politically difficult or impossible to make the appropriate adjustments to the official indexes.

These various deficiencies mean that actual inflation is generally less than inflation as measured by the official indexes. This means that in many countries (especially Japan) actual inflation has of late been not much (if at all) above zero, and at times it has been negative, even when the official indexes still show some increase.

Effects of deficiencies in indexes of inflation

There have been a number of investigations of the accuracy, or inaccuracy, of indexes of consumer prices in recent years. There have been attempts to measure the extent to which productivity increases are under-stated, and price levels over-stated, by the published indexes. (An over-statement of the rate of inflation in the USA of some 1 per cent per annum was estimated by an official committee. An over-statement of about half that figure has been suggested as likely for the UK.) Even if adjustments for quality could be made very frequently, it is likely that there will normally be some time lag before the adjustments are made. If we have to accept that indexes of inflation usually over-state increases in the price level (and this consequently leads to an under-statement of productivity increases) this is a much more serious matter when the rate of inflation falls very low.

For example, if the index in question over-states the rise in the price level by, say, 1 percentage point per annum, this is clearly a relatively much more serious matter when inflation is low than when the rate of inflation is higher. The real rate of interest may be defined (for simplicity – and also because that is near enough to being accurate when inflation is very low) as the nominal rate of interest *less* the actual or expected rate of inflation. The over-statement of the rise in prices resulting from the defective price index could mean that the actual *real* rate of interest could be nearly twice as much as would appear from a mere comparison with the nominal rate and the rate of increase in the published indexes of inflation. This means that monetary policy will in real terms be very much tighter than would appear from looking just at nominal interest rates, or even at nominal rates ± the measured rate of inflation.

The over-statement of inflation in the published indexes also has effects on disposable income after taxes. Interest income is taxed at a very high effective rate when inflation is high (because it is levied on *nominal* income, rather than *real* income). Similarly, the level of taxation on interest receipts falls very low, and may even become (in effect) a subsidy if inflation is really negative. For taxation is then being levied upon a nominal rate of interest that is appreciably less than the real rate being earned.

Similarly, if only nominal interest rate payments are tax-deductible, taxpayers incurring such expenses will incur unintended additional taxation if inflation becomes negative. For their real outlays of interest will then be greater than their (tax-deductible) nominal interest payments, and their tax bill will thus be correspondingly greater than it would be if they were allowed to claim their real interest payments as a deduction. (This is the obverse of the favourable tax treatment of borrowers that occurs in conditions of appreciable inflation because those who incur interest expenses are allowed to deduct nominal interest expenses, when the real rate of interest that they are paying is appreciably lower.)

When inflation was high, business borrowers (and in the USA also households) were able to claim their nominal interest payments as a tax deduction, when the high rate of inflation meant that their real interest payments were correspondingly lower. If actual inflation becomes negative, the effect is that the real interest rate being paid is greater than the amount of nominal interest claimable as a tax deduction. The consequent over-taxation of borrowers paying interest will presumably hit mainly businesses. For consumers are not (in most countries, and for most interest expenses) allowed to claim interest payments as tax deduction. In the USA, however, where such interest payments by consumers are, to some considerable extent at least, tax-deductible, there is no general presumption as to whether it will be consumers or business borrowers that will suffer more from higher taxation if inflation becomes negative.

It is not obvious which income groups would stand to benefit most from the under-taxation of interest receipts when inflation becomes negative (so long as taxation is levied on nominal interest). Presumably higher income groups earn relatively large amounts from fixed interest, and they are also the income-earners best able to diversify into assets where real taxation rates are relatively low compared with the return on equities and property. But many lower-income groups earn most or all of any asset income in the form of fixed interest from bank accounts or other deposit intermediaries. Moreover, income tax rates are highest for the highest income groups. This means that the extent to which their real income from fixed interest earnings stands to benefit from low or negative inflation, coupled with the taxation of nominal, rather than real, income, makes them likely to be to that extent the greater beneficiaries.

There is, however, one form of taxation that may adjust the taxation payable to allow explicitly for inflation. This is capital gains tax (at any rate in Australia – though not generally in other countries, such as the USA). If the index on which this adjustment of taxation is based exaggerates the rise in prices in the relevant period, this over-statement clearly reduces the effective capital gains tax.

Moreover, this over-statement is clearly of greater relative significance when inflation is at low levels than when it is high. This is obviously a more significant matter for high-income groups than for lower-income groups (who, in any event, probably pay little or no capital gains tax).

Policy objectives

The objective of price stability has hitherto in practice been interpreted as holding down or reducing inflation. This objective has been assigned to central banks in recent years. The terms in which this has been done vary: sometimes it has been as a point figure; sometimes as a range (such as 1–3 per cent annual rise in some price index); sometimes as the only central bank objective; and sometimes with varying degrees of concentration on that objective at the expense of others being written into the understanding with the government, or into the legislation.

But what should be the central bank's approach when inflation becomes very low, or when, if correctly measured, it would be zero or negative (even though the price index used for guidance still shows a positive rate of inflation)? Until inflation come down to the point at which the price level is stable, there appears likely still to be some benefits in terms of resource allocation from reducing inflation. But the likely costs of doing so in terms of the objective of high growth or employment will generally become an increasingly important offsetting disadvantage, as the marginal resource allocation benefit from further reductions in inflation decline.

In any case, past a certain point, the ability of monetary policy to operate in an expansionary direction (as nominal interest rates become very low) becomes small, or even negligible. When inflation is low or negative, that constraint on the operation of monetary policy must be set against whatever benefits may follow from using monetary policy to reduce inflation further. When that point is reached, and perhaps before then, it becomes appropriate for a central bank to devote more attention to maintaining an adequate level of demand than when inflation is high or at least positive. One can understand that central bankers, having reduced people's expectations about inflation to a point where something close to price stability is probably widely expected, will be reluctant to risk prejudicing this objective by relaxing monetary policy. Yet if they fail to adopt expansionary policies when measured inflation is zero or negative, they risk inflicting economic losses on the economy by way of lost output and increasing unemployment.

Furthermore, a falling price level can produce some of the same social costs as those that are expected to result from a rising price level of approximately the same order of magnitude. One of the costs inflicted by inflation on the community is that inflation makes it hard for decision makers to decide whether or not a given rise in the price of their products or in that of their inputs reflects a change in the general price level. For it may (or may not) constitute a change in the prices of their products or purchases relative to the general price level. This cost is presumably the same with a 1 per cent fall in the general price level as with a 1 per cent rise in it.

Moreover, what have been called 'menu costs' – the need to change prices frequently to allow for a changing price level – are also as relevant with falling prices as with rising prices. The costs of making price changes when the general price level rises or falls mean that those fixing their prices will not adjust them frequently enough to make full allowance for the changing level of relative costs and prices; and this distorts the relationship between one price and others. This social cost also will presumably be as great with a 1 per cent fall in the price level as with a 1 per cent rise in it.

There is also the 'shoe-leather cost', which arises when inflation leads people to make more trips to the bank (or the automatic teller) to withdraw cash, in order to minimise their losses from holding unduly large amounts of non-interest-bearing currency. Presumably 'shoe-leather benefits' should therefore arise when prices are falling, so that it pays to keep more of one's money in the banks or other deposit intermediaries (that is, to make fewer withdrawals) when the price level is falling. On the other hand, it could be argued that the optimal number of withdrawals (on the basis of other considerations) will occur when prices are stable; so that, on this score, rising or falling prices would be symmetrical in their effects. The reduction in the time and effort spent on 'trips to the bank' would, however, constitute a positive benefit from falling prices, so that there would presumably still be a (probably small) net 'shoe-leather' benefit from falling prices.

If the reason for aiming at price stability is mainly to avoid social costs such as those just mentioned, it is almost as important for a central bank to prevent prices falling as to prevent them from rising.

Policy instruments

The most important aspects of the prevalence of low, zero or negative inflation concern the choice of policy instruments with which to affect the other macroeconomic objectives. In particular, low, zero or negative inflation greatly reduces the scope for using monetary policy to stimulate activity. For nominal interest rates cannot in practice be negative; so that when inflation is low or zero (and especially if it is negative) real interest rates may be high even when nominal interest rates are low but positive. If the available indexes of inflation exaggerate the actual rate of inflation, the real burden of repaying debts, and the interest on them, may be increasing even when inflation as usually measured is moderately positive.

Attempts by central banks to ease monetary policy by buying bonds may in such circumstances be unsuccessful in stimulating activity. People may simply hold the additional money, and interest rates not be reduced, so that activity is not stimulated. This is known as an 'infinitely elastic demand curve for money'.

In the *General Theory* Keynes referred to an old city saying, 'John Bull can stand many things, but he cannot stand 2 per cent'. This was clearly intended to imply that (presumably long-term) interest rates of 2 per cent or less would lead to a lapse of confidence in the bonds bearing such a low rate. (In a period when the general level of prices was thought to be on the average as likely to fall as to rise, one must assume that this was also a minimum *real* rate of interest of 2 per cent.) One may call to mind the disastrous attempt of Hugh Dalton, as Chancellor of the Exchequer in the late 1940s, to reduce the long-term bond rate to about 2 per cent. The result was a failure to sell government bonds at such a low rate. This implies that, in practice, a monetary authority will not be wise to attempt to reduce nominal interest rates to very low levels. The constraint on its actions is therefore much tougher than the fact that nominal interest rates cannot be negative. In fact, even with a zero rate of inflation, presumably the (nominal) long-term rate would not normally be reducible much below about 3 per cent, and perhaps not even as low as that, without precipitating a sharp movement into cash and out of bonds.

Monetary expansion would not necessarily be impaired in a country confronting a perfectly elastic liquidity schedule, if monetary policy is operating through the exchange rate. But if, because of a perfectly elastic liquidity schedule, the central bank is unable to reduce nominal interest rates further (relative to those in the rest of the world), there will not be the outward flow of capital which would in normal circumstance lead to a weakening of the exchange rate. There will thus be no consequent stimulus to the level of domestic demand through depreciation. Exchange rate considerations do mean, on the other hand, that the effect of fiscal policy will be enhanced by the existence of an infinitely elastic liquidity schedule. For the effect of a fiscal expansion, tending to increase interest rates, with a given setting of monetary policy, will not have their usual effect of raising interest rates if there is a perfectly elastic liquidity schedule. For in that case money will be released from speculative balances into transactions balances as the demand for money rises with the fiscal stimulus, without the need for any rise in interest rates (until, of course, the money released from the perfectly elastic part of the liquidity schedule has been exhausted). This means that the strengthening of the exchange rate, which normally follows from a fiscal stimulus unaccompanied by monetary expansion, will not occur. For there will have been no rise in interest rates, and so no increase in capital inflow. Fiscal policy is thus better able to bring about an expansion of demand than it would be in normal circumstances of a somewhat less elastic liquidity schedule. In short, if there is a perfectly elastic liquidity schedule, the efficacy of fiscal expansion is increased. This will be because there will be no rise in domestic interest rates to weaken its direct stimulatory effects. There will also consequently be no additional capital inflow, and so no appreciation of the currency to weaken the stimulus to demand brought about by the fiscal expansion.

It has been suggested that monetary policy may perhaps be made expansionary by creating liquidity even in this situation of very low nominal interest rates. For an expansionary monetary policy may lead people to expect higher inflation – a fall in real interest rates thus being brought about through this route, without a cut in nominal interest rates. If so, this may lead them to spend more freely before the higher prices occur. It may also cause a loss of confidence in the currency on the part of overseas investors. If so, this could lead to capital outflow and a consequent weakening of the exchange rate, providing a stimulus through that route. (This may well, however, be undesirable from other points of view.)

Relevance of fiscal policy

It will be possible for governments to counter-balance the constraints imposed on central banks (especially the difficulty of using monetary policy to raise activity when nominal interest rates are already low) as a result of the existence of low or zero actual inflation by adopting appropriate fiscal measures. But governments will be able to do this only if they are able and willing to operate fiscal policy so as to maintain full employment (on some appropriate definition); and if they take full account of the inability of the monetary authority to move its policy in an expansionary direction when nominal interest rates are already low.

Problems arise, however, if governments are unable or unwilling to operate fiscal policy flexibly enough to deal with this additional problem. There may be political, administrative or other obstacles to their doing so. They may also be averse to measures that involve increasing budget deficits. Furthermore, they may also be averse to adopting the redistributive measures in favour of lower income groups (but paid for by higher income groups) that could be used to stimulate demand without necessarily increasing the budget deficit. If there are such obstacles to a sufficiently flexible use of fiscal policy, it becomes correspondingly more important for central banks to change the emphasis in their policy objectives towards maintaining a high enough level of activity, relative to the weight placed on holding down inflation.

The reasons why governments have been reluctant to use fiscal policy as much as in the past vary considerably from country to country. But a dominant consideration may well be that in the USA, whose influence on economic thinking is dominant, the political system makes it very difficult to vary fiscal measures flexibly, and the predominant fiscal aim has become that of holding down the budget deficit. But in some countries there seems of late also to have been a feeling of scepticism about the efficacy of fiscal instruments – though there was (for example) no reluctance in 1998 among the major industrialised countries to urge Japan to use these instruments in an expansionary direction. A further factor may be antipathy among the more influential observers, and among policy makers, to the use of increases in government outlays, especially those that would benefit lower income groups. This may often be coupled with a preference on the part of policy makers, and those that have most influence upon them, for tax cuts that benefit higher, rather than lower, income groups. In fact, however, a strong fiscal stimulus would always be available (even within the constraint of targeting a given level of the budget deficit) by way of tax cuts for lower-income groups and higher social services outlays that would benefit mainly these lower-income groups. This could be offset (if it were thought necessary in the interests of holding down the budget deficit) by an increase in taxation of higher-income groups. The aim of keeping down the budget deficit is thus not incompatible with the use of fiscal instruments to stimulate demand.

Moreover, in may countries producer prices have been falling in the later 1990s, and these may be the most relevant prices for many production decisions. So long as that is so, it is especially dangerous to leave to monetary policy the task of ensuring an adequate level of effective demand. The reduction in nominal interest rates in Japan to very low levels in recent years, appears to have had virtually no effect in stimulating demand – perhaps partly because they are still relatively high in real terms It is therefore a matter of concern that in so many countries governments appear to have almost completely left the task of macroeconomic management to central banks, despite the fact that monetary policy has now or may in the near future become very limited in its ability to raise effective demand.

Negative inflation and debt

One effect of negative inflation is to increase the burden on debtors (and correspondingly increase the wealth of lenders). Where there is a large amount of debt, and where activity is low, there may result what has been called 'debt deflation'. This comes about because the increased difficulty faced by debtors may lead to widespread distress selling (which tends to make inflation still more negative) and bankruptcies. The consequent downward pressure on economic activity will necessitate strong measures to stimulate demand; and, as we have seen, central banks may well find such measures difficult or impossible when nominal interest rates are already low.

A special aspect of the effect on debtors is that on governments, which are usually large debtors. Negative inflation increases the real burden of the national debt, and so the amount of taxation that will be required to service it. (Of course, it correspondingly increases the real income of those deriving interest from holding government bonds.)

If the monetary policy being pursued by the central bank exerts downward pressure on the price level through a tight monetary policy, it correspondingly increases the real burden of the national debt (even though we are assuming that there has been no change in the nominal budget deficit). Now suppose that the budget deficit is reduced in nominal terms by a tightening of fiscal policy, and that the means whereby this occurs exerts downward pressure on the price level. It is then quite possible for the real level of the national debt to rise even when the budget is moving towards surplus in nominal terms.

By the same token, if the budget deficit is increased, and this is done in ways that tend to increase the price level, the consequent fall in real interest rate costs may exceed the increase in the nominal interest bill resulting from the rise in the budget deficit.

Conclusion

There have so far been only few cases of countries where consumer price inflation, as measured, has been close to or below zero. It is nevertheless important to consider the implications for policy if this situation should become common, especially now that inflation has fallen to much lower levels than in the past and inflation of producer prices has widely become negative. Moreover, if price stability is to be the aim of macroeconomic (or at least of monetary) policy, this implies that, on the average of years, the price level should be falling as often, and for as long a period, as it is rising. The implications for macroeconomic policy when unemployment is high and when inflation is low or falling, are that monetary policy should not be solely concerned with price stability; and that full use should be made of fiscal policy to achieve growth or full employment objectives. For both monetary and fiscal measures will inevitably have effects on all the macroeconomic objectives.

Appendix: Gilbertian Parodies for Economists

After 'The Aesthete' (from *Patience* by W.S. Gilbert)
If you're anxious for to shine in the economic line as a man of expertise
You should just commit to mind lots of jargon words – you'll find that you can use them when you please.
Most people you'll amaze with every jargonistic phrase, and it's nearly always true
That the meaning doesn't matter it it's only idle chatter – and the credit goes to you.
And everyone will say as you pass along your way,
'If that young man expresses himself in a way too deep for me,
Then what a very singularly deep young man that deep young man must be!'

Meet all doubts with stern defiance, keep on blinding them with science, and whenever times are tough,
So that people fear depression, say, 'It's just a growth recession' – and they'll think you know your stuff.
If you show familiarity with ultra-rationality they'll say you are the best,
If you talk of Sims-causation and of spurious correlation they are bound to be impressed.
And everyone will say 'A new Keynes is on his way!
If this young man expresses himself in a way obscure to me,
Then what a quite astonishingly wise young man that wise young man must be!'*

If you're seeking recognition as a bright econometrician you must surely be aware
You can make a great impression with a multiple regression with a high enough R-square.
There's no need for frustration if there's autocorrelation – no need to let them see,
It really shouldn't trouble you to find that the D-W is not what it should be.
And everyone will say as you pass along your way,
'If that young man expresses himself using terms obscure to me,
Then what a quite exceptionally bright young man that bright young man must be!'

---

* The gender-specific formulation is left as it was in the original, mainly because it scans, but also because it may be considered uncomplimentary to the other half of the human race to change it to being non-gender-specific.

Advice to young researchers

(To be sung to the tune of the song of Sir Joseph Porter, First Sea Lord, in Gilbert and Sullivan's *HMS Pinafore*)
(English or Australian version: for American version see below)

(Note that there is in fact no 'Chairman of the ARC': she/he is a 'Chair'. But I object to referring to anyone as an inanimate object; and anyway 'chair' does not scan. I have therefore stuck to 'chairman'. This serves incidentally to emphasise that the whole thing is completely fictitious, and no reference to any real person is intended. Readers in Britain may care to substitute the words 'Chair of the ESRC'. In all other relevant places (in the chorus lines) 'she' may of course be substituted for 'he'.)

When I was a grad my career took off as research assistant to an ancient prof.
I put all his figures on a data base and devised equations to support his case;
   (Chorus) He devised equations to support his case.
I devised those equations so successfully that now I am the chairman of the ARC.
   (Chorus) He devised those equations so successfully that now he is the chairman of the ARC.

The old professor was lazy and slow, his stock of new ideas had run extremely low;
I saw that he was overcome by sloth, and this led me to work out many a new hypothesis.
   (Chorus) Led him to work out many a new hypothesis.
I set down my arguments persuasively – and now I am the chairman of the ARC.
   (Chorus) He set down his arguments persuasively – and now he is the chairman of the ARC.

I soon discovered a decided flair for getting out equations with a high R-square;
And upon my word I declare it's true that all of my D-Ws were close to two.
   (Chorus) Yes, all of his D-Ws were close to two!
Of auto-correlation my results were free, and now I am the chairman of the ARC.
   (Chorus) Of autocorrelation his results were free, and now he is the chairman of the ARC.

I got promoted: as my status rose I wrote research proposals in the finest prose;
I took good care to apply the test of what was thought to serve 'the national interest'
   (Chorus) Of what was thought to serve 'the national interest'.
I sent in proposals with such frequency that at last one was accepted by the ARC.
   (Chorus) He sent in proposals with such frequency that at last one was accepted by the ARC.

My economy-tricks soon acquired such fame a research professor I at last became;
My articles delighted every referee, and a Fellow I was made of the Academy
   (Chorus) A Fellow he was made of the Academy.

The government decided I more use would be if I became the chairman of the ARC.
(Chorus) The government decided he more use would be if he became the chairman of the ARC.
So, researchers all, whoever you may be, if you want to climb up to the top of the tree;
If your soul isn't fettered to a terminal, be careful to be guided by this principle:
(Chorus) Be careful to be guided by this principle!
Just work at your data most assiduously, and you all may be chairman of the ARC.
(Chorus) We'll work at our data most assiduously, and *we* may all be chairman of the ARC.

Advice to young researchers*

When I was a grad my career took off: I became assistant to an ancient prof.
I put all his figures on a data base and devised equations to support his case;
(Chorus): He devised equations to support his case.
I did a most outstanding Harvard doctorate, and now I have become a Nobel lau-re-ate.
(Chorus) He did a most outstanding Harvard doctorate, and now he has become a Nobel lau-re-ate.

I soon discovered a decided flair for getting out equations with a high R-square;
And upon my word I declare it's true that all of my D-Ws were close to two.
(Chorus) Yes, all of his D-Ws were close to two!
My variables would generally co-integrate, and now I have become a Nobel lau-re-ate.
(Chorus) His variables would generally co-integrate, and now he has become a Nobel lau-re-ate.

As a young economist I made such a mark that they soon awarded me the J.B. Clark.
I then got tenure, as my status rose I wrote research proposals in the finest prose.
(Chorus) He wrote research proposals in the finest prose.
With all the big foundations my success was great, and now I have become a Nobel lau-re-ate.
(Chorus) With all the big foundations his success was great, and now he has become a Nobel lau-re-ate.

My economy-tricks then acquired such fame a research professor I at last became;
I soon got a column in a news magazine, and often on the TV screen my face was seen.

---

* American version to be sung to the tune of the song of Sir Joseph Porter, First Sea Lord, in Gilbert and Sullivan's *HMS Pinafore*. My sincere thanks to Max Corden for the idea of making an American version from the original (Australian/British) version, and for the many suggestions incorporated in the above verses. Peter Lloyd also made some helpful suggestions. They should not, however, be held responsible for any infelicities or inaccuracies.

(Chorus) And often on the TV screen his face was seen.
The media often asked me to pontificate, and now I have become a Nobel lau-re-ate.
(Chorus) The media often asked him to pontificate, and now he has become a Nobel lau-re-ate.

My articles delighted every referee, and the Francis Walker medal was awarded me,
They made me a member of the CEA; I then became the President of the AEA.
(Chorus) He then became the President of the AEA.
And then when I had reached the age of eighty-eight I finally was made a Nobel lau-re-ate.
(Chorus) And then when he had reached the age of eighty-eight he finally was made a Nobel lau-re-ate.

So, researchers all, whoever you may be, if you want to climb up to the top of the tree;
If your soul isn't shackled to a terminal, be careful to be guided by this principle:
(Chorus) Be careful to be guided by this principle!
Just churn out research at an impressive rate and you *all* may become a Nobel lau-re-ate.
(Chorus, making horizontal circular motion with clenched hand, as if churning)
We'll churn out research at an impressive rate, and *we* may all become a Nobel lau-re-ate.
Note: In all relevant places 'she' may of course be substituted for 'he'.

I am the very model of a modern macroeconomist*

I am the very model of a modern macroeconomist,
My knowledge of the jargon you would rate as the uncommonest;
I've lots of nice equations, both the linear and quadratic;
At testing their significance I'm really a fanatic.
I understand neutrality, I'm hooked on rationality,
And – helped by Sims and Granger – at assessing non-causality;
I cite with much facility Ricardian equivalence –
But as to its validity my views have much ambivalence.
I love to put in dummies, and I'm really quite fantastic
At saying whether series are chaotic or stochastic
In short, in all my utterances jargon use is commonest;
I am the very model of a modern macroeconomist.
When optimism's running low and people fear depression,
I cheer them up by calling it a 'triple-dip recession';
And urge that every government should aim at price stability,
And tighten up their policies to maintain 'credibility'.
And, furthermore, I urge them to be terribly persistent
In seeing that their policies are always 'time-consistent'.

---

* To be sung to the tune of Major-General Stanley's song 'I am the very model of a modern Major-General', from Gilbert and Sullivan's *The Pirates of Penzance*.

I tell them that the reason unemployment won't decrease is
It's suffering from something that is known as 'hysteresis'*
In short, in all my utterances jargon use is commonest;
I am the very model of a modern macroeconomist.

In fact, when I can say for sure just when's the time for action
To stimulate activity or move towards contraction.
When I can spot each peak or trough and when I've finished learning
To spot a growth recession and identify a turning-
Point; and realised my hope that I shall make a new discovery
That helps to tell the bottom of the cycle from recovery;
When I am sure I really know the way to stop stagflation,
And when I'm sure my forecasts are not merest speculation,
In short when my predictions are more accurate than comic,
You'll say I am well versed in matters macroeconomic.
But still in all my utterances, jargon use is commonest;
I am the very model of a modern macroeconomist.

---

* Hysteresis: a term from electrical engineering, signifying in economics that some quantity, usually unemployment, at a given time is appreciably influenced by its level in immediately preceding periods.

References

Argy, V. (1981) *The Post-war International Monetary Crisis*, London: George Allen & Unwin.

Argy, V. and Salop. J. (1979) 'Price and Output Effects of Monetary and Fiscal Policy under Flexible Exchange Rates', *IMF Staff Papers* 26 (June).

Arndt, H.W. (1985) *A Course Through Life*, Canberra: National Centre for Development Studies, Australian National University.

Barro, R. (1974) 'Are Government Bonds Net Wealth?', *Journal of Political Economy*, 82 (6) (November).

Bilson, J.F.O. (1979) 'The Vicious Circle Hypothesis', *IMF Staff Papers* (June).

Blanchard, O. (1990) 'Suggestions for a New Set of Fiscal Indicators', OECD Department of Economics and Statistics, *Working Paper* 79 (April).

Boskin, M.J. (1978) 'Taxation, Saving and the Rate of Interest', *Journal of Political Economy*, 86(2), Part 2 (April).

Brittan, S. (1993) 'What the Budget Could Look Like', *Financial Times* (27 May).

Carmichael, J. and Stebbing, P.W. (1983) 'Some Macroeconomic Implications of the Interactions Between Inflation and Taxation', in Pagan, A. and Trivedi, F. (eds), *The Effects of Inflation*, Canberra: Centre for Economic Policy Research, Australian National University.

Church, P., Mitchell, P.R., Smith, P.N., Wallis, K.F. and Whitley, J.D. (1991) 'Comparative Properties of Models of the UK Economy', *National Institute Economic Review*, 137.

Clark, C. (1945) 'Public Finance and Changes in the Value of Money', *Economic Journal* (December).

Clark, C. (1964, 2nd edn 1970) 'Taxmanship', *Hobart Papers*, 26, London: Institute of Economic Affairs.

Corden, W.M. (1981) 'Taxation, Wage Rigidity and Employment', *Economic Journal* (June).

Corden, W.M. (1997) *The Road to Reform: Essays on Australian Economic Policy*, Melbourne: Longman.

Corden, W.M. and Dixon, P.B. (1980) 'Tax–Wage Bargain for Australia: Is a Free Lunch Possible?', *Economic Record* (September).

Depta, P., Ravalli, F. and Harding, D. (1994) 'Extended Measures of Investment and Saving', (Australian) *Treasury Research Paper*, 8 (February).

Dernburg, T.F. (1974) 'The Macroeconomic Implications of Wage Retaliation Against Higher Taxation', *IMF Staff Papers*, 21 (November).

Dernburg, T.F. (1975) 'Inflation Indexing of the Personal Income Tax: The Case from the Perspective of Stabilisation Policy', mimeo.

Dernburg, T.F. and McDougall, D.M. (1976) *Macroeconomics*, 5th edn, London: McGraw-Hill.

Dowrick, S. (1994) 'Fiscal Policy and Investment: The New Supply Side Economics', Australian National University Centre for Economic Policy Research, *Discussion Paper*, 322.

Dramais, A. (1986) 'COMPACT – A Prototype Macroeconomic Model of the European Community in the World Economy', *European Economy*, 27.

Fisher, P.G., Tanna, S.K., Turner, D.T., Wallis K.E. and Whitley, J.D. (1988) 'Comparative Properties of Models of the UK Economy', *National Institute Economic Review*, 125.

Fisher, P.G. *et al.* (1989) 'Comparative Properties of Models of the UK Economy', *National Institute Economic Review*, 129.

Fisher, P.G. *et al.* (1990) 'Comparative Properties of Models of the UK Economy', *National Institute Economic Review*, 133.

Friedman, M. (1968) 'The Role of Monetary Policy', *American Economic Review* (March).

Grubb, D. (1986) 'Topics in the OECD Phillips Curve', *Economic Journal* (March).

Hendry, D.E., Pagan A.R. and Sargan, J.D. (1983) 'Dynamic Specification', in Grilliches, Z. and Intriligator, M.D. (eds), *Handbook of Econometrics*, Amsterdam: North-Holland.

Hotelling, H. (1936) 'Relations between Two Sets of Variates', *Biometrica*, 28.

Ironmonger, D.S., Perkins, J.O.N. and Tran Van Hoa (1984) 'Does the Macroeconomic Mix Help to Explain Stagflation in OECD Countries?', paper presented to the 13th Conference of Economists, Hobart, Australia, mimeo.

Jones, R.S. and Perkins, J.O.N. (1986) *Contemporary Macroeconomics*, Sydney: Prentice-Hall.

Jump, G.V. (1980) 'Interest Rates, Inflation Expectations, and Spurious Elements in Measured Real Income and Saving', *American Economic Review* (December).

Knoester, A. (1987) 'Supply-side Policies in Four OECD Countries', University of Nijmwegen, *Research Memorandum*, 8601.

Knoester, A. (1995) 'The Inverted Haavelmo Effect and its Implications for European Economic Policy', Research Centre for Economic Policy, Erasmus University of Rotterdam, *Memorandum*, 9508.

Knoester, A. and Kolodziejak, A. (1988) 'Economic Growth in Europe, Japan and the United States: Policy Options for the 1990s', University of Nijmwegen Institute of Economics, *Research Memorandum* 8804.

Knoester, A. and Van Sinderen, J. (1987) 'Real Wages and Taxation in Ten OECD Countries', *Oxford Bulletin of Statistics*, 49 (1).

Leibfritz, W., Roseveare, D. and Van Den Noord, P. (1994) 'Fiscal Policy, Government Debt and Economic Performance', OECD Economics Department, *Working Paper*, 144.

Lerner, A.P. and Colander, D.C. (1980) *MAP – A Market Anti-inflation Plan*, New York: Harcourt, Brace, Jovanovich.

Lindbeck, A. (1980) *Inflation: Global, International and National Aspects*, Leuven: Leuven University Press.

Malinvaud, E. (1980) *Statistical Methods of Econometrics*. 3rd edn, Amsterdam: North-Holland.

McDonald, I.M. (1985) 'Macroeconomic Policy in Australia since the Sixties', *Australian Economic Review*, 3.

McKibbin, W. and Bagnoli, P. (1993) 'Fiscal Deficit Reduction: An Evaluation of Alternatives', *Brookings Papers in International Economics*, 101 (July).

Muller, P. and Price, R.W. (1984) 'Structural Budget Deficits and Fiscal Stance', OECD Economics and Statistics Department, *Working Paper*, 15.

Nevile, J.W. (1980) 'Economic Activity and Fiscal Policy in Australia: A Survey and Critique', *Economic Record* (December).
Okun, Arthur M. (1978) 'Efficient Disinflationary Policies', *American Economic Review, Papers and Proceedings*, 68 (2) (May).
Organisation of Economic Cooperation and Development (OECD) (1984) *Historical Statistics, 1960–1982*, Paris: OECD.
Otto, G. and Voss, G.M. (1994) 'Public Capital and Private Sector Productivity', *Economic Record*, 70 (209).
Perkins, J.O.N. (1949) Letter to *The Economist* (9 April).
Perkins, J.O.N. (1979a) *The Macroeconomic Mix to Stop Stagflation*, London: Macmillan.
Perkins, J.O.N. (1979b), 'Macroeconomic Policy and Economic Growth', in Adelman, I. (ed.), *Economic Growth and Resources*, Vol. 4 of *National and International Policies: Proceedings of Fifth Congress of the International Economic Association*, London: Macmillan.
Perkins, J.O.N. (1980) 'Using the Macroeconomic Mix to Stop Stagflation', *Journal of Economics*, 7 (1), see Chapter 3 in this volume.
Perkins, J.O.N. (1981) 'Principles of Macroeconomic Policy in a Stagflationary World', paper presented to Tenth Conference of Economists, La Trobe University, Melbourne, see Chapter 2 in this volume.
Perkins, J.O.N. (1982) *Unemployment, Inflation and New Macroeconomic Policy*, London: Macmillan.
Perkins, J.O.N. (1985) *The Macroeconomic Mix in the Industrialised World*, London: Macmillan.
Perkins, J.O.N. (1989a) *Deregulation of the Australian Financial System*, Melbourne: Melbourne University Press.
Perkins, J.O.N. (1989b) 'Some Empirical Evidence about the Macroeconomic Mix in the Open Economy', University of Melbourne Department of Economics, *Research Paper*, 234 (September); see Chapter 6 in this volume.
Perkins, J.O.N. (1990a) *A General Approach to Macroeconomic Policy*, London: Macmillan.
Perkins, J.O.N. (1990b) 'Some Empirical Evidence About the Macroeconomic Mix', *Weltwirschaftliches Archiv*, 126(2) (1990); see Chapter 5 in this volume.
Perkins, J.O.N. (1992) 'Public Finance and Macroeconomic Policy', *Economic Analysis and Policy*, 22(1) (March); see Chapter 7 in this volume.
Perkins, J.O.N. (1995) 'On the Dangers of Targeting the Budget Deficit', *The Economic and Labour Relations Review*, 6(1) (June); see Chapter 9 in this volume.
Perkins, J.O.N. (1996) 'Of Budget Deficits and Macroeconomic Policy', in Nguen, D.T. (ed.), *Queensland, Australia and the Asia-Pacific Economy*, Economic Society (Queensland) Brisbane; see Chapter 8 in this volume.
Perkins, J.O.N. (1997) *Budget Deficits and Macroeconomic Policy*, London: Macmillan.
Pitchford, J.D. and Turnovsky, S.J. (1975) 'Income Distribution and Taxes in an Inflationary Context', *Economica*, 42 (167) (August).
Pitchford, J.D. and Turnovsky, S.J. (1976) 'Some Effects of Taxes on Inflation', *Quarterly Journal of Economics*, 90(4).

Richardson, P. (1987) 'A Review of the Simulation Properties of the OECD's INTERLINK Model', OECD Economic and Statistical Department, *Working Paper*, 47.

Richardson, P. (1988) 'The Structure and Simulation Properties of the OECD Interlink Model', *OECD Economic Papers*, 10.

Richardson, P., Giorno, C. and Thurman, S. (1994) 'Macroeconomic Performance and Fiscal Policy Adjustments in the Medium Term: Alternative Medium Term Scenarios', OECD Economics Department, Working Paper, II (56).

Richardson, P., Giorno, C., and Thurman, S. (1994) 'Macroeconomic Performance and Fiscal Policy Adjustments in the Medium term: Alternative Medium-term Scenarios', OECD Economics Department, *Working Paper*, 148.

Robinson, M. (1996) 'Fiddling the Figures', *Australian Accountant* (May).

Rowthorn, R.E. (1977) 'A Conflict Theory of Inflation', *Cambridge Journal of Economics*, 1(3).

Scarth, William M. (1981) 'Tax-related Incomes Policies and Macroeconomic Stability', mimeo.

Siegel, J.J. (1979) 'Inflation-induced Distortions in Government and Private Savings Statistics', *Review of Economics and Statistics* (February).

Stephens, J. Kirker (1980) 'Inflation, Unemployment and the Macroeconomic Policy Mix', University of Oklahoma Center for Economic Management Research, Norman, Oklahoma.

Stephens, J. Kirker (1984) 'Some Tentative Results on Causality and the Macroeconomic Mix', *Midsouth Journal of Economics*, 8.

Taylor, C.T. and Threadgold, A.R. (1979) '"Real" National Saving and its Composition', *Bank of England Discussion Paper*, 6 (October).

Theil, H. (1958) *Economic Forecasts and Policy*, Amsterdam: North-Holland.

Tinbergen, Jan (1952) *On the Theory of Economic Policy*, Amsterdam: North-Holland.

Van Hoa, Tran (1985) 'A Canonical Representation of the Macroeconomic Policy Mix', University of Melbourne Institute of Applied Economic and Social Research, *Paper* 85/5 (September).

Van Hoa, Tran and C. Harvie (eds) (1999) *Causes and Impact of the Asian Financial Crisis*, London: Macmillan.

Van Hoa, Tran and Perkins, J.O.N. (1987) 'Towards the Formulation and Testing of a More General Theory of Macroeconomic Policy', *Weltwirtschaftliches Archiv*, 123(2); see Chapter 4 in this volume.

Turnovsky, Stephen (1977) *Macroeconomic Analysis and Stabilisation Policy*, Cambridge: Cambridge University Press.

Wallis, K.F. and Whitley, J.D. (1991) 'Large-scale Econometric Models of National Economies', *Scandinavian Journal of Economics*, 93(2).

Wallis, K.D., Fischer, P.G., Longbottom, A., Turner, D.S. and Whitley, J.D. (eds) (1987) *Macroeconomic Models of the UK Economy*, Oxford: Oxford University Press.

Weale, M., Blake, A., Christodoulakis, N., Meade, J. and Vines, D. (1989) *Macroeconomic Policy, Wealth and the Exchange Rate*, London: Unwin Hyman.

Wilson, T. (1980) 'Robertson, Money and Monetarism', *Journal of Economic Literature* (December).

Zellner, A. (1962) 'An Efficient Method of Estimating Seemingly Unrelated Regressions and Tests of Aggregation Bias', *Journal of the American Statistical Association*, 57.

Index

ADAM, model, 139
Argy, F., 27, 197
Arndt, H.W., 126, 197
Australia
 monetary policy, 175
 wage indexation, 160

Bagnoli, P., 134, 135, 136, 137, 198
Bank of England, 173
 model, 76, 77, 97, 98, 114, 119
Barro, R., 52, 197
Bilson, J.F.O., 27, 197
Black, John, 28
Blake, J., 200
Blanchard, O., 143, 197
BOF4, model, 139
Boskin, M.J., 52, 197
Britain, *see* UK
Brittan, S., 144, 197
budget deficit
 as 'constraint', 151–2
 cyclical adjustment, 13, 59, 60, 64, 67, 145, 149
 definitions, 144
 and expectations, 41–3
 and inflation, 13–14
 and national debt, 11–13, 43–4, 148–9
 as target, 13, 50
 and taxation, 43–4

Canada, effects of macro instruments, 79, 80, 81, 89, 90, 91, 93–4, 115, 121, 132
Carmichael, J., 126, 197
Christodoulakis, N., 200
Church, P., 197
Clark, Colin
 views on government spending, 111–12
 views on taxation, 109–12, 116, 123–6, 197

Colander, D.C., 161, 198
COMPACT, EEC model, 81–2, 99–100, 102, 197
Confucius, 126
consumption, and interest rates, 174
controls, over capital, 49
Corden, W.M., 8, 155, 163–5, 194, 197
cyclical adjustment, of budget deficits, *see* budget deficits

Dalton, Hugh, 187
'deflation', definition, 180–1
Denmark, 139
Depta, P., 150, 197
Dernburg, T.F., 70, 197
Dixon, P.B., 8, 162, 164, 197
Dorrance, Graeme, 155
Dowrick, S., 150, 197
Dramais, A., 80, 81, 99, 100, 116, 120, 134, 197

EEC, effects of macro instruments, 76, 80, 85, 96, 99–105, 115, 116, 134–5, 138
Eltis, Walter, 28

Finland, 139
 and inflation, 54, 69, 81
fiscal policy
 and deregulation, 167, 168–9, 171–2, 188, 189, 190
 and inflation, 54, 69, 81
 in USA, 188
 see also budget deficits, government spending, national debt, taxation
Fisher, P.G., 86, 97, 114, 198
France, effects of macro instruments, 78, 79, 81, 89, 90, 91, 93, 115, 121, 132, 133

201

Germany, West, 89
  effects of macro instruments, 79, 81, 89, 90, 91, 93, 94, 115, 121, 132, 133
Gilbert, W.S., 192, 194, 195
government spending
  and current account, 45–8, 84–6, 119–23
  and inflation, 6–7, 25–6, 36–7, 42, 45, 62–4, 67–70, 76–84, 111–12, 114–17, 124, 127, 132–9, 147, 152–5
Grubb, D., 197

Harvie, C., 70, 200
Hendry, 61, 66, 197
Her Majesty's Treasury, model, 76, 97, 114, 119
Horne, Jocelyn, 155
Hotelling H., 66, 197
hysteresis, definition, 195

IMF, and intermediate targets, 152
interest rates
  and capital flows, 19, 46–7, 169–72
  and consumption, 173–4
  and current account, 84–6, 87–106, 169–71, 176
  and deregulation, 168–75
  and fiscal policy, 168–9, 171–2
  and inflation, 11–13, 20–3, 29–39, 44, 62–4, 67–8
  and investment, 52, 84–5, 88, 149–50
  and low inflation, 183–8, 190–1
  and output and employment, 30–41, 52, 76–81, 167–76
  and productivity, 8
  real and nominal, 20–3, 183–4
  and resource allocation, 8
  and wages, 8, 158
INTERLINK, OECD model, 131
Ironmonger, D.S., 53, 61, 197
Italy
  effects of macro instruments, 79, 81, 89, 90, 91, 93, 115, 121, 132, 159
  wage indexation, 160

Japan
  effects of macro instruments, 79, 81, 89, 90, 91, 93, 115, 121, 132, 133
  low inflation, 2, 79, 80, 88, 89, 90, 93, 114, 120, 131, 132, 152, 177, 178, 181, 188, 189
Jones, R.S., 27, 53, 58, 70, 198
Jump, G.V., 27, 198

KESSU, model, 139
Keynes, J.M., 187
Keynesian, ideas, 6, 24, 26, 51, 74
Knoester, A., 126, 147, 198
Kolodziejak, A., 147, 198
KOSMOS, model, 139

Latin America, and inflation, 177
Leibfritz, W., 153, 154, 198
Lerner, A.P., 161, 198
Lindbeck, 26–7, 197
Lloyd, Peter, 194
London Business School, model, 76, 97, 114, 119

Malinvaud, E., 65, 198
'MAP,' 162–3
Market Anti-inflation Plan, see 'MAP'
McDonald, I.M., 28, 53, 109, 117, 122, 198
McKibbin, W., 134, 135, 136, 137, 198
Meade, J.E., 200
Mitchell, P.R., 197
MODAG, 139
monetary policy, see interest rates
mortgage rates, 172
Muller, P., 60, 65, 198

NAIRU, 72
national debt, 13, 15, 25, 43, 144, 146, 190
National Institute of Economic and Social Research, model, 76, 97, 114, 119
negative inflation, and debt, 190
Nevile, J.W., 27, 198
Nguyen, D.T., 127

1930s, macroeconomic problems, 2, 3, 4, 6, 28, 178, 179–80
1940s, macroeconomic problems, 178
1960s, macroeconomic problems, 4
1970s, macroeconomic problems, 7, 20–3
1980s, macroeconomic problems, 11
non-accelerating inflation rate of unemployment, *see* NAIRU
Norway, 139

OECD
  bond rate, 22, 23
  effects of macro policy instruments, 63
  interest rates, 20, 22
  in the 1970s, 9, 20
  in the 1980s, 20–3
  tax rates, 20, 21
  see also INTERLINK model
Okun, Arthur M., 198
Organisation for Economic Co-operation and Development, *see* OECD
Otto, G., 150, 199

Perkins, J.O.N., 27, 30, 58, 70, 117, 125, 126, 167, 198, 199, 200
Phillips curve, 50, 113
Pitchford, J.D., 51, 199
Porter, Sir Joseph, 194
Price, R.W., 60, 65, 198
productivity, and tax cuts, 38
Public Sector Borrowing Requirement, *see* budget deficits

'rational expectations', and tax, 43
Ravalli, F., 197
resource allocation policy, and macroeconomic policy, 16–18
Richardson, Pete, 79, 81, 84, 90, 115, 132, 133, 135, 152, 199, 200

Robertson, D.H., 24, 200
Robinson, Marc, 128, 200
Roseveare, D., 198

Salop, J., 27, 197
Scarth, William M., 160, 161, 200
Siegel, J.J., 27, 200
Smith, P.N., 197
South Korea, low inflation, 2
South-East Asia, and inflation, 177
Stebbing, P.W., 126, 197
Stein, Jerry, 166
Stephens, J. Kirker, 53, 64, 70, 85, 200
Sweden, 139

Tanna, S.K., 198
targets intermediate, 13, 50, 64, 66, 72, 142, 143, 150, 151
tariffs and quotas, 48
taxation
  and current account, 45–8, 50, 84–6, 88–106, 199–23
  and inflation, 9–12, 20, 29–39, 56, 61–4, 67, 76–85, 109–11, 112–17, 122–6, 130–9, 152–5, 157–63
  and investment, 52, 85, 87–9, 91–3, 120–3
  and output and employment, 14–16, 29–33, 61–4, 67, 76–84, 130–9, 146–8, 152–5
  and unemployment, 61–4, 67–9
tax-based incomes policies, 161–2
Taylor, C.T., 26, 27, 200
Thatcher, Mrs., 25
Theil, H., 61, 200
Threadgold, A.R., 26, 27, 200
'thrift', *see* wealth, net
Tinbergen, 61, 200
'TIP', *see* tax-based incomes policies
Turnovsky, S.J., 61, 200

UK
　effects of macro instruments, 79, 80, 81–9, 90, 91, 92, 93, 97–9, 114, 115, 119, 121, 132–3
　models, 76, 81, 82, 95, 97–9, 114, 119
unemployment, and inflation, 5–6, 28, 51, 61–4, 68
United States, *see* USA
US, *see* USA
USA, effects of macro instruments, 79–81, 88, 89, 96, 115, 121, 126, 132–3, 135–8, 174–5
　fiscal policy, 188
　low inflation in 1997–9, 182–3, 178–9

Van Den Noord, P., 198
Van Hoa, Tran 53, 66, 70, 71, 200
Van Sinderen, J., 198

Vines, D., 200
Voss, G.M., 150, 199

wages
　Corden's proposals, 163–4
　and government outlays, 158
　'MAP', 162–3
　and monetary policy, 157–9
　and taxation, 158, 159–60
　'TIP', 161–2
Wallis, K.F., 85, 139, 197, 200
Warwick, University
　simulations, 75–7, 80, 81, 86, 96–97, 114, 119
　see also Wallis, K.F.
Weale, M., 117, 121, 126, 126, 200
wealth, net, 88–9, 91–3, 99–104, 118, 120, 126–7, 130, 131, 136, 139–41, 143, 148–50
Whitley, J.D., 139, 197, 200
Wilson, Thomas, 24, 200

Zellner, Arnold, 200